MW00817920

Receive Our Memories

RECEIVE OUR MEMORIES

The Letters of Luz Moreno, 1950–1952

José Orozco

OXFORD
UNIVERSITY PRESS

OXFORD
UNIVERSITY PRESS

Oxford University Press is a department of the University of Oxford. It furthers
the University's objective of excellence in research, scholarship, and education
by publishing worldwide. Oxford is a registered trade mark of Oxford University
Press in the UK and certain other countries.

Published in the United States of America by Oxford University Press
198 Madison Avenue, New York, NY 10016, United States of America.

© Oxford University Press 2017

All rights reserved. No part of this publication may be reproduced, stored in
a retrieval system, or transmitted, in any form or by any means, without the
prior permission in writing of Oxford University Press, or as expressly permitted
by law, by license, or under terms agreed with the appropriate reproduction
rights organization. Inquiries concerning reproduction outside the scope of the
above should be sent to the Rights Department, Oxford University Press, at the
address above.

You must not circulate this work in any other form
and you must impose this same condition on any acquirer.

Library of Congress Cataloging-in-Publication Data
Names: Orozco, José, author.
Title: Receive our memories : the letters of Luz Moreno, 1950–1952 / José Orozco.
Other titles: Letters of Luz Moreno, 1950–1952
Description: New York City : Oxford University Press, [2016] | Includes bibliographical
references and index.
Identifiers: LCCN 2016025407 (print) | LCCN 2016047158 (ebook) |
ISBN 9780199340439 (pbk. : alk. paper) | ISBN 9780199340422 (hardcover : alk. paper) |
ISBN 9780199340446 (Updf) | ISBN 9780199340453 (Epub)
Subjects: LCSH: Moreno, Luz, 1877–1953—Correspondence. | Mexican American
families—Correspondence. | Moreno family. | Fathers and daughters—Correspondence. |
Moreno Rivera, Francisca, 1901–2002—Correspondence. | Sharecroppers—Mexico—
San Miguel el Alto—Biography. | San Miguel el Alto (Mexico)—Social life and
customs—20th century. | Synarchism—Mexico. | Poor—Mexico—Correspondence. |
Poor—Mexico—Attitudes.
Classification: LCC E184.M5 O7855 2016 (print) | LCC E184.M5 (ebook) |
DDC 306.874089/6872073—dc23
LC record available at https://lccn.loc.gov/2016025407

9 8 7 6 5 4 3 2 1

Paperback printed by Webcom, Inc., Canada
Hardback printed by Bridgeport National Bindery, Inc., United States of America

To the admissions committee at University of California, Santa Cruz
for allowing me into their community
and to Jonathan Beecher, Herman Blake, and Roberto Crespi
for, among other things, taking the time to speak with me.

CONTENTS

Plaza de Armas, San Miguel el alto, c. 1945. Courtesy of Obdulia Orozco.

ACKNOWLEDGMENTS

This book would not have been possible without the generosity of my aunt Obdulia Orozco Moreno (Lula). She gave me the shoebox that contained Luz Moreno's letters and photos and entrusted me with their fate. Over the years, she has been the first person I called when I got confused or feared that I had gotten something wrong about her grandfather, the Moreno family, San Miguel el Alto, or her life. With unfailing good cheer she answered my questions and often gave me much more information than I asked for. When Lula was not available, or when she could not answer one of my questions, I turned to my parents José Orozco Moreno and Elida Barba Orozco. They were especially helpful in helping me decipher some of the colloquial expressions that Luz used in his letters but I could not find in the dictionaries I consulted. I also want to thank the many people who helped me over the many years I have worked to complete this book. My colleague and friend Laura McEnaney read many of my "shitty first drafts" (God bless Anne Lamott!) and helped me make them less so. Roger Mensink helped tame an early draft of a rambling first chapter. John Womack Jr. read some of the letters and early drafts of the book; he helped convince me that they would be interesting and significant to people beyond my immediate family. Enrique Ochoa read an early version of the manuscript and suggested that it would be easier to use the letters in an undergraduate course if they were organized into thematic chapters. He was right. Roy Márquez, the best friend a person could ever ask for, helped me edit the translated letters. Roberto Gutiérrez read the first draft of the book and said he loved it. That was enough. My aunt, Sidonia Moreno Márquez, had several conversations with me about her father Bonifacio Moreno and her grandfather, Luz Moreno. My cousins Luz Delia, Martha, Judith, Lourdes, Yesenia, and Gema Orozco kept me company, and in good cheer while I was in San Miguel doing research. Thanks to them I met local historians, who helped me with various aspects of the book. Among these were José de Jesús Ortega Martín and Juan Alonso Hernández Delgado. Students at Whittier College, too many to name, but especially Manuel Román and

Liz Rubalcava, helped me with translations and engaged me in conversations about how to make the letters more accessible to undergraduates. Rebecca Overmyer-Velázquez encouraged me to complete the project and reached out to her brother, Mark Overmyer-Velázquez, who in turn gave me the name of an editor at Oxford University Press. Brian Wheel at OUP graciously took the time to talk with me about the project, and then agreed to consider the manuscript for publication. Susan Ferber kindly and ably edited the book for publication. Whenever my writing glided into esoteric corners of academese she reminded me that my audience would not follow. She was right. Maya Bringe and her team expertly crafted the final production of the book, and did so with great sympathy and good cheer.

To Emilio Kourí, Kathryn Burns, Brodwyn Fischer, Aurora Gómez Galvarriato, and Charles Romney for being professional inspirations and great friends.

Finally, to my cobbled-together family: Irma, Spencer, Santos, Nicolás, and Naima. Mbs.

The illustrations that grace this book are by the artist José Lozano. Lozano was born in East Los Angeles, raised in Ciudad Juarez, Mexico, and has lived most of his life in Fullerton, California. He earned his MFA from California State University, Fullerton and has spent most of his professional career painting, drawing, and writing children's books that capture that culture of his transnational existence and the aesthetic qualities of the art forms he loves best: good French cinema, bad lucha libre movies, and the tantalizing gossip he heard from the women who raised him. Inspired by the visual quality of Luz Moreno's letters and the way they reminded him of his favorite novel, Juan Rulfo's *Pedro Páramo*, Lozano used Luz's correspondence and the Moreno's family photographs to create the black ink images that are included in this book. Other drawings, including the family tree and the maps, represent Lozano's fanciful depictions of Luz Moreno's imagined world. All the images reflect back on the text while transforming it into a visual medium that values expressive rendition more than literal fealty.

The drawings and their pairing with Moreno's letters are meant to honor and reflect the lexical-visual collaborations undertaken in the 1930s and 1940s by Mexican artists like Miguel Covarrubias, Diego Rivera, and José Clemente Orozco with radical American writers like Frank Tannenbaum, Stuart Chase, and Carleton Beals.[1] These transnational collaborators, most of them political radicals with socialist affinities, favored naïve, sensuously drawn black ink images that emphasized the supposed nonmechanized, primitive, and subversive power of the Mexican peasant and Indian populations.[2] Culled from the iconography of the Mexican Revolution, this imagery, full of sombreros, donkeys, cacti, and peaceful Indians, was popular among a segment of Americans who, tired of economic depression, social unrest, world wars, and the alienation of modern industrial society, flocked (or dreamed of going) to Mexico to find a more authentic way of life.[3] Their collaboration was one that was hopeful and sunny. Moreno's letters and Lozano's drawings represent a multigenerational, transnational collaboration that elegizes the darker, emotionally gloomy experience of Mexican families who, finding that Mexican primitivism does not fill one's belly, decided to migrate from rural idylls like San Miguel el Alto to live and work in industrial cities like Stockton, Fullerton, and East Los Angeles.

Receive Our Memories

Introduction

The history of a family begins when a person leaves home.

Leslie Chang, *Factory Girls: From Village to City in a Changing China* (2008)

Francisca (Pancha) Moreno Rivera was born in 1901 in the Mexican town of San Miguel el Alto in the central-west state of Jalisco. When she died in California, in 2002, she was 101 years old.[1] No one who knew her was surprised by her longevity. In San Miguel, Pancha's small body moved through space and time with a kinetic energy that was admired by her friends and family. As the eldest of seven children, she was a seamstress and the comatriarch (along with her mother, Secundina) of the Moreno family. She provided her large and poor family with emotional and financial stability, as well as the hard hand of discipline that kept it a functioning, and often loving, entity. She was also a Catholic revolutionary who participated in the two biggest movements mounted by the Catholic Church and its lay partisans against the Mexican State in the twentieth century, the *Cristero* Rebellion (*La Cristiada*) of the late 1920s and the *Sinarquista* movement of the early 1940s. In 1950, at the age of forty-nine, she married her childhood sweetheart, Juan Rivera, and left Mexico to live in Stockton, California. In Stockton, she found work in the rich agricultural fields and the fruit and vegetable canneries of California's Central Valley. She labored in the canneries until she was sixty-five years old and remained in Stockton until she died almost four decades later. While she often visited her family, and was eventually buried in San Miguel, Pancha never returned to live in Mexico.

During the 1970s, Pancha, her husband Juan Rivera, and my aunt Obdulia (Lula) Orozco made regular trips from Stockton to visit their extended family in Southern California. I always looked forward to these visits from my two aunts. Pancha was the saintly aunt who had raised my father, José, after his mother died. Lula was my father's older sister. Both Lula and Pancha were kind, gentle, and generous with their time, affection, and the bricks of government cheese they brought us from Stockton.

Every night after dinner, when the family sat around the living room television set to watch Spanish-language soap operas, my two brothers and I would sneak off to another room to play with our *tía* Lula. Because she didn't have children, and, I assume, because she knew that she would leave us in a day or two, our *tía* Lula lavished attention on us. We talked, she told us stories, and—when our father was not paying attention—she wrestled with us. During her visits, our small house shook as my brothers and I clambered all over Lula. We pummeled her, and our poor aunt would writhe in dramatic displays of pain that rivaled the theatrics of the "real" wrestlers we idolized.

Very little could pry us away from our daily wrestling matches. Little, that is, except for the professional wrestling matches televised from the Los Angeles Olympic Auditorium. On Saturday evenings, the English-language station, KCOP, channel 13, televised wrestling. On Wednesdays, *lucha libre* was televised by the local Spanish-language station, KMEX, channel 34. On those evenings, our whole family was absorbed by the drama of the black-and-white gladiators that tumbled across our television screen. My reserved and well-mannered parents watched but did not comment. My brothers and I gazed silently into the glowing television set, took mental notes, and imagined ourselves applying the holds and aerial maneuvers we were seeing on each other and on our hapless aunt. Lula would give us sly looks from across the room and feign fear. She knew what we were thinking; and, in the best tradition of all *rudos* (the Mexican wrestling world's bad guys), she was conveying contempt for our hubris and challenging us to prove our skills.

Everyone sat before the television set in silence. Everyone, that is, but Pancha. Pancha loved *lucha libre*; while she was not quite convinced that it was real, she was also not quite convinced it was not. This doubt was enough to draw her into the spectacle as an excited participant who was never shy about fulminating at the deaf figures whose play violence so enthralled her. Being a good Catholic and a true wrestling fanatic meant that Pancha always cheered for the good guys and booed at the *rudos*. Her sense of justice dictated this alliance with good; it is what made her such an extremely devout Catholic, and it is why she almost never attended wrestling matches

Obdulia Orozco (far left) and her brothers Jesus and José Orozco c. 1940.

in person: On one of the few occasions when Pancha actually went to see a wrestling match, our *tía* Lula had to restrain her from throwing a folding chair at one of the bad guys.[2] She believed the *rudo* had gone beyond the limits of respectable wrestling etiquette, and felt that a chair thrown on top of his head was not only justified, but also called for.[3]

Pancha remained an avid wrestling fan until 1994, when she suffered a series of strokes that effectively ended her romance with the sport and her life as a practicing Catholic. While incapacitated she remained alive for another eight years. Tended to by Lula, Pancha remained in her room on a hospital bed, beneath a crucifix and surrounded by the many plastic dolls and plaster Catholic saints she had spent a lifetime collecting, fussing over, and making clothing for. In its semiconscious state, Pancha's body—the first link in the chain of migration that eventually brought many of the Orozcos and Morenos to the United States—became the object of much reverence and propelled members of her family, all of whom lived in Los Angeles, to make pilgrimages to Stockton. For Christmas, Thanksgiving, Easter, throughout the summer, and especially for her birthday, the Orozcos and the Morenos trekked up the Golden State Freeway to be with Pancha and Lula. During these visits Lula and her guests sat around Pancha's bed and reminisced about their shared history, gossiped about family members who were not there, and sang old *ranchera* songs and *Cristero* anthems ("*Viva Cristo Rey! Viva Cristo Rey!*") to Pancha's inert body.[4] Invariably, someone would take out a camera and invite the whole group to assemble around Pancha's bed for a family portrait. Parents held their infants aloft near Pancha and young children were encouraged to pose with their great-great aunt.

In 1996, Lula organized a party for Pancha's ninety-fifth birthday. Many members of her extended family, including myself, attended. Along with her aging friends—mostly Mexican and Filipina cannery and agricultural workers—her family gathered to celebrate her long life and their presence in the United States. It was a joyous affair that began with a Mass and continued with a party. At the end of the festivities, after all the guests had left and we had cleaned the house, Lula called me over and said she had a gift for me. From a closet located next to a framed photograph of President John Kennedy and his wife Jacqueline, Lula pulled out an old shoebox and handed it to me. Inside the box I found several bundles of old letters. Each bundle had been lovingly preserved and tied with a red ribbon. Lula glowed with pride as she explained to me that her grandfather Luz Moreno (Pancha's father) had written these letters to Pancha in the years following her departure from Mexico in 1950. Lula said she hoped the letters would help me in my studies (I was then in graduate school) and that by reading them I would come to understand a little about our family's history.[5]

It was nearly midnight when I laid down on the turquoise blue Naugahyde couch that was my makeshift bed. As I squirmed trying to get comfortable, I opened Pancha's shoebox. I took out the bundles of letters and discovered a small collection of family photographs. Among these photographs was one of Pancha taken in the 1940s during her time as a Sinarquista activist. Pancha is standing with five other Sinarquista women in front of two homemade, hand-painted flags. The first flag is the Mexican national flag. The second flag, red with the silhouette of the Mexican nation in a white circle, is the flag of the Sinarquista Party. The women, resolute about their ideas and their politics, look confidently, almost threateningly, into the camera. They hold their right arms stiffly across their chests (a gesture that bears

Executive Board (Mesa Directiva) of Sinarquista Women: Francisca (Pancha) Moreno (President) is the fourth from the left. San Miguel el Alto, c. 1940. Courtesy of Obdulia Orozco.

more than a passing resemblance to the German Nazi and Italian Fascist salutes) and seem ready to strike against anyone who dared threaten their version of conservative Catholicism and the spiritual security it provided their community at a time of great change.

Pancha—who in all likelihood not only sewed the flags but also the dresses she and her comrades are wearing—stares out through and beyond the camera. The force of her presence seems to flow from her disciplined body, through her chiseled jawline, and out her steely eyes; her visage and posture highlighting her confident and combative spirit. Seeing a Mexican woman enact such a defiant stance in public—one that is at odds with prevailing ideas of Mexican femininity, especially conservative Catholic femininity—defies traditional expectations.[6] But Pancha's attitude, and the political convictions that fortified it, had been hard-earned through her participation in both the Cristero Rebellion and the Sinarquista movement. During the Cristiada, when a ragtag army of Catholic partisans violently resisted the revolutionary federal government's attempts to wrest many of the social and political privileges that the Catholic Church had enjoyed since the sixteenth century, Pancha smuggled arms for the rebels and tended to wounded soldiers. She also took it upon herself to remove dead Cristero combatants from the public spaces where the federal troops had left them hanging or shot as warnings to the insurgents.[7] In the 1940s she and her uncle helped organize the local chapter of the *Union Nacional Sinarquista* (UNS). The UNS was founded in 1937 to continue the Church's resistance to the secularization of Mexican society through a mass, explicitly nonviolent movement. Pancha and most of the women in the photo were veterans of the Cristiada and members of the Sinarquista's women's auxiliary group. Away from their familial responsibilities and the strict gender roles that circumscribed their access to public spaces and public activities, these women, like many Mexican women before them, created for regular and spiritually sanctioned spaces, activities, and relationships away from their husbands, brothers, and children. Pancha and her *comadres* held regular evening meetings where they and the parish priest organized the annual festivals to commemorate the town's patron Saint Michael; they held *kermeses* (the equivalent of today's bake sales) to procure the money they needed to pay for the buses that would take them to León, Guanajuato, or Guadalajara for the next Sinarquista rally; and they joined together in sewing circles to make flags and the uniforms that their children wore at Sinarquista rallies. Some of their husbands may have suspected that their wives had less-than-pious reasons for absenting themselves from their homes and their domestic duties, but the women, backed by their local priest, could counter with the obvious: they were doing God's work.[8] And if the men still refused to let their wives participate, Francisca Moreno, the town's toughest Catholic, would pay them a visit.[9]

Beneath the photograph of Pancha was a black-and-white postcard of her father, Luz Moreno, taken during a visit to Guadalajara, the capital of Jalisco. The photograph captures Moreno in his *campesino*-visits-the-big-city attire standing awkwardly in front of a cement bench. He is holding a straw hat with his right hand and is wearing a *sarape* over his left shoulder. From his skinny, rather gangly body hangs a white cotton shirt and a pair of denim slacks. The *huaraches* on his feet had seen better days, but the rest of his clothes were his Sunday best. Prominent ears and a hint of a buck-toothed grin dominate his face, and although the photograph makes his skin look dark, his family remembers him as a light-skinned man with light-colored eyes—blue, some swear. The photograph is undated, but it must have been taken sometime between 1950 and 1953.

Pancha's departure to Stockton in 1950 changed Luz Moreno's life. When she left, Luz was seventy-three years old, and it was the first time anyone in his immediate family had moved away. Pancha was not only his favorite daughter, but also his most stalwart ally in the contentious family

Luz Moreno. Agua Azul Park, Guadalajara, Jalisco, c. 1950. Courtesy of Obdulia Orozco.

politics that often pitted Luz against his daughters Victorina and Ysabel, and all of them against the destructive behavior of the hard-drinking male Moreno siblings. Luz missed his daughter and understood that her move to Stockton had illuminated a path to a world his increasingly restless family would find hard to resist. Even if Pancha's departure did not mark the beginning of the Moreno family's history, this event placed its members into an alternative historical trajectory. For a family whose life chances were severely restricted by poverty and the rigid social and political structures of their small town, her move opened new venues for long-term social and economic advancement. It also exposed the Morenos to many of the centrifugal forces (immigration, money, Los Angeles) that eventually tore them away from each other and from their birthplace. Indeed, while Luz Moreno and some of the older members of the family hoped that Pancha's absence would only be temporary, most of the younger Morenos plotted to find a way to join her in the promised land of *El Norte*. Like the ubiquitous cows of San Miguel's countryside who, as popular lore has it, always face north, Luz's children's minds, dreams, and bodies were now oriented toward the United States and away from him.[10]

This new world and its many possibilities both excited and saddened Luz. Too old to emigrate himself, the elderly patriarch turned to the only practical way he had to bridge the physical and emotional distance that had suddenly separated him from his daughter—letter-writing. Thinking about his life in the context of the void left by the departure of his favorite daughter, and using pens made from sharpened pieces of wood, along with paper, ink, nibs, envelopes, and postage purchased at the expense of essential items such as food, Luz Moreno wrote about 170 letters between 1950 and 1952. His compulsion drove his uncomprehending family to question his sanity: Why was he writing so much? What was he saying about us? Why doesn't he spend his money on food? Why, after having lived his life in silence, was he opening up to Pancha?[11] But Pancha appreciated these tangible reminders of her life in Mexico, and she dutifully tried to respond in kind by writing to her father as often and as meaningfully as she could. She sent him news and photographs of her life in Stockton, tried to calm his worries, proffered him messages of tenderness, and every once in a while mailed him money.[12]

Although Pancha's letters to Luz have been lost or destroyed, the fact that we have so many of Luz's letters highlights both how prolific a writer Luz was and how much Pancha cherished these material reminders of her father's affection. Academics interested in uncovering the voices of that segment of humanity that Eric Wolf once characterized as the "people without history" also believe that these types of letter collections are invaluable.[13]

Although immigrant letters constitute "the largest single body of first-person writings by ordinary people historians possess," many historians caution that there are limits to what we can expect from letters written by people with little education and less motivation to comment on the great historical forces and events that they were a part of. The historian David A. Gerber argues that the "reflective mood" is often a passing and ephemeral part of most letter writer's personality and condition and that most immigrants, primarily interested in using letters to keep in contact with their families, "seemed no more willing or able than most people in any time or place to stand far above their lives, look down at them, and explain themselves."[14] While Gerber's argument is empirically true for the much-studied European context, and makes intuitive sense about the much-less-mined correspondence sequences of the Mexico/US immigration context, Moreno's letters to his daughter are different in several ways.[15]

Like other immigrant letter sequences, Luz Moreno's letters are remarkable if only for the fact that they still exist. More than six decades after they were penned, the existence of the letters, which capture Moreno's aura in ink and paper, is a small miracle that should not go unnoticed.[16] That his letters survive, whereas Pancha's were lost or destroyed sometime after Luz died in 1953, underscores historian David Fitzpatrick's point that the canon of immigrant letters available to historians is inevitably "defined by preservers rather than writers or readers."[17] Because the lives of those who stayed home were generally more stable than the often unpredictable lives of the immigrants who wandered out into the world, the survival rate of letters is skewed heavily in favor of the immigrant letter sent from abroad but kept and preserved by families in Mexico.[18] This means that in all likelihood correspondence sequences from the Mexican diaspora, will, like those from the European context, tell the story of immigration from the perspective and life experiences of the young to the old, of men to their wives, from the mobile to the inert, from the future to the past. Luz's fragile artifacts construct a narrative that flows in the opposite direction. They are the imaginary peregrinations of an old man who lived in a poor and small town in Mexico to a daughter who wandered out to live in the wealthiest nation in the world. In this way, this collection of letters adds to an emerging literature that conceives of the "immigrant experience" as encompassing the lives of both *los que se fuerón y los que se quedarón* (those who left and those who stayed behind).[19] While traditional studies of los que se fuerón, including the very rich canon of work based on immigrant letters, has helped illuminate what people risked when they left home and family, what they hoped to gain, what they lamented losing, and how they felt about and dealt with their exile, the emotional landscape and epistolary voice of those who stayed, especially the elderly, remains opaque.[20]

This correspondence is also notable because Luz Moreno's letters reveal the most sensitive parts of his interior life. In many of his letters Moreno writes about the holy trinity of Alteño rural life—cows, corn, and clouds. But when he was in a reflective mood—which, given his age, was often— he wrote extended passages of unexpected beauty and introspection. His reports on the crops and the weather glided into pondering the eschatological questions that weighed on him at the end of his life: Is life worth living? What is death? Will I be rewarded or punished in the afterworld? What does it mean to live a moral life? Luz did not meditate on these questions in an existential vacuum. Pancha's departure and the newspapers he read brought the world to Luz and framed his meditations within a transnational context defined, among other things, by the Cold War, the contract labor agreement know as the Bracero Program, the Korean War, and the nuclear arms race. So while most of the immigrant correspondences that have thus far been discovered and studied reveal that migrant-written narratives are mostly "contained within the 'little kingdom' of the family," Luz's letters plumb a wider and deeper world.[21]

Finally, Luz's letters are noteworthy because, in addition to challenging established notions about the content of immigrant letters, they challenge assumptions about the intent and ability of poor people to construct a story about their lives that aspires to narrative beauty. Most letter writers in any immigrant circuit, regardless of class and education, had neither the talent nor the desire to write letters that were anything other than functionally informational (to provide news) or sentimental (to share the blues).[22] Luz Moreno's prose, on the other hand, displays a conscious and persistent literary intent and skill that he believed was the material manifestation of a long-repressed, God-given gift.[23] Divinely inspired or not, Luz's letters are shining examples of a vernacular literary form that is not only useful as a primary document for historians, but also sometimes the source of a deeply satisfying aesthetic experience.[24] Indeed, what the Mexican critic Carlos Monsiváis says of the Mexican writer Juan Rulfo is also true for Luz Moreno. Like Rulfo's short stories and his novel *Pedro Páramo*, both of which are lauded for their portrayal of the interior monologue and language of Mexico's rural population, Luz's letters reveal "the intimate logic, ways of being, and the secret and public poetry of peasant villages and communities, marginalized by the forgetfulness that so defines power."[25]

While Luz was a remarkably expressive writer, he was not a formally educated one. He does not mention any schooling in his letters, and when his youngest son, Cecilio Moreno, was questioned on the matter, he stated that, as far as he knew, his father had had only a couple of years ("*unos años*") of schooling. If we take Cecilio at his word, and if we agree with scholars who argue that for a working-class person like Luz "a little education [could go] a long way," it is not difficult to be confident that even with *unos años* of education, Luz was capable of writing the letters collected in this book.[26] The fact that Luz was literate made him an anomaly in a community that in 1900 (when Luz was twenty-three years old) had a literacy rate of about 23 percent.[27] His letters, though, betray Luz's lack of formal education. For example, while he rarely spelled words phonetically or split words into syllables (telltale signs of marginal literacy), he consistently used the letter "b" instead of "v" to spell words like *vaca* (cow) and did the opposite (used "v" instead of "b") in words like *bien* (good), which he spelled as *vien*. More significantly, Luz used a limited range of the signposts that formally educated people use to pace the reader's eye. He read the newspaper daily and understood that sentences were building blocks of ideas that needed to be separated from each other and that a collection of these sentences constituted larger units of thought, or paragraphs. While he employed periods rather deftly, he just did not have the formal education that would have allowed him to punctuate his sentences using a full range of pauses that are available to more tutored writers. Instead, Luz, transposing a sense of pacing derived from speech, used capital letters at the beginning of a sentence and spaces within sentences to indicate the types and duration of pauses that periods, commas, colons, parentheses, and other forms of punctuation usually suggest to the reader.

These "defects" do not diminish the power or beauty of his prose, nor did they impede the conversation between Luz and his daughter. Indeed, because they carried an element of intimacy not present in more grammatically precise prose, these letters must have been especially meaningful to the correspondents, who saw the authentic hand of their loved one in every imperfection.[28] Yet the very aspects of these letters that helped endear the writers to each other—idiosyncratic spelling and nonstandard grammar and punctuation, the shared language of local or more intimate idioms, the inclusion or absence of context about the people, places, and events that the writer assumes are familiar to the reader, and the anxiety and relief that attended the rhythm of writing and receiving letters over long distances and across seemingly interminable time lapses—tend to impede other people's understanding of much of the information and affective import that this correspondence had in its original context.[29] I attempted to alleviate some of this confusion in several ways. In addition to translating the letters from Spanish to English, I consulted family members to fill in the context about the events, people, and places Luz wrote about but that I could not find in primary and secondary sources. Family members also kindly shared with me the type of biographical information about Pancha and Luz Moreno and their relatives that most historians who study immigrant correspondence sequences simply do not have.[30] Not all of the letters in the correspondence are included in this book, and those that appear have had punctuation added, and repetitive sentences or passages removed.[31] Hopefully this increases the readability of the letters while retaining the substance, form, and meaning of Luz's writing.[32] Also, while most of the letters are dated, some are not. I used the information in the letters, the color of the ink, the type of paper, and the letter's location relative to others in the stacks that had been kept in the shoebox to approximate the date that Luz wrote that particular letter.

The first chapter begins with a brief history of the region of Los Altos and the town of San Miguel el Alto where Luz Moreno was born in 1877. This introduction is followed by a brief history of the Moreno family from the late nineteenth century to 1950, when Luz began his correspondence with Pancha. Many historical events and processes shaped the lives of the Moreno clan during this time, but the most significant were the antigovernment, social Catholic movements that convulsed the region. These movements were formative in shaping the language and ideology that Luz employed to talk about, understand, and vicariously explore the world in which he and his family found themselves in the 1950s. The chapter explores the political and social context of so-called Social Catholicism and highlights the way it formed Pancha and Luz Moreno's worldviews. After delineating this context I trace the events that led up to Pancha's marriage, her departure from San Miguel, and the beginning of her and Luz's correspondence. Pancha's departure was momentous not only because it turned her father's life upside down, but also because it gave him the opportunity to pen his thoughts, something rarely done or imagined in a town where most people lived and died in the place where they had been born.

What follows the historical context for the correspondence is a compendium of eighty or so letters organized around five themes. Each chapter begins with a brief introduction that frames one or two core themes of the collected letters within a broader historical and cultural context. These are not intended to exhaust the potential interpretations and insights that could be gleaned from the correpondence, but rather to guide the reader to aspects of Luz Moreno's writings that shed light on the role of letter-writing among nonelite people in the context of immigration during the middle part of the twentieth century. The thematic organization is facilitated by the formula Moreno used to structure his letters. He began most of his letters with a salutation to his "Beloved Children" or "Absent Ones," and usually ended them by sending his regards to Pancha and asking her to remember her family in San Miguel. In between these quite standard components of immigrant correspondence, most likely learned from one of the many writing manuals available in Mexico during this time, Luz sprinkled endearments and dutifully reported the affairs of his family and town. Then he frequently plunged into more heady discussions about domestic and international affairs: the fate of the poor in a world structured to benefit the rich, the fortunes of the American military in the Korean War, and the machinations of the Soviet Union and their designs, as Luz saw it, on world domination. Mixed into these ruminations are diary-like entries in which the nostalgic septuagenarian philosophically recounts vignettes of his life, the lessons he gained from those experiences, and the feelings of dread that often overcame him as he dealt with old age. Together, these elements—the formal, the quotidian, the philosophical, the affective, and the political—structure Luz's letters and provide the organizational scaffolding for this book.

Chapter 2 highlights the manner in which Luz and Pancha attempted to build, maintain, and repair the affective bonds that sustained their relationship in its new, transnational context. It is sometimes assumed that keeping in touch with absent loved ones is an easy and natural activity. But, as the letters in this chapter highlight, while the writing of one letter is born of sorrow and inspired by affection between *los ausentes* (absent ones),[33] the creation of an epistolary culture—the establishing of the habit of reading and writing, the structuring of one's day to accommodate these activities, and the immersing of one's self in a timetable and rhythm that is not physically intimate or temporally immediate—is one that must be constantly created, sustained, and repaired. This chapter examines how Luz and Pancha created this epistolary culture when immigration reconfigured their relationship.

Chapter 3 calls attention to the centrality of religion and religious expressions in Luz Moreno's life. In the decades following the Cristero Rebellion, the region of Los Altos de Jalisco developed a reputation as the cradle of Mexico's most Catholic populace. Alteños became famous for embodying a rebellious and atavistically pure Catholicism that was not only free from Indian spiritual and ritual influences, but also the weapon they used to keep the modern world and its corrupting influences at bay. While the image of the righteous religious warrior was comforting to many Mexicans living in an era of often vertiginous change, the reality of Alteño religiosity, at least in the case of Luz Moreno's faith, was more complicated. As the letters in this chapter show, what characterized Moreno's religion-mediated encounter with modernity was a chronic emotional uncertainty and intellectual hybridity that is very different than the ideological purity, political clarity, and self-assuredness of purpose and method that is commonly believed to characterize Alteño religiosity. Rather than being exceptional, Luz Moreno's religiosity did what it did for poor Catholics in Mexico and elsewhere: it explained the world, contained the anxieties caused by forces beyond his control, and gave him hope that the next world would be kinder to souls like himself. These are tender human desires rarely expressed in the trenches of religious social movements, but fully and touchingly evident in the pages of Luz's correspondence with his daughter.

Chapter 4 highlights the passages in the correspondence in which Luz writes about himself as a poor person. In addition to his religious identity, his self-conception as a member of a transnational community he calls *el miserable pueblo* (loosely translated as "the wretched of the earth") shaped how he conceived of and acted in the world. Luz saw himself and his family as a part of this community and he believed that they, and other like them across the globe, suffered not only the indignities of material poverty, but also the emotional poverty that comes with being ignored, discounted, and forgotten. Usually, the reactions of *los de abajo* (the underdogs) of Mexican society to the abuses they suffer only register on the national or international consciousness when they organize and take to the streets in protest, strikes, or outright rebellion. Luz's letters, however, reveal at a very intimate level the bruised and battered affect of a poor person who experienced abuse not only at the hand of his social betters, but also from his family and neighbors. Indeed, as he got old and was less able to meet the social and financial expectations they had of him, it was the microaggressions from those closest to him that seemed to hurt Luz the most.

Chapter 5 focuses on how important letter-writing and reading newspapers were to Luz Moreno. I speculate not only on the character and source of his literacy and the effect it had on him and his family, but also try to contextualize his love of reading and writing within a local culture of literacy made up of other *letrados* who, like Luz, were committed Catholic activists. I also highlight how Luz's literacy connected him to other poor, literate people in Latin America. The most important of these was Carolina María de Jesus, the Afro-Brazilian woman whose diary was published to great acclaim in 1960 and is one of the few published texts written by one of Latin America's *miserable pueblo*.

Chapter 6 is organized around Luz's meditations on his old age, his declining health, and his increasingly marginalized position within his family and community. It is often taken as an article of faith that Mexican families provide their elderly with a warm and inclusive environment that salves the physical and emotional losses of old age and alleviates their anxieties about dying. Luz's letters complicate this perception by showing just how existentially challenging his old age and looming death were for him, in spite of his religious beliefs and the love of a caring, yet frustrated family. The letters in this chapter also highlight how Luz prepared for a dignified death in the void left by Pancha's departure and his perception that the world was at the end of times.

Luz's expression of his convictions and doubts opens up the emotional and social landscape of a man who, with very little formal education but with a mind full of curiosity and dread, articulated his love for his daughter, accounted for his life, lamented the changes the world was bringing to his little corner of Mexico, and wondered at the marvels he was witnessing. In many ways he was an insignificant man who was born and died in the same small town and who wished that things would stay the same. Yet, as the writer Nathaniel Philbrick comments about Moby Dick, Luz Moreno's correspondence reveals "as much about the microclimates of intimate human relations as it is about the great, uncontrollable gales that push and pull all of us."[34] There is no other collection quite like it. And it all began when one person left and another decided to take pen to paper and tell her how much he loved her—among other things.

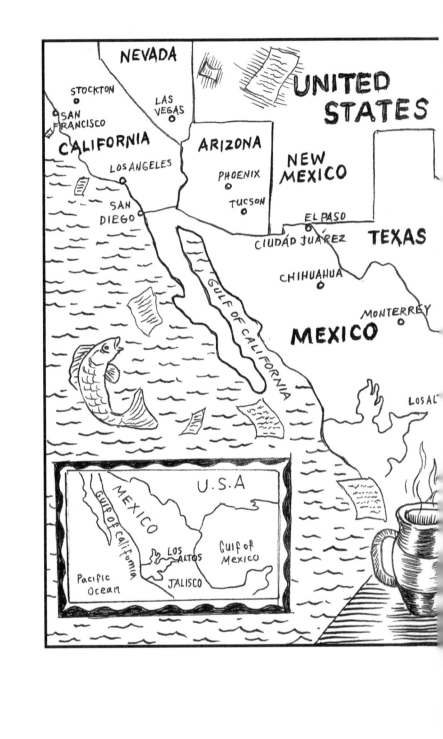

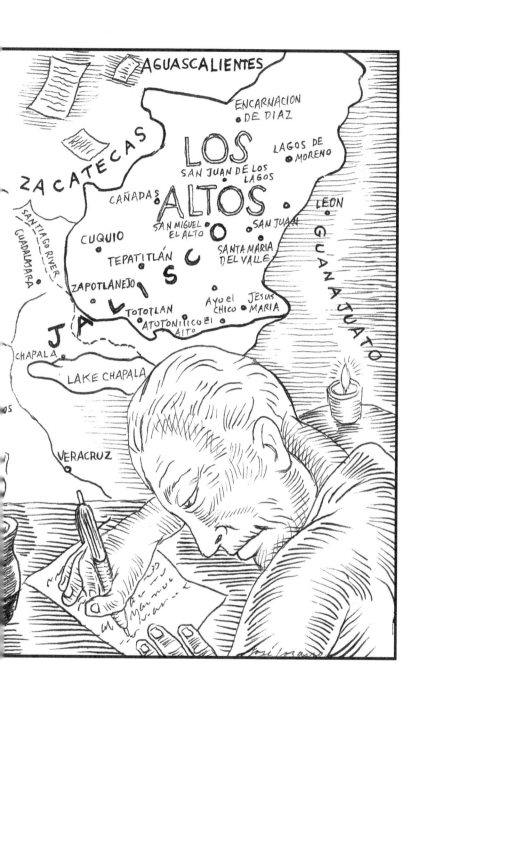

CHAPTER 1

The Morenos of San Miguel el Alto

A single person is missing for you, and the whole world is empty.
Philippe Ariès, *Western Attitudes Towards Death* (1980)

San Miguel el Alto, the town where Luz Moreno's family had lived in for generations, is located in the region of Los Altos de Jalisco, a plateau in the central-west state of Jalisco, Mexico. Sparse and hauntingly beautiful, the vistas of the region are dominated by the juxtaposition of the crystal-blue of the big skies of the plateau with the rust-red of the oxidized soil and the blue-green of the magueys that are used to produce the region's most famous agricultural product: tequila. It is three hundred miles north of Mexico City and 1,500 miles from the United States. Surrounded by the states of Zacatecas and Aguascalientes to the north and northeast, San Luis Potosí and Guanajuato to the east and southeast, and Michoacán to the south, San Miguel is in the heart of Mexico's most prolific emigrant-sending region.

San Miguel was founded as a *pueblo de indios* named Atoyanalco in the sixteenth century by Franciscan missionaries in the wake of a massive indigenous uprising called the Mixton War (1540–1542).[1] Indian towns were segregated settlements socially monitored and spiritually ministered by the Catholic Church. The Spanish Crown hoped the *pueblos de indios* would keep the indigenous population away from the corrupting influence of the Europeans, Africans, and *castas* (people of mixed race). The Crown and the Catholic Church also hoped that these towns would provide them with a space in which they could militarily control, Christianize, civilize, and economically exploit the indigenous population. In Los Altos, where the local Indian population had proven itself a military threat, antithetical to Christian doctrines, suspicious of a settled, non-nomadic life, and hostile to the idea of laboring for the benefit of the Spanish, these Christian towns were key to the expansion and stability of the Spanish empire.

By the late nineteenth century San Miguel had become a small town of about three thousand mixed-race people surrounded by a municipality of rural households (a community of about another nine thousand people) who were dedicated to agriculture (corn and beans) and animal husbandry (cattle and horses).[2] Over the course of three hundred years the community had acquired and internalized many of the material markers and cultural and mental habits valued by the conquering European Catholics. Despite early resistance by the mostly nomadic Indians who occupied the region, the people of San Miguel were, by the time Luz Moreno was born in 1877, a largely mestizo population of non-nomadic, agricultural workers whose primary, if not only, way of understanding their world was derived from the Catholic Church and its doctrines.

Like most of their neighbors in San Miguel during the late nineteenth century, Magdaleno Moreno and Teodora Lozano Moreno, Luz Moreno's parents, Pancha's grandparents, were sedentary agricultural laborers who organized their lives around the practices and rituals of their faith and their labor. Among the more fortunate families in San Miguel, they were the owners of a small rural property, a rancho called *La Tinaja*.[3] For Magdaleno and Teodora, their way of life was the same as their parents and it was how they imagined their children—José Luz Moreno, Francisco (Pancho) Moreno, Francisco (Panchillo) Moreno, and Zenón Moreno—would live out their existence.[4]

At La Tinaja, the Moreno children began their working life at a young age. Luz delivered food to his father in the fields at age seven. At nine, he tended to the family's animals and farmed his own plot of land. In 1900, when he was twenty-three years old, he decided to marry Secundina Román. He believed that his many years of service to his father had garnered him enough favor to ensure his continued use of La Tinaja for the benefit of his new family, so Luz was bitterly disappointed when his father informed him: "You no longer fit in La Tinaja—you must find somewhere else to farm." (October 22, 1951). Luz was the victim of a rural strategy known as *desconocimiento* (literally, to not recognize) that allowed the head of the rural household to not acknowledge some children, usually the youngest, as legitimate heirs. Landowners with large families often ignored legitimate heirs to prevent the fragmentation of their land and to preserve the economic viability of their rural properties. Although

Magdaleno Moreno's decision may have been an economically sound and culturally justifiable strategy to deal with the fact that he just had too many children and too little land, it devastated Luz. He was the oldest son, had labored long and hard for the benefit of his parents, and had only imagined his life as a landowner. His father's decision not only ended this illusion, but also forced Luz and Secundina to move into a house owned by Secundina's sister, Angelita, in San Miguel.

Luz never felt at ease living in his sister-in-law's house. Secundina, on the other hand, was happy to leave La Tinaja; she did not get along with her mother-in-law and hated the indignities that accompanied living in her in-laws' house. When Luz protested about their living conditions and the emasculation he suffered at the hands of his overbearing sister-in-law, Secundina ended the conversation by stating, "Either you want a mother, or a wife."[5] Every day Luz walked from San Miguel to La Tinaja, where he continued to work for his father and his brothers as a landless rural worker, a *peón*. To supplement the 37 cents a day his father paid him, Luz also labored on other people's land as a sharecropper.[6] Despite the fact that land in the municipality was readily bought and sold,[7] Luz Moreno was never able to purchase a rural property for his family.[8] He spent the next five decades in a state of grinding poverty barely alleviated by the money earned by his daughters and sons, who held a variety of jobs ranging from dressmakers to musicians, and the wages earned by his wife, who cooked for wealthy families in San Miguel and was one of the principal midwives in the municipality.

San Miguel's population grew from about 12,500 in 1900 to 17,028 in 1950 despite increased out-migration, two civil wars, an outbreak of typhoid fever in 1916, and the Spanish influenza, which killed six hundred of Luz's neighbors in 1918.[9] The population growth in San Miguel, however, reflects a larger trend in north central Mexico. While in the nineteenth century the population of the region had grown by one percent annually, by the 1920s its growth had more than doubled annually. Rather than doubling every hundred years as it had in the nineteenth century, the population of the region was doubling every thirty years.[10]

The Morenos were no exception to this trend. What they lacked in material wealth, they made up for in children: four daughters—Francisca (Pancha), Ysabel, Micaela, and Victorina—and three sons—Isidoro (Lolo), Bonifacio (Chito), and Cecilio (Chilo). The Moreno brothers became musicians, fiercely dedicated to their craft, their family, and too often to the consumption of alcohol. The Moreno women worked selflessly, but not always without rancor, for the betterment of the family as cooks in the homes of San Miguel's wealthier families, midwives, and seamstresses.

They were also fervent Catholics whose lives were inextricably bound to the rituals and calendar of the Church. They helped organize the annual festivals for the patron saint of the town, sang in the choir, and cooked and cleaned for the parish priest. Catholicism was a vibrant part of their daily lives, a link to their past, and the promise of a new world order so, when duty called, as it often did during the three decades following the Mexican Revolution, they helped organize and actively participated in several social movements whose members sought to protect the Church and its privileges from the encroachments of the Mexican state: the *Cristero* Rebellion (1926–1929), the second Cristero Rebellion (mid 1930s to early 1940s), and the *Sinarquista* Movement (1937–c. 1950).

To many people in Los Altos the Mexican Revolution is not the revolution of Pancho Villa and Emiliano Zapata.[11] *Alteños* of a certain generation think of the Mexican Revolution as the Catholic Church-inspired armed revolt against the central government known as the Cristero Rebellion.[12] The rebellion was precipitated when President Plutarco Elías Calles (1924–1928) and a cadre of radical anticlerical governors launched a campaign to defanaticize Mexico's populace in the 1920s. Calles and his modernizing associates endeavored to curtail the power of the Catholic Church by severely limiting its ability to own property, prohibiting religiously affiliated political parties, outlawing public displays of religiosity and ritual, closing churches, burning idols, limiting the number of priests and registering them with the state, and, as in the extreme case of the state of Tabasco, forcing all clerics to marry.[13] Most of these anticlerical laws and actions had roots in the nineteenth-century wars of reform between Liberals and Conservatives, but had not been a prominent part of the Mexican political landscape since President Porfirio Díaz, the dictator overthrown in the revolution of 1910, had forged a peace between Mexico's two most powerful institutions that lasted almost four decades.[14] While the two postrevolutionary presidents that had preceded Calles had maintained the *modus vivendi* established by Díaz, Calles worried his enemies were conspiring with Church leaders to overthrow him and began to apply the anticlerical provisions of the Constitution to counter the machinations of, as he said, "the political priest, the scheming priest, the priest as exploiter, the priest who intends to keep our people in ignorance, the priest who allies with the hacendado to exploit the campesino, and the priest allied with the industrialist to exploit the worker."[15] In reaction to Calles's provocations, the Archbishop of Mexico, José Mora y del Rio, declared on February 4, 1926 in the newspaper *El Universal* that Mexican Catholics "did not recognize and would fight against" the anticlerical articles of the 1917 Constitution. Calles, who rightly saw the archbishop's statement as a challenge to his authority, briefly detained Mora y del Rio. The President then expelled scores of foreign priests, closed down religious schools, and limited the number of Catholic priests to one per six thousand Mexicans. In reaction, lay Catholic associations organized economic boycotts against the government, prepared for armed conflict, and urged the Catholic hierarchy take a more militant stance against Calles. With the Vatican's acquiescence, Mora y del Rio complied with the demands of the grassroots organizations and announced a religious strike. On July 31, 1926 the Catholic hierarchy shuttered all the churches in Mexico. The country's priests took their vestments and whatever holy accouterments they could carry with them and went into hiding. Some went into the hills to prepare for a holy war against the state, but most moved into the homes of rich patrons. For the first time in over four centuries Mexico's Catholic faithful, especially the poor, were unable to attend mass or receive their sacraments.

Meanwhile, President Calles, an ex-school teacher and a politician with a firm belief in progress and the redeeming power of modernity, was so confident that the religious strike would be the death knell of Catholicism in Mexico that he predicted that "each week without religious ceremonies will cost the Catholic religion 2 percent of its faithful."[16] Between 1926 and 1929 tens of thousands of armed Catholic peasants all over central-west Mexico proved him wrong.[17] The so-called *Cristeros* organized themselves into guerrilla cells and fought the federal government, at the time also attempting to deal with an economic crisis that lowered Mexican GDP by 30 percent, to a stalemate. When three years of civil war and the loss of 100,000 lives did not resolve the conflict, the Church hierarchy, hoping to reestablish a *modus vivendi* with the revolutionary government, agreed to a truce in 1929. The so-called *arreglos* (agreements) ended the civil war, but left many of the participants of the Cristero Rebellion—including Pancha and her family—resentful of the Catholic hierarchy's capitulation, angry at the government's continued attempts to "defanaticize" the Mexican population, and ready to continue defying the state's revolutionary edicts.[18]

Resistance to the government in the postcristero era was most clearly manifested in the popular rejection of both President Lázaro Cárdenas's agrarian reforms and his plans to indoctrinate Mexico's schoolchildren with a curriculum of "socialist education." Ironically, it was ex-president Plutarco Calles's *Grito de Guadalajara* speech in 1934 that energized Catholic resistance against the presidency of Lázaro Cárdenas (1934–1940). In the speech, Calles, out of office but still perceived as the autocrat who actually pulled the strings in the Mexican government, declared, "We ought to seize the consciousness of the children, the consciousness of the youth, because they belong and should belong to the Revolution. . . . It is absolutely necessary to take the enemy out of that trench where the clerics are, where the conservatives [are]. I am referring to the schools . . . With all skill reactionaries state that children belong to their homes and the youth to the family. This is a selfish doctrine, because the children and the youth belong to the community, and it is the Revolution that has the absolute right to seize their consciousness, to root out the prejudices, and to shape a new national soul."[19]

While individual and communal acts of subversion ranged from boycotting government schools to killing government teachers, resistance against socialist education and the redistribution of agrarian land coalesced in Los Altos with the resumption of guerrilla activities known as _La Segunda_ (the Second Cristero Rebellion, 1934–1938).[20] The Segunda was an armed rebellion led by veterans of the first _Cristiada_, foremost among them Lauro Rocha. It was an ideologically incoherent movement lacking popular support from Los Altos' rural population. Still, the armed rebellion worried the moderate wing of the Catholic hierarchy for several reasons. First, they could not support or control the independent action of the guerillas. Second, they feared that the guerrilla's activities would reenergize the more militant sectors of the clergy and their lay supporters. Third, the members of the Church's moderate hierarchy worried that the inflamed passions of these militants had the potential to re-ignite a conflict with a Mexican government that, especially after 1936, had taken a more conciliatory tone towards the Church.[21]

These issues—and a genuine fear that Cárdenas's socialist education and massive land redistribution policies were removing the Mexican peasantry from the control of the Church—encouraged the Catholic clergy to support the creation of _La Unión Nacional Sinarquista_ (UNS).[22] The UNS was organized in 1937 in León, Guanajuato, by social Catholic activists, mostly young lawyers and the sons of wealthy land owners, who were aided and encouraged by the clergy through two poorly understood organizations, _La Legión_ and _La Base_.[23] The goal of the UNS leadership was to continue the struggle against the Mexican revolutionary government, but this time as a social movement that eschewed both institutional politics and armed struggle.[24] Rather than wage a military campaign against the government, or challenge the ruling party at the ballot box, the leadership of the UNS put their faith in a process of moral regeneration in which struggle, faith, and sacrifice would return Mexican society to a premodern Christian idyll that, in spite of the fact that women made up a large percentage of the party's rank-and-file members, they always understood as a masculine space:[25]

> You want bread, justice, and happiness for your children. We want the same thing. You want the land to be yours. YOURS ONLY, like a woman with whom

you are in love, like a woman who has won your heart. And the land must be yours, ONLY YOURS, only yours! Like [a] woman. Not of the politician, not of the leader, not of the cacique, not of the exploiter, No! Yours! . . . Peasants of Mexico: Come to sinarchism, the movement of the men from the fields, the movement of those who love the land and defend it and with it defend the Fatherland.[26]

In this new/old world order the laws of Christ would infuse every aspect of Mexican society. This Catholic Integralism, what Sinarquistas called the Christian Social Order, was meant to restore the social balance and peace of a golden era they believed had existed between the sixteenth and nineteenth century when Mexico had been a colony of the Spanish Catholic crown. According to the Sinarquista version of history, colonial society had been characterized by its Hispanic culture and organized around the Christian medieval principles of tradition and hierarchy. In the intervening centuries, or so the Sinarquistas believed, Mexican culture had been corrupted by waves of foreign influence. The first wave came in the late eighteenth century with the introduction of Enlightenment ideals by the Bourbon kings and their Mason viceroys. This fall from grace continued in the nineteenth century when postindependence liberals, especially the reviled Benito Juárez, further transformed Mexican society by curtailing the power of the Catholic Church and establishing the power of civil society and republican institutions. According to party radicals like Salvador Abascal, who was one of the founders of the UNS,[27] the latest transgression was being perpetuated on Mexico by a revolutionary government whose leaders were mere puppets of both Soviet Communism and North American capitalism: "Soviet Communism and North American capitalism are manifestations of the same revolution . . . whose body is located in fanatic Judaism, whose branches are extended in masonry and Protestantism, and whose fruits were brought forth in the French Revolution, in the Mexican Revolution, and in the Russian Revolution."[28] As was typical of corporatist political movements during this time in Latin America, the Sinarquistas called for the creation of an internally unified nation that followed a "third way" between liberalism and socialism. They wanted to create a nation in which private property was sacrosanct and evenly divided, in which industrial production was abundant, and in which the state, imbued with the spirit of the Catholic faith, intervened to fashion peaceful and just relations between the classes and ensured that the Protestant faith and its materialistic culture was kept north of the US border.[29] This "Christian third way" was reflected in an anthem sung by Sinarquista youth: "The happy victory that we desire is found neither in Moscow nor in *el Norte/* It is Christ's, our flag is God's and it will wave on Mexico's highest peaks./ Worker participate in the factory and in the countryside, [we want] land as property. Marx can have his proletarian world. We want property owners! And there will be peace."[30]

Once in the movement, Sinarquista men were instructed to lead a life of sacrifice, danger, and abnegation. They were to remain convinced in the righteousness of their struggle and, as the document *Ten Norms of Conduct for Sinarquistas* exhorted, confident that in spite of moments of personal insecurity, they had history and God on their side: "If you feel small, unfit, and weak, recover all your strength thinking that God is with you and that he will never abandon you if you know how to wait for everything from him."[31] Throughout the country, the "small, unfit, and weak" people of Mexico responded to the *Sinarquista* call with a torrent of enthusiasm that increased the membership of the organization from 90,000 militants in 1939 to 560,000 members by 1943.[32] Party leaders organized these militants along a strict hierarchical model based on the military. At the top of the hierarchy was a supreme chief who was aided by several subchiefs and a secret committee of about ten people. Below the national leadership, regional committees were usually in charge of administering individual states. Under the regional committees were the municipal committees and the rural subcommittees.[33] The leadership of each municipal committee, like the one Pancha and her family were a part of, consisted of seven people: a municipal chief, a secretary of assemblies, a treasurer, a secretary of propaganda, a secretary of organization and statistics, a secretary of youth, and a secretary of feminine action.[34]

Even though most of the Sinarquista leaders were ultranationalists, their movement became an international phenomenon that was exported by emigrants and *braceros* to the United States and Central America. Nowhere, though, was *Sinarquismo* as fervently and energetically embraced as it was in the Mexican region known as the *Bajío,* which includes the state of Jalisco.[35] Here, as sociologist Nathan Whetten noted in the early 1940s, the recent struggles of the Cristero Rebellion, the revolutionary government's failure to alleviate the economic hardships brought on by ten years of civil war, and an agricultural economic policy that emphasized technology over jobs and favored large Northern farms over land grant communities (the so-called *ejidos*), and small ranchos, created conditions especially conducive to both emigration and the growth of a mass social movement such as *Sinarquismo.*[36] As was true in the rest of Mexico, *Sinarquismo* in the Bajío largely bypassed big cities. Most of the 20,000 Sinarquistas who lived in Jalisco in 1940 resided in small provincial towns.[37] This meant that while the regional committee responsible for organizing the state was located in the capital, Guadalajara, the heart and soul of Sinarquismo was located in municipal and rural subcommittees, like the ones in San Miguel el Alto.

Located less than 100 kilometers from León, Guanajuato, the birthplace of Sinarquismo, San Miguel provided fertile ground for its growth.[38] Social Catholic organizations had been active in the municipality since 1918 when the local clergy and active laypeople, inspired by the doctrines of *Rerum Novarum* and the example of European lay Catholicism, began to organize themselves to "restore Christian social order in Mexico."[39] The term "social Catholicism" connotes a collection of ideologies that enjoyed great popularity in Mexico during the first half of the twentieth century. In spite of many ideological and strategic differences, the individuals and groups that were part of the social Catholic movement in Mexico shared two beliefs: they wanted to maintain the social, economic, and political privileges that the Catholic Church had enjoyed prior to the Mexican Revolution, and they believed that in order to do so, they had to organize themselves and fight against the encroachments of a modernizing (sometimes liberal, at other times socialistic) Mexican state.

Social Catholic activism seems to have started in San Miguel in 1918. In that year the interim governor of the state of Jalisco, Manuel Bouquet Jr., issued decrees that limited the number of priests to a ratio of one per five thousand inhabitants and required them to register with the state government. Failure to do so would result in one to eleven months in jail and a fine of ten to two hundred pesos. The decrees, as well as the arrest of Archbishop Francisco Orozco y Jiménez, elicited a statewide response from Catholics. One anonymous flyer titled "Be Alert Catholics: The seven plagues or capital sins of the Carrancista Government of Jalisco" listed reasons why the decrees were harmful to Mexican Catholicism and its priesthood: 1) they limited the number of priests in the state; 2) when registering, priests would have to be photographed like common criminals, "*rateros*"; 3) priests would be punished with penalties usually reserved for delinquents; 4) suppressing the Catholic Church would open the door to "heretical cults"; 5) they would establish the grounds for the state government to harass priest; 6) the municipal government would be empowered with the authority to monitor local priests; and 7) the police could monitor priests as if they were "bands of dangerous criminals." The flyer also listed seven "virtues" or actions that Catholics should take to counteract the government's anticlerical laws. These included not sending children to schools "without God," not patronizing movie theaters and other "immoral diversions," not attending mass until priests were able to freely conduct the business of the Church, boycotting the purchase of "luxury" items at clothing stores, and not paying taxes.[40] San Miguel's Catholic activists heeded the call to action by protesting in the streets and sending the state government two letters of protest (1,096 *Sanmiguelenses* signed the petition dated September 5, 1918) demanding the repeal of the new law. They made this request as Mexican citizens who had the inalienable right to petition their government (Article VII of the 1917 Constitution) and as Catholics whose "individual liberty of conscience" had been "injured" by the decrees. Beyond the question of individual religious freedom, the signatories insisted that the state's laws "profoundly injured the religious sentiments of almost all the population who has been led to believe that it is free and sovereign." In other words, what was at stake for Catholics was, beyond how many priests the state allowed in their town, the very important issue of who was going to define the moral, individual, and public culture of Mexican society.[41] Catholic protests around Jalisco and an organized boycott forced the state government to rescind the decrees in February 1919, but it was a conflict that both parties (using similar strategies) were destined to replay in 1926 during the lead up to the Cristero Rebellion.

The militancy of Catholic social activism in San Miguel coincided with, and was energized by, a shift in land tenure that made agricultural land more difficult to acquire. Indeed for poor families like the Morenos, the first two decades of the twentieth century brought many unsettling changes: revolution, emigration, local and national political instability, state-sponsored anticlericalism (including the expropriation of Church buildings to establish public schools in 1914), and the arrival of typhoid fever (1916), the Spanish influenza (1918), electricity (1919), and the automobile (1920). These changes radicalized Catholic notions of the relationship between their faith, justice, and the world outside their small town.[42] In the context of these changes, social Catholicism's emphasis on Catholic traditionalism, and its opposition to liberalism, modern ideas, and the redistribution of land, resonated among San Miguel's lower classes and small property owners and prepared them for their subsequent participation in the Cristiada and Sinarquismo.

In the postcristero era, social Catholic activists in San Miguel organized themselves into a potent civic force around a charismatic shoemaker named Gregorio Román. Román was Pancha Moreno's uncle; he was an ex-cristero and a fearsomely energetic man who after the Mexican Revolution channeled his love of the Catholic Church and his hatred of the revolutionary government into organizing Catholic militancy in his hometown. In 1939, Román and some like-minded people, including his *compadre* Jesús Delgado, organized a *Sinarquista* municipal committee in San Miguel. Román was chosen to be the chief of the committee while Delgado ran weekly education meetings from his house where Sinarquistas gathered to strategize and learn the tenets of their movement. Neither man was new to the social Catholic movement; both had helped organize a Catholic worker's union in San Miguel in 1918, the same year they signed the petition to repeal the laws that limited the number of priests in Jalisco.[43] In the intervening years, Gregorio Román and Jesús Delgado's continued activism legitimized their positions as lay Catholic leaders in the municipality of San Miguel.

During this turbulent time, Pancha had also become a force in the social Catholic movement. So much so that her uncle Gregorio appointed her the Secretary of Feminine Action for the Sinarquista Party. Their familial connection and the fact that Pancha was a thirty-eight-year-old single woman with almost twenty years of experience as a Catholic activist made her an ideal choice for the position. She in turn appointed her niece and nephew—Obdulia and Jesús Orozco—cosecretaries of the Children's Action Committee. Her parents, Luz Moreno and Secundina Román Moreno, and two of her sisters, Victorina and Ysabel, also joined the Sinarquistas—but only Pancha was part of the *Sinarquista* leadership. Thanks to the efforts of Gregorio Román, Jesús Delgado, Pancha Moreno, and a wide range of working people in San Miguel, Sinarquismo became, by the early 1940s, a social movement whose growing popularity worried local authorities. This concern is highlighted in a report written by San Miguel's municipal President to the region's military commander in 1940:

A *Sinarquista* group, that though small in number, works against the social and political interests of the Government, [and is] supported in moral form by the sympathizers of *Almazán*, has organized itself [in San Miguel]. On the 24th of March [1940] . . . there took place a *Sinarquista* public meeting in the *Plaza de Armas* of this town. During the meeting those who spoke insulted the authorities of the country and were attempting to disorient the people about the ideological and social principles established by [our government]. On the 28th of this month, this group once again organized a public meeting in the above-mentioned place during which, in addition to affirming the above-mentioned concepts, they nearly incited the public (which certainly numbered around fifty percent of the population) to rebel against the government.[44]

Pancha was at this rally, as she was for the many public protests she helped organize in and around San Miguel. While the Sinarquista's national male leadership attempted to limit women's participation in the movement to gender-appropriate activities, Pancha's energy and intelligence earned her

Executive Board of Sinarquista Girls: Obdulia Orozco (President) is the second from the left. San Miguel el Alto, c. 1940. Courtesy of Obdulia Orozco.

Executive Board of Sinarquista Boys: Jesús Orozco (President) is the first from the left. San Miguel el Alto, c. 1940. Courtesy of Obdulia Orozco.

the respect of the municipal committee's inner circle and enabled her to participate in the movement beyond the limits set by the Sinarquista's *Ten Norms of Conduct for the Sinarquista Women*. These norms circumscribed female Sinarquista participation to traditionally gendered roles. Women were instructed to "cultivate in the heart of the man and the child a great love for the Fatherland"; to not "betray your beautiful destiny as a woman by undertaking manly tasks"; to not "rest until all the members of your family participate in Sinarquista action; [and to] not protect cowardice or indolence."[45] Pancha both observed and flouted the gender restrictions of her male superiors. As a first-rate *modista* (seamstress) she sewed the Sinarquista and Mexican flags that militants carried during the marches that were the focal point of Sinarquista political action. A vocal and confrontational force during public rallies, she undertook the "manly task" of organizing the marches, monitoring discipline, and confronting government soldiers who stood in the way of the advancement of the Sinarquista crowds.[46] She also helped cook meals to feed the rank and file, participated in the education of Sinarquista children activists, and sewed the outfits her nieces wore when they handed out water and lemons during Sinarquista rallies.[47] But just as frequently, Pancha traveled with her uncle around San Miguel's ranchos to recruit peasants and small property owners for the movement. In this role she was invaluable to the male Sinarquista leadership. Pancha facilitated party recruitment efforts because she was intimate with both the terrain around the town and the rural families who knewand respected her because she and her mother had delivered many of their children.[48]

For Pancha both types of political labor (those that more closely hewed to the gender expectations of the Sinarquista leadership, and those that did not) were the natural extension of her life as a dutiful Mexican and a good Catholic woman. Like many lay members of the social Catholic movement, especially other women, private virtue was bound to public displays of faith. Indeed, it was women's assumed religiosity, innate moral superiority, and their central role in socializing children that helped the Church justify the establishment of women's Catholic organizations such as the Union of Mexican Catholic Ladies during so-called Second Reconquest of the early part of the twentieth century.[49] In the small towns of the provinces the creation and maintenance of this "extra-domestic" space gave women like Pancha a role in public life, a political voice outside their homes, and a crucial place in the militant organizations and forms of resistance (from boycotts, to unions, to armed rebellion) that Mexican lay Catholicism had creatively absorbed from the revolutionary tumult of the 1910s and 1920s.[50] This was especially true during the Cristero Rebellion and thereafter, when the crisis of the Church–State conflict opened up the possibility for lay Catholics to shoulder more responsibilities for keeping and administering aspects of the Church's ministry that had normally been the domain of men or priests.[51]

Women were so important to lay Catholic organizations that they invariably attracted the attention of the radical anticlerics who came to prominence in the late 1920s and exerted political and social influence in Mexico throughout most of the 1930s.[52] To these mostly male, rationalist, progressive, and materialist revolutionaries, Catholic women were the embodiment of the irrationalism and obscurantism that they believed prevented Mexico from becoming a modern, industrialized nation. Because they shared with their Catholic counterparts the belief that women were the transmitters of family values, education, and religious morality, anticlerics made Catholic women (and their children) the targets of their modernizing zeal. Indeed, while their attack on the Catholic Church and on religious education was ostensibly a cultural offensive developed by modernizers to change the habits and minds of all Mexicans, in practice, as the historian Patience Schell notes, "anticlericalism was a program developed by men and aimed at women and children."[53]

In addition to her work with the Sinarquistas, Pancha was one of the main organizers of the town's annual religious festivals. These celebrations commemorate the crucifixion and resurrection of Jesus Christ during Holy Week and honor the patron saint of the town, Saint Michael, in late September. Pancha tailored the costumes for the women and children who posed as angels, holy virgins, or Roman soldiers on the parade floats (*carros alegoricos*) and the popular *cuadros plasticos*, a local version of the *tableau vivant*. She also used old Sears catalogues to pattern hundreds of tailor-made dresses for the women of San Miguel to parade around in during "*las fiestas*."[54] These activities were important in a town where clothes could not be purchased off the rack. Inside the Moreno household Pancha's income helped support her extended family and provide material comfort for her aging father. Because Secundina Moreno's job as a midwife took her away from home for days on end, Pancha, when she did not accompany her mother, was often left to cook for Luz, listen to his worries, wash his clothes, and take him to political rallies.

Between 1940 and 1950, life for the Morenos had settled into a predictable, if not peaceful, pattern dominated by the habits and rituals of the family, work, politics, and the Catholic Church. Secundina Moreno continued her work as a midwife. Pancha, Ysabel, and Victorina managed the Moreno household, produced women's clothing, participated in the church

Religious float (*carros alegórico*), c. 1947. Courtesy of Obdulia Orozco.

choir, helped organize the town's festivals, and kept attending Sinarquista meetings, even though by the mid-1940s the movement had squandered most of its energy in political infighting, financial mismanagement, and utopian colonization schemes.[55] The Moreno men, mostly politically apathetic, continued to dedicate themselves to music, agriculture, shoemaking, and dreaming about life in the United States.[56] In his seventh decade of life, Luz retired from his work in the fields. His son Bonifacio (Chito) lent him a donkey that Luz used to gather, transport, and sell potting soil from the surrounding countryside to the people of San Miguel. At home, the elderly patriarch of the Moreno clan dealt with his mounting physical ailments and an interminable series of familial dramas comforted by the

Religious float, c. 1947. Courtesy of Obdulia Orozco.

unquestioned belief that he would spend his remaining years surrounded by the family he loved.[57]

In 1950, this calm was suddenly and irrevocably shattered when Pancha, then forty-nine years old, married her childhood sweetheart, Juan Rivera, and left San Miguel. Juan, a dark man with African features, a sharp mind, and a controlling temperament, had spent his early years in San Miguel working as a barber, a shoemaker (with Pancha's uncles), and—despite being a fervent anticleric—helping his father make the rosaries the family sold during the Lenten season. In 1916, Juan met the fifteen-year-old Pancha at her uncle Gregorio's shoemaking shop. After secretly courting her for several months, Juan asked Luz and Secundina Moreno for their oldest daughter's hand in matrimony. The Moreno family—fearful of his temper, repelled by his anticlericalism, and worried by his reputation for being lazy—refused to let the young couple marry.

Furious at the repudiation, Juan immigrated to Santa Barbara, California, where he moved in with his sister, Petra. After spending a couple of years there, he moved north to Stockton, California. Long a center for provisioning gold miners with goods and transportation, Stockton's elite turned to exploiting the rich soils of the San Joaquin River Delta in the late nineteenth century. While farming machinery was manufactured there (the company that became Caterpillar was founded in Stockton in 1883), the elites' wealth was more dependent on their access to cheap immigrant labor. Chinese, Italian, Japanese, Punjabi, Filipino, and, increasingly, Mexican immigrants came to Stockton and its surrounding areas attracted by the promise of jobs that paid more than those in their impoverished home countries. Their presence in and around Stockton made the community one of the most ethnically diverse regions of California.[58] But by World War II Mexican workers began to replace other groups as the preferred labor force in the fields of the Central Valley. Several factors account for the shift from a primarily Filipina/o labor force before the war to one in which Mexicans made up over half of the workers in Stockton's fields and canneries in the 1960s. Among the most important of these were the opening of the Port of Stockton in 1933 and the influx of government investment for the construction of transportation infrastructure, military munitions factories, shipbuilding facilities, and a naval depot to supply the Pacific fleet during World War II. These factors diversified Stockton's economy and opened up work opportunities for Filipina/os as soldiers and industrial workers. The region's agriculturalists felt the Filipina/o absence so acutely that when the Bracero Program was initiated in 1942, as a binational agreement to provide contract Mexican workers to the United States to alleviate wartime labor shortages in the agriculture and railroad industries of the American Southwest, the first contingent of braceros contracted and processed by the US Department of Agriculture was assigned (five hundred strong) to Stockton farms. Their labor saved the asparagus crop, weakened the influence and militancy of Filipino labor unions, helped the region's larger farmers consolidate their power over smaller producers, and accelerated the flow of Mexican immigrants (both documented and not) into the San Joaquin Valley.[59] Among these migrants was Juan Rivera.

During his time in the United States, Juan never forgot his childhood sweetheart or the slight to his honor he had received at the hands of her family. In 1950 Juan, then fifty years old, and working as an itinerant fruit and vegetable vendor in Stockton, decided it was time to return to

Mexico to marry his girlfriend.[60] Juan's reappearance in San Miguel set off a series of drunken episodes by Pancha's brothers, who rightly saw him and his plans to marry Pancha, their beloved and most productive sister, as a threat to their family.[61] Out of a wrong-headed sense of masculinity and a fear of losing Pancha, they "protected" their older sister's honor as if she were still the teenager Juan had courted three decades earlier. Pancha was hardly in need of her brothers' protection.[62] She loved Juan, had secretly corresponded with him over the years, and wanted to get married.[63] Still, her brothers threatened Juan with violence. They drank themselves into self-righteous rages, hounded Juan, and attempted to guilt Pancha into abandoning her plans by telling her that "it would be better if you took a gun and killed your parents" (c. June 1950). Juan refused to back down. He was not leaving San Miguel this time without marrying Pancha. At an impasse, one of Secundina's uncles prevailed on Luz and his wife to give Pancha and Juan their blessing. He convinced them that if they did not graciously accept the marriage, the determined couple would leave San Miguel without their approval.[64] Fearing the shame that elopement would bring their family, knowing how strong-willed Pancha was, and anxious not to hurt their favorite daughter's feelings, Luz and Secundina reluctantly acquiesced. Juan and Pancha were married in February 1950.[65] At the reception, her mother served the turkey *mole* she normally prepared for visiting dignitaries, and her brothers played music.[66] Luz attended the ceremony, ate mole, and then retired to his room.

After the wedding, which Juan paid for with the money he received from selling his parent's house in San Miguel, he left for Stockton to start the process of getting his new bride's immigration papers in order.[67] Pancha followed him several months later. In Stockton, she settled into a life dominated by her work in the canneries, her domestic duties, her commitment to the local Catholic Church, and her responsibilities, financial and otherwise, to the family she left behind in Mexico. Each aspect of her life in San Miguel had an equivalent in Stockton, but rather than expanding her horizons, life in the United States seems to have diminished her existence.[68] The Catholic Church still provided her with a home for her spiritual life, one that was even more important to her in the overwhelmingly Protestant country she had immigrated to. But attending church in Stockton, which she tried to do daily, could not inspire the spiritual passion, piety, and revolutionary praxis, much less replicate the public sociability that her cristero and Sinarquista activities in Mexico had. At almost fifty, Pancha was proud that she had managed to get and keep a job, especially because she had to wrest assent for working outside the house away from her extremely domineering husband.[69] But having her life revolve around the temporal needs of the agricultural cycle of California's Central Valley and the industrial rhythms of the canneries was a poor substitute for the sense of personal accomplishment and financial independence that she had enjoyed in San Miguel. She made more money in the canneries, which allowed her to continue supporting her family in San Miguel.[70] But the trade-off—living two thousand miles from her close-knit kin—hardly seemed worth it. In Stockton, Pancha's relationship to her family was mediated by the rather more cold and tenuous links that money, memories, hopes, and letters provided. Even the singing birds that she kept seemed to announce to her that her life had become a little less vibrant. In San Miguel, Pancha and her sisters kept caged *cenzontles* (mockingbirds) on their patios. In Stockton, Pancha replaced these aristocratic and voluble masters of song with less-talented canaries. The canaries reminded Pancha of her life in San Miguel, but they also reminded her that life in the United States was but a fainter, paler version of her previous existence.

Pancha's age and sudden departure set tongues wagging in San Miguel, but the fact that she had immigrated to California could not have come as a surprise to the peripatetic San Miguelenses. Pancha's neighbors in San Miguel and in their corner of Jalisco had been leaving their homes to work in the United States since the late nineteenth century,[71] and most of them understood the allure of the United States and appreciated the advantages that came with selling their labor for dollars instead of pesos.[72] Indeed, after

Panch and Juan sitting in the backyard of their home on East Market Street, 1958. Courtesy of Obdulia Orozco.

Pancha left, her brothers started to plot their exodus to the Promised Land. The first one to leave was her youngest brother, Cecilio. Chilo, as he was called, left San Miguel several months after Pancha in 1950 to work picking cotton in Arizona as part of the Bracero Program.[73] He was one of the estimated 4.6 million Mexican braceros contracted during the program's existence from 1942 to 1964. The program was immensely important in shaping a culture of emigration in regions like Los Altos and small towns like San Miguel.[74] Such movement had been a fact of life for Alteños since the railroad that connected the US border with Guadalajara was finished in 1888.[75] Not only did the railroad allow Alteños to travel north, it also facilitated the presence of American recruiters who penetrated the interior of Mexico to enlist laborers.[76] The so-called *enganche* system was weakened as Alteños, wary of its abuses, began to avoid recruiters and learned from returning emigrants how and where to travel to work in the United States. In the early part of the twentieth century several key events energized large-scale emigration, both legal and illegal. One of the most important was the Cristero Rebellion. During the three years that the war between the federal army and the cristero soldiers engulfed the region, many municipal authorities forcefully concentrated the rural population in the municipal capitals as a way of keeping the guerrilla cristeros from their rural allies.[77] These *reconcentraciones* exacerbated the effects of the military battles by increasing economic and social insecurity and creating the conditions that fostered an epidemic of smallpox in 1928.[78] They also drove many Alteños who had chosen not to fight into temporary or permanent flight. This exodus was commented on at the time by the newspaper *Excelsior*: "We have seen that in some days there have not been enough buses and automobiles . . . to transport the passengers who leave. As for the peasants, it is obvious that as soon as they finish harvesting their crops, which are bought by the speculators [*acaparadores*] at a very low price, they go elsewhere, especially to the United States."[79]

Many of these immigrants were repatriated during the Great Depression, but their presence, their knowledge, their stories, their stuff, and the glimmer in their eyes when they talked about el Norte, while initially ridiculed by those who had not left, soon fired the collective imagination of the region and helped normalize the idea of leaving the country as a life strategy.[80] Since the turn of the century they had been recruited by American agents or migrated on their own using the information given to them by other migrants. The Bracero Program changed these patterns. Coming at the precise moment when a shift in the local rural economy from subsistence farming and animal husbandry to one increasingly centered on the less labor-intensive production of dairy products was making it more difficult for Alteños to sustain themselves and their families through agricultural work,[81] the program systematized the inchoate movement of brave and desperate individuals into a mass social, economic, and cultural phenomenon.[82] Most Alteños stayed in Mexico; but many, like most of the Morenos, eventually migrated to the United States.[83] As Luz Moreno reveals in his letters, they did so willingly with a headstrong desperation that was energized and tempered by the machinations of larger economic and political structures, but never solely defined by them. Their government may have been, at times, glad to see them go, low wages, high inflation, and low employment may have pushed them out, and the industrialized agricultural behemoth of the American Southwest may have been an irresistible attraction, but in many ways Alteños migrated because they wanted to.[84]

Such was the Alteño enthusiasm for the Bracero Program during the post-WWII era that while Luz and his generation could only imagine themselves working the land as their parents and grandparents had, a large segment of men and women in the municipality could not imagine a future that did not involve migration to the United States. In his letters to Pancha, Luz Moreno characterizes the enthusiasm that his neighbors in San Miguel had for the Bracero Program as a form of collective insanity (April 21, 1951; July 14, 1951; September 11, 1951; October 22, 1951). The insane and desperate workers of Los Altos, though, could only become braceros if they participated in a bureaucratic game that favored very few with a golden ticket to the US. Every year, the municipal government held a lottery in the central plaza for men interested in the program. A state commission (*La Comisión Intersecretarial Encargada de los Asuntos de los Trabajadores Emigrantes*) allotted a certain number of permissions for each municipality and only men who were unskilled laborers, unemployed, and between the age of twenty and forty were allowed to apply. Men who were public employees, or who had received an ejido land grant from the government, were expressly prohibited from applying. The commission put these restrictions to ensure that local economies were not deprived of skilled laborers and that the United States received workers who were both motivated and in the prime of their working lives. In 1947, 688 men applied for one of the forty spots that the commission had allotted to the municipality of San Miguel. This number, which included all three of Luz's sons, his son-in-law, and his brother-in-law, represented about 35 percent of San Miguel's male population between the ages of twenty and thirty-nine. In 1948 the Commission apportioned the municipality fifty-four spots but only 325 men, about 16 percent of San Miguel's eligible men, applied to the program.[85] Of this subset of the population, 68 percent lived in town of San Miguel; the rest lived in the countryside (26 percent), or in one of the smaller towns in the municipality like San José de Reynoso (6 percent). The average age of the applicant was thirty years.[86]

Mexican and US officials had hoped the Bracero Program would reduce illegal immigration, but one of the consequences of the disparity between the small numbers of permissions allotted every year to municipalities like San Miguel and the desperation of poor workers was an increase in the flow of undocumented workers to el Norte.[87] In 1943, a year after the Bracero Program was implemented, 8,860 Mexicans were deported from the United States; ten years later the number of deported undocumented workers soared one hundred times to 885,587.[88] Luz was pessimistic about this culture of migration and the attendant affective and materialist desires it created among the poor. He saw emigration as a threat to his religion, to the coherence of his family, and to the viability of a way of life that he once believed was immutable. It was not only that people were leaving; it was that people were changing, and with them, and because of them, his town and his family was changing also. Emigration, as he continually reminded Pancha, was reorienting the culture and priorities of everyone around him: "Many go illegally to that Promised Land in search of the Dollar and they give more importance to it than to tending the corn in their own country. Compared to the Dollar, everything seems to be stacked against corn . . . What shall we do? Shall we only eat Dollars?" (September 15, 1951).[89]

Luz, Pancha, and thousands of Mexicans had become cristeros or joined the Sinarquistas to prevent, or at least mitigate, some of the most pernicious effects of a modern world that valued mobility more than rootedness, and secularism and materialism more than religious spirituality and ritual. Seeing his daughter move to Stockton and the wanderlust that consumed his sons and his nephews highlighted for Luz the fact that in very tangible ways, they had failed. Like the people of the town of San José de Gracia, Michoacán, San Miguel's desperate but optimistic men "rubbed their hands in anticipation" of immigrating to the United States, and "no power on earth could stop them."[90] All Luz could hope for was that not all his children would leave, that Pancha would return periodically to visit him, that she would send money to support him and his large extended family, and that their epistolary embraces would be strong and warm enough to keep their relationship alive across the great distance that separated them.[91] Pancha, for her part, must have hoped for many of the same things. Then, in the moments of sheer desperation that must have come over her as she realized how difficult it was to live in a strange land with strange people, as she pondered the obligations that came with answering the letters her father wrote her, and as she weakened under the weight of the responsibilities that came with maintaining the happiness and financial well-being of such a large family, she must have just sat down and cried.[92] She loved her father and her family, but sometimes she just tired of wrestling with her obligations to her absent ones.

Moreno-Román Family tree, c. 1950.

CHAPTER 2

"Follow Your Path My Beloved Children, Go in Peace"

On Saying Goodbye and Keeping in Contact

Which of the two lovers suffers the most sorrow
The one who stays, or the one who leaves?
The one who stays is left crying
The one who leaves, goes sighing

"The Farewell"[1]

As a man of seventy-three, Luz Moreno had expected that his oldest daughter, Pancha, would be present to see him through his last years on Earth. It was not an outrageous expectation. While people in San Miguel had been migrating to the United States for decades, including Pancha's *novio* (boyfriend) Juan, the only person in Luz Moreno's extended family to leave prior to 1950 was his brother-in-law, Hilario Román. Hilario fought in Pancho Villa's army during the Mexican Revolution, and then moved to Oregon, where he worked as a lumberjack and as a bootlegger during Prohibition. Eventually his undocumented status and his illegal activities captured the attention of local authorities, who sent him back to Mexico. In San Miguel Hilario joined Jalisco's ruling party, the Revolutionary National Party (*Partido Nacional Revolucionario* or PNR), and, like many veterans of the Revolution, used his political connections to get a state job. He became chief of police in the municipality of San Miguel: it was an odd

Hilario Román, membership card for the National Revolutionary Party, 1933. Courtesy of Obdulia Orozco.

fate considering his law-breaking past, but one that fit his authoritarian personality, his military experience, and his penchant for legally suspect activities.

Pancha, though, was not Hilario. If Hilario was prone to risks, illegal activity, and flight, Pancha was constitutionally made for staying put, obeying the rule of (God's) law, and fighting. These qualities made her, in fact, if not in name, the *mandamás* (the shot caller) of a large and fractious family where none of the men, including her father, were strong-willed and responsible enough to question or usurp her authority. She was the primary breadwinner, she helped take care of and feed a growing brood of nieces and nephews, and she assisted her sisters and sisters-in-law in the seemingly never-ending job of keeping her often-inebriated brothers out of trouble. She was, as anyone in the family will affirm, *la ley*—the law—but she was also Luz's most intimate confidant. The titular head of the Moreno family loved his firstborn because she listened to him when others in the family ignored him, tended to his physical ailments when others tired of his complaints, and gave him spending money when others thought he was foolish to spend his allowance on newspapers. Pancha anchored Luz Moreno's life as old age made him less capable of controlling the world around him. But then Pancha married a man most of her family detested and moved to a country that he, Pancha, and all their fellow Sinarquistas saw as the source of many of the evils that had befallen Mexico since its independence in 1821. Her departure left Luz sad and the Morenos in an emotional pall and bewildered state that Obdulia Orozco describes as form of blindness: "When Pancha left, we were left blind."[2] The Morenos had lived in San Miguel in the warmth of each other's physical proximity enacting roles that had long been defined by their shared sense of family, culture, tradition, history, and hopes for the future.[3] Pancha's departure severed the seemingly natural and reciprocal link between place (San Miguel el Alto) and the family's understanding of itself. The sudden insertion of two thousand miles of "empty space" between daughter and family reconfigured the Moreno clan into a transnational entity linked by affect, imagination, memory, money, the written word, and the impersonal bureaucracies that carried their correspondence across great distances.[4] Like many people separated by the growing Mexican diaspora, Pancha and Luz Moreno depended on letters (which he wrote every eight days and seem to have taken two weeks to arrive) to transcend the "blue distances" that separated them (March 7, 1951).[5] But building a transnational relationship—one in which the very definition of what it meant to be a father or a daughter was fluid and vulnerable—does not happen naturally. Rather, defining familial roles, managing absence, forging affective bonds, and leveraging memories to do so requires modes of thinking, doing, feeling, representing, and behaving that have to be consciously and constantly negotiated and maintained by all the parties involved. Even the most mundane aspects of creating and sustaining an old, but often fragile and rapidly changing, relationship—finding the time, place, and energy to sit down and write a letter, budgeting the money to buy postage, paper, ink, and nibs and deciding where, when, and how often to write—requires mutually agreed-upon commitments and individually refined skills. While most of the Moreno siblings were literate, it was Luz who set out to write the letters that he hoped would keep the Morenos a family. The first order of business on this account was overcoming the hurt and anger that Pancha and Juan felt as a result of the abuse they had endured in the weeks prior to their marriage.[6]

Luz is nothing if not thorough in his self-appointed task as the family's epistolary clerk: he revisits the events surrounding Pancha's departure and apologizes for his family's behavior; he tells her that he loves her, that he remembers her, and that he, her extended family, and many people in San Miguel miss her. He advises her to forgive her brothers who were only acting out because they loved her and because they were drunk. He also tells her that he is not upset that she has married; rather, he is upset that she has moved so far away and that all he wants is to "live in peace, communicating constantly . . . [in order] to endure this cruel separation that causes us harm" (c. May, 1950; c. September, 1950; c. June, 1950; c. 1951).

The use of the plural "us" is interesting. Luz is acknowledging the contract that he hopes will sustain his correspondence with Pancha, but also implicitly including Juan Rivera. The inclusion of the formerly reviled Juan reflected the fact that Luz was using his letters to repair his relationship not only with his oldest daughter, but also with his new son-in-law. To this end, Luz addressed his letters not to his daughter, but to "Juan and Pancha" or to his "Beloved Ausentes [Absent Ones]." He also tried to endear himself to the couple by using rhetorical strategies that were at once obsequious and strategic: he referred to Juan by his diminutive, Juanito; he asked for forgiveness for past offenses;[7] he lauded Juan's personal qualities;[8] and he insisted that the Morenos, most of whom he says love Juan,[9] were better off for his presence in their lives: "Ever since Juanito became a member of our house, God's mercy has been admirable. For as long as Juanito is Juanito and Pancha is Pancha we . . . will live securely" (October 20, 1952; c. 1951).

Luz's epistolary Juanito seems to have very little in common with the man who showed up in San Miguel, unannounced and unwanted, to marry Pancha. When Obdulia Orozco was asked about this incongruity, she offered a practical explanation: "Pancha married Juan, if he [Luz] did not establish a friendly relationship with him, Juan could have made Pancha's life difficult."[10] Luz understood and respected the rights and privileges that patriarchy conferred on Juan. Even though Pancha had not been submissive to anyone while she was single, Luz understood that she had abdicated this independence when she got married. Luz also understood that it was Juan, not Pancha, who had lived among the American infidels for thirty years; it was he who knew English, it was he who could drive a car, and it was he who had all the social connections in Stockton that Pancha needed to live and work. Luz conjured Juan into Juanito because the loving father could hardly afford to alienate the man who had power to shape Pancha's new life in the United States;[11] without Juan, Pancha was without language and without family; a voiceless stranger in a hostile land. This, along with the demands of civility, explains why Luz Moreno also reimagined the narrative of Pancha and Juan's tumultuous union into a romantic epic—a love story in which the Morenos went from being the victims to becoming the bad guys who almost impeded a relationship sanctioned by God: "Because there is never anything that is good that is also not coveted, from the most tender of ages Juanito loved her. If they did not get together early on it was in order not to contradict [our] weak opposition. Still, that love resurfaced later with an unstoppable resolution. The merits of her new life, who can say? Let Juanito, who is her breath of life, who feels the palpitations of her heart, who is one with her, who will die with her united in the Lord, [let him] speak on these matters" (c. November 18, 1951).

Francisca Moreno, c 1925. Courtesy of Obdulia Orozco.

This imagined courtship is only one example of the inventive and touching ways Luz used his correspondence to envelop Pancha and Juan with a constant flow of affect, useful information, creative narratives, and invented characters (Juanito, Papá Luz, *los ausentes*) that he hoped would bridge the miles between them. If Pancha could not be with her family in San Miguel, Luz was determined to use his correspondence, as the following excerpt clearly and movingly shows, to convey to his daughter a sense of the places and people she was missing:

I would like to take you through the countryside, over the hills, to the little hill of *Cristo Rey*, to el *Cerro Grande* (the Big Hill), to el *Cerro de la Llave* (the Hill

Juan Rivera, c. 1920. Courtesy of Obdulia Orozco.

of the Key), and to *el Cerro de las Bateas* (the Hill of the Washtub): [I would like to take you] to the towns that surround San Miguel so you could see how the rainy season approaches: how [the sky looks] so full of clouds, so full of heat, and how a mist almost completely covers the hills. [I would like you to] hear the songs of the little birds—the happiest of them, the Mockingbird— and to hear the bees, also. The trees are blooming and look very green; the cacti are full of tunas. It rained on the plain only once and it is blooming once again. The bishop's weed flowered in beautifully. In March they flowered after only a slight rainfall. [Oh, if you could only] see the *campesinos* on the hills working on their fallow land. On Sundays, there is only talk of the sowing. Imagine yourselves here in your town surrounded by all the human bundles that make up your family. From the oldest to the infants who are still in their mother's arms, so full of life, so talkative . . . Just imagine yourself here. (May 26, 1951)

The excerpt conjures up a Chagall-like image of Luz Moreno holding his daughter's hand while flying through the night sky across the rural landscape of San Miguel. This flight of fancy, along with others where he dreams of growing wings so he can fly to Stockton, may appear to be quaint and inconsequential; but they are extremely important because it is through memories and images of the places and times that they shared that Luz attempts to "lift" Pancha "out of conventional time-space" and give both of them a phantom sense of physical intimacy.[12] Pancha reciprocated Luz's evocations of space and memory by sending her father postcards and photographs of the United States—and, on one occasion, a photograph of worn-torn Korea (c. April 1951). These visual stimuli helped Luz imagine the material and social landscape of Pancha's new life (her house, her dog, Stockton, and San Francisco), temporarily closed the distance between them, and, as he wrote, "calmed [his] desires to see" her (August 7, 1951, c. July 14, 1951). Letters, photos, gifts, and money also reinforced fragile memories by confirming the absent loved one's continuing presence in the world.[13] Every time Luz touched the objects that Pancha had touched, he could say to himself: "My daughter (who I am now imagining in a factory canning tomatoes) placed these dollars in this envelope." Conversely, with every letter that appeared in Pancha's hands she could think to herself: "My father (who I now see sitting in his room hunched over scribbling on this paper) inked these words, folded this paper, and licked this seal."[14]

Often, though, the imaginary encounters that the postcards, photographs, and letters facilitated between Luz and his absent ones only increased their anxiety. While these offerings gave Luz and Pancha a measure of the human contact they craved, the memories that were engendered by the missives weighed on the writers because they were melancholic reminders that their best, happiest moments were in the past.[15] This was especially true for the elder Luz, for whom the past tense "it was" was more meaningful than the present "it is" or the future "it will be" (March 7, 1951). This haunting, and the anxiety it produces, seems to be inherent to the letter-writing process. This is because epistolary discourse and the technology of the postal service make it impossible to speak in the present. A time lag "haunts epistolary language," and even the most committed correspondents have a difficult time using letters to smooth out the immense discontinuities that space and time impose on their relationship.[16] Indeed, the necessarily serialized nature of the written correspondence creates an alternative and extremely personal, but very fragile, time dimension whose rhythm and chronology are defined by several unstable factors: the transnational nature of the relationship between Pancha and Luz, the efficiency and affordability of the technology they used to convey their sentiments, the mode of transportation used in the United States and Mexico to deliver the mail (planes, trains, trucks, bikes, and humans), and the dedication of each writer to the correspondence.[17] While letter-writers can control some factors in this machinery, they cannot control, for example, the efficiency and honesty of the national postal services, the punctuality of the local postmaster, or the vagaries of inclement weather.[18] A failure at any of these junctures could disrupt the rhythm of the epistolary relationship so that it ceases to resemble the type of conversation that correspondents like Pancha and Luz craved. Luz Moreno feared interruptions in communication and unexpected silences because they were reminders that Pancha's presence could not be assured beyond the date of her last letter. Letters lean forward toward hope and life, but the loss or delay of a letter resulted in what father and daughter feared most—a silence that, as Luz writes, extinguished hope with intimations of despair and death: "If there is anything that [would] oblige us to keep silent or to suspend our mailing of letters, whether it be because of illness, or for whatever motive, it would be good to know. Silence can occur for many reasons. . . . Here, if only eight days go by without you answering our letters we become very worried. But if you tell us the motives [for this silence] we will rest easily, or not, depending on the reason [for the interruption]."[19]

Once Luz had apologized to Pancha and Juan for the Moreno's many indiscretions, once they had developed epistolary versions of themselves and integrated them into an evolving, collaborative narrative about their separation, and once they had accepted that no matter their dedication there was no effective way of totally mitigating the effects of their physical separation, time became the ausente's enemy. Things were happening in San Miguel that Pancha was not there to witness and could only be informed about days or weeks after the fact. Luz used his letters to keep her in time with the place, people, and traditions she left behind (March 9, 1952). In some letters he narrates the natural changes in Pancha's immediate family and closest friends: family members were growing older, friends were dying, nephews and nieces were maturing into young adults, and his body and mind were declining. In other letters, Luz offers his daughter descriptions of the environmental pulsations of San Miguel: the capriciousness of the weather, the changing of the seasons, and the cycles of the cultivation of corn and the breeding of cattle. Luz, though, spends most of his epistolary efforts chronicling the rhythms of the institution that he, and most San Miguelenses, felt was the beating heart of their community, the Catholic Church. The celebrated Mexican author Agustín Yañez recognized this feature of Alteño towns when he wrote that in his hometown of Yahualica "ecclesiastical time ordered existence." People, he noted, awoke in the morning, were called to mass, summoned to rosary, reminded of the daily prayers for the departed souls, and cautioned about the evening's curfew by a regime of ringing bells whose varied melodies and spiritual authority everyone understood and obeyed.[20] Yañez believed that this regime was so hegemonic that all of Yahualica's citizens orientated themselves in time and space by referring to the liturgy of the Catholic Church and its religious events: "In the Plaza, in the stores, in the streets, in the homes, on the roads we hear expressions such as these: 'My mother is already doing her housework when the first call for mass is issued.' 'I will lend you money; but you will repay me before the day of San Miguel.' 'God willing, he will arrive during Holy Week'."[21]

All this accounting of time and its passage was unnecessary when Luz and Pancha lived together in San Miguel. Before she left Mexico, Pancha's consciousness of community (of "we") was defined by the entanglement of a cluster of temporal, spatial, and spiritual markers such that "when" (now/yesterday/tomorrow) was linked not only to a bounded sense of "where" (San Miguel, Mexico), but also to an unshakeable certainty about "whom" (God).[22] But when Pancha left San Miguel she moved to a space with different time sensibilities. Luz's anxiety over the fact that Pancha no longer resided in a place ordered by the rhythms and logic of God's time is one of the reasons he continually writes to her about the rituals, visual signs, and oral resonances that the Catholic Church employed to orient the temporal existence of Catholics in San Miguel. Yet, while the tolling of the church bells and the rituals related to Advent, Christmas, Lent, and Easter were important to Luz, none of the liturgical or ritual practices seemed ....re significant in marking the passage of both secular and religious time in San Miguel than the town's *fiestas* for its patron saint, Saint Michael. Moreno repeatedly reminds Pancha of the beauty and the pageantry of the fiestas, which took place every year during the last two weeks of September and culminated on the 29th of that month. In doing so, he emphasized the sacred role that the events had in bringing together and defining the religious community of San Miguel as a social and spiritual organism under the patronage of God's most trusted angel.[23] Moreno also emphasizes his descriptions of the fiestas because he wants to highlight Pancha's absence, underscore his loneliness, and remind her that even though she is living in the United States, she is still a member of the community they share. If, as he does in the following excerpt, Luz can use the fiestas and his suffering to entice Pancha (with not a little guilt) into coming home, so much the better: "The time in which we wished to see our absent ones has come and gone. [We did not wish you here because] the festivities were extraordinary, but because this season is traditionally so unusual and full of memories. You cannot imagine how the passing of the time and the changing of the seasons [increases] the emptiness that no one, if not my adored absent ones, can fill. You were missed not only on the day of San Miguel, but every instant since the first moment that you departed more than a year ago" (c. October 1, 1950).

Pancha needed little convincing. She missed her father and wanted to return to San Miguel during the last two weeks of September. The fiestas had always been her favorite time of the year; not only because of the festive atmosphere that enveloped the town with music, fireworks, and religious pageantry, but also because so much of her identity—as a worker, as a sister, as a daughter, as a Catholic, and as a citizen of her town—had been expressed most intensely during the fiestas. During this time she and her sisters made hundreds of party dresses for the town's women; she gave some of her hard-earned money to her father so that he could enjoy a Sunday afternoon bullfight; and she designed and sewed the costumes for the biblical characters who stood on the parade floats that she and her sisters helped design and build. These floats were living tableaus that affirmed the town's Catholic identity and its dedication to its patron saint, Saint Michael. Pancha and her friends, Eufrosina Padilla, Lupe Tostado, and her *compadre* Jesús Delgado, hand picked the members of the community who would have the honor of portraying the saints, virgins, Roman soldiers, and deities that were paraded around San Miguel during the town's fiestas. Pancha's niece, Obdulia Orozco, remembers the selection process as very much a human affair: "Sunday was the day that the people from the countryside came to town to attend mass and buy their supplies for the week. Pancha and her friends went to the most popular masses and waited till the crowds poured out of the church. They waited until they saw the prettiest *ranchera* girls and then they would ask their parents to allow their daughters to be part of the *carros alegóricos* [parade floats] or *cuadros plastico* [*tableau vivants*]. They only picked the prettiest, whitest girls. I always wanted to be an angel, but Pancha explained that people would say that she was being unfair by choosing her niece . . . It bothered me, a little. But I knew, the whole town knew, that only the best, the prettiest girls could be on the floats."[24]

These activities had defined Pancha's role in the civic-religious life of her town. But now Pancha lived in a country where washing, sorting,

Tableau Vivant (*Cuadro Plastico*) representing the arrival of Cristopher Columbus and the missionary work of the Franciscans in the Americas, c 1940. Courtesy of Obdulia Orozco.

packing, cutting, and canning fruits and vegetables left little space for communal religious celebrations.[25] As the maturation cycle of tomatoes competed with saint's days as markers for the passage of time, Luz and Pancha despaired. She had left San Miguel in April 1950, and both she and her family had hoped that she would come back to San Miguel during the festivals in September. The demands of her new life made this impractical. Much to her father's despair, Pancha was not able to return to Mexico until late November 1951—after the tomatoes were canned, and around the day of Santa Cecilia, her brother Chilo's saint namesake. Luz celebrated the news of Pancha and Juan's imminent return to San Miguel with a series of ecstatic letters: "In regards to your parents, your brothers and sisters, and nieces and nephews, and all your friends, how to describe the joy and happiness that we will experience when we receive the telegram [that lets us know] you are on your way? We will wish to fly where you are and accompany you on your way back in order to defend you from all harm" (November 5, 1951).

Pancha and Juan spent four months in San Miguel, from December 1951 to March 1952. During this time there is a break in the correspondence. Luz resumed his letter-writing in March 1952 with a series of letters that followed an established familiar thematic cycle: the first letters are lamentations in which Luz highlights his love for his daughter and his gratitude to her for all the material and emotional kindness that she and Juan have extended to him and the rest of the Moreno clan (March 1, 9, 19, 1952). These letters are followed by missives in which, among other things, Luz begins a campaign to convince Pancha and Juan to visit San Miguel again (August 21, 1952) [Among these letters is one that presents a very curious side of Luz's personality, his relationship with Pancha, and the continuous self-creation that he engaged in when he wrote to her] In the letter dated March 19, 1952, Luz asks Pancha for forgiveness. Apparently, after writing dozens of letters and thousands of words lamenting his loneliness and pleading with Pancha to come home to visit, when she finally did come back to San Miguel Luz did not speak with her as much as she would have expected, especially given the heart-wrenching tenor of his pleading letters.[26] Instead, Luz spent Pancha's visit in bed "tossing and turning, day and night" (March 19, 1952). He knows that, given the tone and tenor of his missives, it was a peculiar way to behave, so he apologizes, he offers excuses (he was not mad at anyone, he was sick, he knows he is dying), he asks for her forgiveness, and promises to continue sending his "memories and the memories of everyone."

Though her father regretted his behavior, Pancha was most likely not surprised by her father's silence. According to Obdulia Orozco, Luz Moreno was a shy and introverted man who, as he affirms in one of his letters, did not like to have long conversations with people.[27] The epistolary version of her grandfather, on the other hand, was a voluble, philosophical man who took full advantage of his letter-writing to express himself. This Papá Luz, as the Mexican essayist Carlos Monsiváis has written about women letter-writers in the eighteenth century, used his letters to make and "feel [himself] a character in his own words."[28] Through this medium, Luz Moreno developed a literary version of himself who could express ideas, emote (often with a sentimentality associated with women and the elderly), and project opinions about his past, his present condition, his family, and his world that he could not express in person.[29] While the fragile Luz hardly spoke to Pancha during her visit, the epistolary Papá Luz enveloped his beloved daughter in words of consolation, instruction, and love.[30] This required a heavy investment of time, effort, and money. It also necessitated the creation of empathy that was devoid of physical cues, constructed through words, committed to paper, and flowing slowly across two thousand miles. Indeed, as bureaucracies like the postal services of two countries increasingly mediated his relationship with his flesh and blood, Luz became increasingly more capable of disassociating the different personas that he and his daughter had become. In a letter included in chapter 4 he responds to Pancha's request that he not address his letters to her with the honorific title "Doña," by arguing: "You ask me not to write 'Don Juan' or

'Doña Francisca' on the envelopes? Well, I do it because in the [post] office I speak with the employees and inside the envelopes I speak with my children" (c. April 1951).[31] On the envelope, and to all the eyes of the postal workers in both Mexico and the United States, Pancha was Doña Francisca, and Juan was Don Juan. Inside the envelope his oldest daughter was alternatively Pancha (as she had been in San Miguel), Precious Ausente [Absent One] (what she became when she left her home), or his beloved child (what Pancha was and would always be regardless of age or place of residence). Each name indicated a different paper and ink version of the person that Luz's epistolary self communed with. Luz still dreamed of reuniting with his children; he fantasized about the possibility of Juan sneaking him over the border illegally and daydreamed and, as the following passage indicates, of using other modern conveniences to transport him to Stockton: "I see that the radio transmits news instantly. I see that airplanes fly like little birds. I see the quickness with which trains, like cars, travel without becoming tired and I realize that with that same quickness, as if in a dream, and without believing it, I could be in your presence . . . But I would need money in order to see you. If I had one thousand pesos I would grow wings, and just like that I would be with you" (May 17, 1951).[32]

Not owning a car, nor having the funds to pay for train or air passage, Luz was left to create the ties that would bind him to his daughter with his imagination, his memories, and his letters.[33] He hoped that his description of the fiestas, the depictions of the beauty of their town and its people, and his woeful accounts of his health would either entice or guilt Pancha and Juan to come home for a couple of months every other year. When that was not enough, Luz, Pancha, and the rest of the Moreno family would have to be content to live their relationship in letters as paper-and-ink people scattered across two countries, multiple work cultures, and several time regimes. It was not ideal, but when the letters became not merely the medium that allowed Luz and Pancha to maintain their relationship, but "the relationship itself," what more could they hope for?[34]

All my misfortune in life—I don't want to complain, just make a generally instructive observation—derives, one might say, from letters or from the possibility of writing letters. People have hardly ever deceived me, but letters always have, and as a matter of fact not those of other people, but my own. In my case this is a particular misfortune which I do not want to discuss further, but it is nevertheless also a general one.

Franz Kafka, Letters to Milena[1]

April 8, 1950 we departed from Mexico and my father
Luz Moreno gave this to me.[2]

My beloved children,

When I contemplate the thought of you leaving our side, I am overwhelmed! After so much time, diligence, and sustained work you have finally realized your wish to walk side-by-side to see those far-off lands to seek out a better life. I see that you take special care and precaution to take in your luggage all the documents and passports so that there will not be any difficulties with either Mexican or American authorities.

There is no doubt in my mind that you take with you, and will safeguard with great care, those things that are most worthy of care, like the matters of the soul. That nation that you are headed to is very materialistic . . . it is very rich in material possessions, but very poor in spiritual matters.

Many of those people have not received the Sacrament of Baptism; this is enough so that although they may look happy while they live, they shall be doomed when they die—not just for one day, but for eternity. The doorway to heaven is Christian Baptism, which can only be received in the Church founded by Christ. Consequently, those who pretend to live well and think that they will be saved [without it] are greatly mistaken.

As you attempt to live in those lands you should live with great precaution so as to not give in to the influences of those godless beings. Take care of that precious treasure that is your faith; with it, and the practice of all the Virtues, you will be great in the eyes of God. However, if in trying to please your friends or, if for material benefit, you heed the Devil, the world, or carnal desire, you shall be damned.

With these recommendations I send you off and wish you much happiness. When you reach El Paso [Texas], write to us. When you have reached

---

1. Franz Kafka, *Letters to Milena*, trans. Philip Boem (New York: Schoken Books, 1990), 223.
2. Pancha wrote this on the letter.

your destination, also write to us in as much detail as possible and send us the address and a general description of the terrain. I wish I could be like your body's shadow so as to not be separated from you. I wish I could be like the wind that sweeps through our bodies so that we can say many things to each other. I wish I could be the sun that illuminates the Universe so that I could see you by day and the stars to comfort you at night ... Follow your path my beloved children; go in peace ...

Luz Moreno April 8, 1950

c. June, 1950

To my beloved children,

For 5 months this house has suffered a mortal agony; a shock very far from our control, and we don't know what will come of it. If we had been forewarned, it would not have surprised us as much as it did. It struck like lightning. Cresencio Romo told me: "The priest is looking for you." "What does he want me for?" "I don't know." "Then who would know [if not you]?"[3]

Later the priest came and told me: "Don Luz, they are going to ask for Pachita's hand in marriage." "Who is asking?" "An old boyfriend," [the priest told me]. "What do you think?" [he asked.] "Well, I would rather they didn't. Is he [Juan] in a hurry?" "Well, yes; he wants to go to *el Norte*," [replied the priest.] "Well then, Ok, right now, just let me take this donkey back." "Listen," [the priest] said, "are you saying you are not opposed? Well, then continue with your work." Then he left. In the blink of an eye everything was done, as it was only a question of asking [for her hand]. Every one protested. But all was lost. The one who protested the loudest was Lolo, who took advantage of the situation to get drunk. He showed up drunk and everyone thought he was crazy. How can you compare what Lolo did and said when he was out of his mind [drunk] with what his brothers did sober? It is clear that his brothers are more responsible [for their words and actions]. You, Pancha, who harbor hurt feelings because Lolo told you that it would be better if you took a gun and killed your parents, [keep in mind that] he did so because he loved you and because he was out of his mind. What good is it to hold on to these feeling if they undermine our family?

3. Cresencio Romo was Juan Rivera's cousin, a friend of the family, and an ex-Cristero soldier.

Pancha, those bad feelings between siblings have fatal consequences; this is why I don't want either you or Juan to hold on to them. There are many things I could tell you, and I could show you, [to convince you] that there is no reason to be fighting now that what we [really] want is to be close to each other in order to see each other and console ourselves.

Pancha, my daughter, the fourth of June is your 49th birthday. I am very happy that you have gotten to this age and that you find yourself accompanied by a good man. Your life has returned to form in an admirable and prudent manner. It appears that God has wished to reward your many years of suffering with a rich and happy life. But, don't become like the Pharaoh's cupbearer who forgot [Joseph's] prophesy after seeing himself reestablished at the Pharaoh's side. . . .[4]

Pancha and Juan and his sister Petra and her husband and their family, receive our many thanks and salutations. And just because we do not send letters, do not stop sending them.

Luz Moreno

❦

c. May 1950

To my much beloved children.

God willing that upon reaching your hands these words find you . . . as well as can be expected in this mortal life. I greet you with the sincerest affection; [please] communicate this greeting and this remembrance to [Juan's] sister and her family who reside in Santa Barbara, [California].

Next, we let you know that only Ysidoro is ill. Although he is not as ill as when it began, he is still very weak and cannot sleep well or eat. We do not know anything about Coco.[5] As for the illness among the old ones—if its not one thing it's another, though the palpitation has worsened a little. As for the rest, the maladies are fleeting.

We have received your very lovely and very comforting letters, they are our only consolation. I hope to God that this solace endures. I think we will not tire

---

4. The Old Testament story of the Cupbearer and the Baker comes from Genesis 40. In the story, the Egyptian Pharaoh's cupbearer is jailed for having offended his master. In prison he meets Joseph, the son of Jacob, who has been sold into slavery. The cupbearer has a dream that Joseph interpreted. Joseph tells the cupbearer that in three days the Pharaoh would release him from jail and restore him to his old position in the royal court. Joseph asks the cupbearer not to forget him and implores him to ask the Pharaoh to release him from jail. The cupbearer promises to advocate for Joseph, but does not.

5. Coco is Socorro Moreno, Ysidoro Moreno's daughter.

of communicating through this medium. Here, many people have been touched by Pancha's absence. They ask with much insistence: "What has happened to Pancha?" We convey your memories to all your friends and acquaintances.

Pancha, I very much appreciate the money that you sent me as you have always helped me. God will repay your kindness and good disposition. Pancha and Juan: you should remember that May 5 is the day that your parents will celebrate their 50 years of marriage. I don't know if we will do anything special or if it will be a day like any other. What is certain is that if we look at our circumstance, it is like a miracle that we have arrived to this age.

In order to mitigate the pain of our absence, I have always wanted us to take a family portrait at our house with a vista of the horizon that surrounds us.

I would not want to remember the affronts that we perpetrate on each other while our family issues are sorted out. What matters at the moment is that we look forward, not back. That is to say, that we forgive each other if we ever had any resentments. For my part, I am not upset because my daughter, Pancha, got married; what upsets me is that she is so far away.

Let us live in peace, communicating constantly, and let us make an effort to endure this cruel separation that is so harmful. Let us remember that even though our bodies are absent [from one another,] our souls are together.

c. September 1950

[To my beloved ausentes [absent ones],]

No person knows what another knows. When this began . . . no one knew what it could possibly come to.[6] Two people loved each other from early on in their lives. That affection grew. Bad times came, the Revolution, and that affection kept on growing.[7] It received affronts, insults, and much opposition. That love would not tire. One of them [Juan] left, but the other stayed.

Who has created these problems? Who preserves these kinds of loves? What is the nature of this affection? Who will guide them on those roads? What goals will they pursue? Who will assure them that they will accomplish what they want? And if they accomplish their goal, how long will they have it? Will it hurt them or help them? Will those who saw them begin, see them end? Will those who saw them leave, see them return?

6. "When this began": Moreno is referring to the relationship between Juan and Pancha and their eventual departure from San Miguel in 1950.
7. Here, the reference to the revolution is to the Cristero Rebellion (1926–1929).

As time passes the world fills with confusion. What to do? Talk or remain silent? Is this not the same world of yesterday, of today, of tomorrow? Is this not the ground upon which our parents tread? Is this not the earth that past generations baptized with the name "the vale of tears"? How can one make those who are silent in death speak so that they may tell us how one [is supposed to] live and how one should die? How can one explain that Man, being the king of Creation, lives a more base existence than spiritless creatures? The mountains and men who witnessed the water that flooded the world, where are they? What is everlasting life? Because it is sad to be alive one day, only to die the next. [It is sad] to be rich, but to have no security in life.

To understand these questions, it is necessary to comprehend that they refer to some ephemeral thoughts of a higher sense. You, my children, are undoubtedly the ones who carry those figures and symbols full of mystery and mysticism. I think of you engrossed and content. You are in those strange lands, working bravely, but fulfilling the destinies of Providence. All your deeds (both internal and external) deserve the praises of men and God's blessing. The perfection of a person does not lie in achieving great things, nor does it lie in the fame that comes by performing miracles: it lies in fulfilling the obligations that come with one's station in life.

I have no doubt that the memories of your past life, and the desire to participate in everything that happens in your homeland, must be, in spite of your feigned disinterest, an unsupportable agony. But if you offer [these sufferings] to God, He will give you the patience and resolve so that as the days go by the temptation [to be here] will diminish. If in these moments you were offered the ability to see what is happening here, [while] leaving your partner and the help you give each other behind [in Stockton], I am sure that you would prefer to deprive yourself of seeing all [that is here] over seeing yourselves separated, one here [and] the other there.

Receive the regards of all of us who live here, family and friends, and know that it hurts us not to be able to see you in these days of happiness. May God and Saint Michael bless you.

Luz Moreno

⟨design⟩

c. September 1950

My children,

In all the time that has passed since you departed, I would not want one moment to pass without speaking to you. I would like for you to continue to be aware of what is happening in your homeland, just as we would like to know what is happening in that American land. There is no mystery about what is happening here. The fiesta is characterized by the peace that every family has; if there is a dispute, all is bitter. In this life, only friendship can give tranquility. Show me a rich family without friendship and it resembles Hell more than a home. In contrast, show me a poor family with friendship and it will appear happier than a rich [family].

I think of you in that place and I consider you happy because I believe you have friendship. You are not happy because you have money, nor because one of you bosses the other around, nor because you dominate in social dealings with criteria that is intelligent and prudent . . . Although it is logical that all of this helps and contributes to forming the moral qualities a person of good birth should have, if friendship is not in a home, it is as if there is nothing because the important things [in life] will be seen without respect. Even what one eats [will] cause harm because what one eats while angry is not nourishment, it is poison.

Friendship should be in homes, in towns, and in nations. Friendship is peace. If friendship is so necessary, the obligations to have it and conserve it must be serious. A man in his house is the king. In his kingdom he must have vassals, and these will be his children. Not his wife. Because her nature is the same as his, she shares the same crown. They are rooted and united in such a way that only death can separate these two beings. The virtues that nourish the ground so that the flower of friendship can blossom are many: humility, patience, gentleness, purity, the Grace of God, to be with God, Christian worship, Christian faith, Christian baptism, and perseverance till death.

On the 21st of this month, we received some letters and some very beautiful postcards from San Francisco, California. What beautiful and elegant places! Is it possible that the war will one day destroy that culture? What poor person might be allowed to walk on those streets? Only the rich from those lands are worthy of their nation.

Receive our regards and our regret that you are not coming to the Fiesta. All are well; only Papá continues to suffer from his stomach, palpitations, and headaches. The novenary[8] is on schedule, like every year. The bullfights are 5 pesos for a seat in the sun, 10 in the shade, 3.50 for seats on the roof of the portals. Chilo went to Mexico on the 19th, he will return on the 24th. They bring Chito many donkeys from San Julian.[9] They also promised

8. The novena is period of nine days of praying or mourning.
9. Chito killed, skinned, and butchered the donkeys. He used their flesh to make jerky-like meat that was popular in the area. For more details see letters dated February 15, 1951 and February 20, 1951.

to bring him some from Aguascalientes, but they have not. If you cannot get enough people to pray the novena with you, invite your little animals.

Luz Moreno

～ଓ୨～

c. 1951

To my children,

My children, on the 25th of this month I received a very worrisome letter [in which you tell me that you believe] that your father is still holding on to the hurts that arose from your nuptials. No, I don't even want to remember them. It is one thing that I cannot stand not seeing you, and it is another [to believe] that I am cursing the hour in which you married. I am not even cursing the hour you left. Yes, I feel your absence; this is natural. That I need my Panchita, who would say otherwise? And now I not only miss my Panchita, but also my Juanito because since they married they are one being. And not just any being, but a being that has dignified itself by its laudable conduct. That is why I always write "My Children" at the beginning of my letters. Is it strange for a father to address his children with the most filial of love? I well understand that I don't deserve to be called Father because, while I am your father by nature and by grace, I do not have the dignity that I should have. My poverty, my illness, [and] my old age have me at the edge of an abyss. I see the sons and daughters who surround me here in the middle of a destitution that afflicts me [and I am saddened.]

I have found in many of your letters and in people's opinions that we should not fear the war; that I should not think about it because it only makes my heart condition worse. Yes, it is true. But at the moment when a thought hits me, no matter the thought, it is like a mosquito [that buzzes around] until it sucks my blood. Those who are strong, well good for them; everything comes easy. I speak to you about war, insofar as I understand such things. It is not my intention to deceive or frighten anyone; everyone should believe and do what they want or can do. Me, they have me pegged for a simpleton because I believe what the newspapers say; [they say] that it is a waste to give them my money because I am so poor. I see that lately more newspapers are being sold. Why should that be? War is ugly in and of itself, not because the newspapers tell us it is.

Many nations are represented in the front. Soon, at the behest of the Russians, they will open another front: one in Germany and the other one in Korea. [The Americans] will find themselves like me when two dogs got a hold of me. I wanted to defend myself from one while the other came at me.

One threatened me from the front as the other attacked me from behind and bit my rear.

Receive my salutations,
Luz Moreno

~⚬≳⚬~

c. October 1, 1951

Beloved children,

The time in which we wished to see our absent ones has come and gone. [We did not wish you here because] the festivities were extraordinary, but because this season is traditionally so unusual and full of memories. You cannot imagine how the passing of the time and the changing of the seasons [increases] the emptiness that no one, if not my adored absent ones, can fill. You were missed not only on the day of San Miguel, but every instant since the first moment that you departed more than a year ago. But our hopes to see you do not die, even though my health threatens me with death at any moment. Even so, I do not want to alarm you; live with your faith in God and pay no heed to my weak state and my fragile nature. Let us give thanks to God that He has kept us all alive; although [some of us as if] by a miracle like Lolo and Hilario and Lolo's Lupito and Coco, and you even you [because you] live in those American territories where all the ambitions of the world are concentrated.

While you, like Chilo, arrived in *el Norte* believing that there was no danger . . . you should not doubt [that danger] exists. Chilo has already been in *el Norte* for many days. Arizona Avondale P.O. Box 102. This is the address so that you can write to each other and visit. He is with Pablo Trujillo, Gaudelio, and 8 more from San Miguel. They earn 6 Dollars.

The Novena is over and the bullfights are over, your Papá Luz did not go to any bullfight. I was not in any mood for bullfights. I am not healthy enough to think the way I used to when you, Pancha, would kindly give me money with no strings attached. [While] they tell me to go to the bulls [they do not give me money.] I know that if I have money I go. If I do not have money, I will not. The Fiesta and the Novena were good, more or less. The first day [they did not] have any fireworks. On Sunday the 23rd, it was the Sinarquista's turn [to pay for the evening's fireworks]. That is what the program said, "Sinarquistas from here."[10] There were lots of fireworks

10. During the Novena leading up to the day of Saint Michael on the 29th of September, there is a fireworks display each night. Different families, civic groups, and religious organizations sponsor the fireworks.

[that night]. The last day, Father Lupe Padilla preached. They put a car with a loudspeaker on [its roof] aimed at church's plaza; [Padilla's sermon] was heard in practically the whole town. I would like to tell you what he said: [He preached about] the creation of Angels and the battle in the Heavens; the creation of Adam and Eve [and] the temptation in Paradise; the creation of humanity and its ingratitude toward God. The creation of the modern world [and] the founding of the Catholic Church. [He spoke about] the struggles that good and evil have waged, from the first battle in Heaven to the ones that are taking place today—[Battles] in which San Miguel has always taken part in. [He said] the town should make itself worthy of the protection that this parish receives from such a powerful patron [San Miguel], because in reality there is much ungodliness and corruption [here].[11] The multitude surrounded the vehicle in the portico. Receive my poor information. Let's see what else I can tell you.

May 17, 1951

Beloved and never forgotten children,

You are so far that even sharing the simplest parts of our lives [is difficult]. Not even the faintest beatings of our hearts, or the signs of health or illness are insignificant [bits of information] because all things start off small and lead to greater things. And this is the quite natural order of things. It is the inconvenience that I lament. I see that the radio transmits news instantly. I see that airplanes fly like little birds. I see the quickness with which trains, like cars, travel without becoming tired and I realize that with that same quickness, as if in a dream, and without believing it, I could be in your presence . . . But I would need money in order to see you. If I had one thousand pesos I would grow wings, and just like that I would be with you.

I see what is happening to Anita Becerra and it horrifies me.[12] They took her to Guadalajara for treatment only after she was gravely ill, supposedly to remove a tumor. She paid the hospital for the operation. The doctors assured her she was fit enough to survive the operation. [But once at the hospital,] they discarded her, paying her no attention. My *compadre* arrives and he sees her dying. He signals to her to see if she wants to go [back] to

11. Saint Michael was the military leader of God's forces in the battles to banish the devil from heaven.
12. Anita Becerra was María Moreno's (Ysidoro Moreno's wife) grandmother. Tiburcio was Anita's son.

San Miguel. With a nod she indicates yes. Then my *compadre* and Ysabel send word to Tiburcio to come in a car to take her to San Miguel.[13] This was on the 16th; they arrived with her at 10 o'clock on the same day. She will die [in San Miguel], but [at least] it will be in her home. I asked Ysabel, my daughter, if [any of Anita's family from Mexico City] were coming. "Oh," she says, "don't you see what it is costing them [for Anita's medical care]?" "Ah," I said, "isn't it more costly to be apart from one another?"

My most beloved children, living apart may be [economically] beneficial but like others things, it comes at a price. . . .. Here, the cost is a moral and material privation. Being away from each other is what increases the value of our love. And if it were not for our letters, I am not sure how we would

13. Tiburcio Vasquez was the undertaker in San Miguel.

manage. How is the weather? Here it only gets cloudy, but it does not rain. Where it did rain was in Monterey, but it was hail and it destroyed the crops.

Receive our regards,
Luz Moreno

~e9~

May 26, 1951

Most beloved children,

On the 23rd and on the following day we received letters where we found out that you are doing well, that you are no longer cold, and that it is getting warmer. [We also found out] that you are witnessing with compassion [the plight] of the immigrants and that you want to know if we received the small gifts you sent. I believe so. Mamá Cunda's postcards and the ribbons, as well as the money [you sent] have arrived, thank you. You want to know about what is going on in our lives, about our health, and our town? Oh, how I would like to show you your town, your countryside, your sky, and everything else so that you could see it as if you were here, looking at all your friends and relatives who eagerly ask about you. You would [also] be able to see your marketplace, so full on Sundays that the stands hardly fit and must be moved outside in front of the temple [so the vendors can sell their] fruit, potatoes, chilies, and onions. Inside [of the marketplace you would see] Margarito's refrigerator, 3 butcher shops, 3 carnitas vendors,[14] 3 taverns, 3 small shops, and in the plaza a lot of traffic and a lot of people coming out of 11 o'clock Mass. During the week, it is quiet [throughout the day, except] very early [in the morning] and at night.

I would like to take you through the countryside, over the hills, to the little hill of Cristo Rey, to el Cerro Grande (the Big Hill), to el Cerro de la Llave (the Hill of the Key), and to el Cerro de las Bateas (the Hill of the Washtub).[15] [I would like to take you] to the towns that surround San Miguel so you could see how the rainy season approaches: how [the sky looks] so full of clouds, so full of heat, and how a mist almost completely covers the hills. [I would like you to] hear the songs of the little birds—the happiest of them, the Mockingbird—and to hear the bees, also. The trees are blooming and look very green; the cacti are full of *tunas*.[16] It rained on the plain only once and it is blooming once again. The bishop's weed flowered in beautifully. In March they flowered after only a slight rainfall. [Oh, if

---

14. *Carnitas*: deep-fried pork.
15. These are all hills that are near San Miguel.
16. Prickly pears.

you could only] see the *campesinos* on the hills working on their fallow land. On Sundays, there is only talk of the sowing. Imagine yourselves here in your town surrounded by all the human bundles that make up your family. From the oldest to the infants who are still in their mother's arms, so full of life, so talkative . . . Just imagine yourself here.

Pancha, one of Marina's sons died of intestinal fever. The doctor bathed him to break his fever, but he died. . . . The dollars and everything you sent arrived.

Chito wants to write to you, but he doesn't have time. He is struggling to get the feed [for his donkeys], which is more expensive every day. I am watching over all my sons and daughters, may God's Providence protect them and give them patience to overcome the struggles with their children [and] life's troubles—such as the lack of work, [and] the high cost of living. The government promises to ease the people's hunger, but it has not been able to do it. [It promises] that it is going to give *campesinos* plenty of money for planting, [and] trucks to haul seed; [that it is going] stop the greedy and the communist leaders, [that it is going] to eliminate bad government officials, [and that it is going to] attend to the poor, orphans, [and] widows. To complete the Alemanization of Mexico, [the government] has ruled that all schools must teach the Alemán doctrine, which is nothing more than a Godless doctrine.[17]

On the 27th the [Sinarquista] newspaper *Orden* will [be published] for 40 cents. I did not see anyone from here go to León (Guanajuato).[18] Around here Sinarquismo is in sad shape. The Corpus celebration will take place in the plaza.

There is no place we can hope to live securely. All groups, political parties, unions, syndicates, no matter what kind, have the goal of ensuring our well-being. [But] because there are different opinions, because there are many ways of feeling, and because there is freedom, it is natural that the results are unequal. [This inequality] is the source of all displeasure. All that is unequal cannot be apportioned without causing displeasure. We see in the world people who are happy, and others who are wretched: To whom

17. Luz is referring to Mexican President Miguel Alemán (1946–1952). The Alemán Doctrine is a set of educational guidelines set out by Department of Public Education in the pamphlet *Pro-Mexico*. It included twelve propositions that teachers were required to incorporate in teaching. Among them: "The government is and must be considered 'essentially democratic,'" and "the government is and must be considered honest." Stephen R. Niblo, *Mexico in the 1940s: Modernity Politics, and Corruption* (Wilmington, DE: Scholarly Resources, 1999), 223–224.

18. León, Guanajuato, the birthplace of the Sinarquista movement. Every year the Sinarquistas held a rally in León to commemorate the birth of the movement.

can we complain? From birth, we notice the difference between a rich person and a poor person. Why ask why? Why the fights? Why the wars? The hills, the entrails of the Earth, the depths of the sea have so many riches and yet, we still see people die of hunger. For whom was so much wealth created? For a few greedy [people]? For the strongest? It seems that the only ones who have the right to live are the ones who have their hearts in their heel, or [those who] do not have a heart. Oh, beloved children, why reflect on [these matters], it will not stop the killings in Korea, nor [bring down] the high cost of living, nor will it stop the plague of Protestants [who continue to come to Mexico], [nor will it stop] the opportunists or those criminals who live like animals and die as if they had no soul to be saved.

Receive our regards.

⁓℮℀⁓

c. February 1951

[My dear children,]

We cannot let a moment pass without paying attention to all four corners [of the world] because the problems that concern us are many. And while we worry about some, we ignore others. The seasons and changes brought on by the passing of time bring many issues that require our special attention: lawlessness, discord, the demands of the government and society, sickness, poverty, worries, sadness, uprootedness, and separation from our homeland. To live among strangers. Hate and its consequences. Deep sorrow. To cry alone, to look for solace without finding it. To ask for favors and not receive them. To have and to have not. To expect rights, yet live like slaves. To be rich, yet live like a poor man. To be the light of one's home, but darkness in the street. To live like an immortal, yet to be mortal. To boast that you are a man, yet cry like a child. My children, Juan and Pancha, objects of my worries, may peace be with you. As I watch God's sentence over us mortals, I see with horror how humanity walks blind among the light, and deaf, unable to hear the thunder of divine justice. The voice of the Shepherd is not heard by the sheep.

I imagine an American house, and as if only by wishing it, all things were possible, [I am there].[19] "May God keep you, my daughter," I tell a woman who comes out of the house, dressed in two dresses in order to not die from the cold. And just like that, with a surprising movement, I embrace and kiss

19. Moreno is relaying a dream he had.

her. "Where is Juanito?" "He is at work." "How is life treating you?" "As God has ordered it," responds my daughter with an air of resignation. "What do you think of the way we have treated you?" I ask her. "You have done all that you could. Just as when it is cold and overcast and those small chicks gather where they can [for warmth], that is how it is daily." "And you," [she asks]: "Do you bathe like you used to?" At that moment, Juanito arrives looking as if he were mourning. I hugged him and showed him my tearful eyes. My heart was beating hard because I found what I was looking for. Today is one year, my absent ones, since you began to take the necessary steps to get married. Receive our regards. We are fine despite the occasional fleeting misfortune. Do not forget to visit us. Receive my blessings.

Luz Moreno

～∾ℰ∾～

August 7, 1951

Beloved children,

After greeting you, becoming acquainted with your health, and sharing with you information about ours, I tell you [that] our health varies greatly, depending on the person. Hilario, is as always. On the 20th, Papá Luz suffered palpitations for 4 hours; on the 18th he purged and it seems that his digestion and appetite were fine, but [he was] very much without energy. On the 20th, the attack [heart palpitations] began at 6:30 in the evening and did not stop until 9:30 at night. Mamá Cunda cannot seem to get better; she is very restless and her foot hurts very much when she wears shoes. I have told her that Juan wants her to write to you; even though she gets lazy, she has promised to [fulfill] her duty [and write to Juan], even if it is a little. If you could only see her when she starts making tortillas—she makes them so fast that if someone else helps her, and there is a good flame under the griddle, it is amazing to see how quickly she serves them up, so full of air. Because I know how much you care for her, I would like to highlight for you the great work that she does, in and out of the house.

There are no more sick. The rainy weather continues to be good; there were eight calm days and in these days a lot was accomplished [in the countryside]. Scarcity is on the rise. Corn is at 80 and 90 [centavos] a kilogram and it is said that they will raise it to a peso. The necessities are the most expensive. On the 20th they robbed the *Mercado* [central market] of San Miguel. They broke one of the bars on the door on the east side, but neither the police nor anyone else has any clue about who was responsible. All the people were shocked, making a thousand comments, but not even one policeman was present at the Mercado. . . . The news did not even catch the police's attention. [It is said that] if it did not catch their attention, it was because they are trying to hide their negligence . . . [or] because they may have taken part in the robbery.

We received your photos and we looked at them with much satisfaction; they eased our desire to see you a bit. We imagine you full of good health and life—robust and cheerful. The image of your faces, so full of happiness and joy, [enliven those of us] who are in the middle of such misery. We see a future that is yet darker and filled with horror. We received the dollar that you sent Papá Luz at the beginning of July, we are extremely grateful.

You tell us my children that your little house is turning out very nicely, although it has come at a high price. That labor speaks very highly and with an incomparable eloquence [about what you are achieving there]. [That house represents] all of your sacrifices. It houses all your desires. Upon entering your [house] your eyes will scan over all the space that is encompassed by your walls, and with a scrupulous examination you will look at your belongings and . . . imagine the adornments with which you desire to decorate your house. This is the spirit of progress. This desire is very unique and uncommon. How many men go through life living in other people's homes suffering the disdain and accusations that they receive from the home's owner? [Men who] before they have had a chance to warm the place where they sleep must leave to another place because the owner has snapped his fingers [and sent them on their way].[20] That is sad and lamentable. But [worse yet] is to conform oneself to a lack of energy and character. God gave man freedom, [and with this freedom] he can travel the whole world and do a thousand somersaults and shake off that apathy, that inertia, that lack of ability, in order to equalize oneself with those men who have a strong spirit and who attract so many types of happiness to themselves. Juan and Pancha, when you enter your little home keep this in mind. This material home must be [made] in the image of the spiritual home that we have committed ourselves to build when we joined our destinies as Christians and members of a civilized nation, Mexico. And you will not be ashamed to admit your dignity before your friends and strangers.

Peace is so difficult to achieve that if the Korean question is not solved, the war will get worse. They have already spent 9 days in discussion and have been able to fix nothing. On the one hand, they are negotiating for peace; on

20. Luz is not so obliquely referring to himself and the fact that he lives in his sister-in-law's home.

the other, they are killing each other with such resignation that it seems more likely that they are crazy. Who can feel at peace under such a government?

JUAN AND PANCHA, do not pay attention to the laments of this new Jeremiah who predicts the destruction of this modern Jerusalem.[21] All I want is for you to have serenity and firmness; in this way you will give valor to your Father and your Cunda and to all of your family, the way you have done so until now. If you would do so, The God of Abraham, of Ysai [Isaiah] and Jacob, The God of Israel, The Invincible Father, The love of the Son and the grace of the Holy Spirit [will be] with you now and forever, Amen.

Luz Moreno

❧

September 28, 1951

My very beloved children,   *h·Z IS ≈ 74 Y/.*

[W]here do you find the space to concentrate your energies to pay so much attention to us?

Work is difficult. One hour of fatigue requires good nourishment, [and] a satisfactory rest. The human body does not only need physical strength, it needs moral peace. If one does not have this peace, the regular functioning of the human body is destroyed. When the bile spills [out into the body] it converts the blood into clear filthy water that does not circulate. [This condition] produces anemia, tuberculosis, loss of appetite, and whatever you eat causes you harm. Pleasure, grief, [and] anger create bile. A worker who does not allow himself to rest is liable to suffer a disruption in his [vital] energies: headaches, nerves, and a shortening of their life. The human body is not made of rock, it is very sensitive as it is made of flesh and bones and, as such, it needs rest to conserve itself. For these reasons we should see, understand, and put into practice [my suggestions.]

[About Juan's] job, let those who have gone to perform it under the watchful eye of [the boss] talk about it. This job requires one to be on time when one enters work [in the morning] and when one leaves [in the evening.] The worker must have a continent of good humor to show the boss that [he is worthy] of the job that that poor soul performs, this is the only way that the bracero can assure his job over there. How, my dear Juan, have you put up with this for 30 years, living that job and suffering such harsh cold and heat?

---

21. Jeremiah was a seventh-century prophet who was born, lived, and prophesized around the city of Jerusalem. He has been called the "weeping prophet" and is famous for prophesizing the destruction of Jerusalem at the hands of the Babylonians.

Working freely I already feel myself without energy; if I would have been obligated to work those jobs in those temperatures I would not have lasted 15 years. I praise your perseverance and resolution, especially because you have dedicated a considerable part of the fruit of your sweat to help your family. [We] expect you to come to your land together so that you can receive a hug from those of us here who live grateful [of your efforts.] My beloved children, receive this poor gift that your poor old man offers you.

Luz Moreno

～❧～

c. November 18, 1951

My Children,

God has granted us life in order to see you return, just as you promised . . . I would like to know when you are leaving in order to calculate the day you will arrive.

The 18th we received one of your letters that tells us you are no longer working . . . that the day you arrange your affairs you will come. On the 18th, Baudelio was married; there was a dance and Pablo, the father of the bride, went in peace and played music.[22] Julia went, but not José. I did not go to the dance as I was sick and only went to the mass. They did not give me a piece of bread nor a drink of water. I went [to the countryside] to get soil and while I was out there the palpitations got me. They lasted 5 hours; they went away, then came back and lasted another 2 hours.

On Sunday the 19th in the morning the Romans are going to march through town, and in the evening there are going to be floats and a theater group from Ocotlán performing. There is going to be a tridiuum for Santa Cecilia and a party in the salon on the 22nd.[23] Pancha and Juan, Chilo was born on the 22nd of November and he expects his congratulations.

Many people ask me, when is Pancha coming? It is an obstinate question and one of great interest. Pancha is a woman who has created around her an aura that only those who have known her since she was a child can understand what it has been, what it is, and what it will be in the future. In the past she was a learned child. With the passing of time she continued to unfold an accumulation of science and virtue rarely seen. In the first place, was her obedience to and love for her parents. She loved her siblings. She

22. Pablo, "the father of the bride," was a member of Chilo and Lolo's musical band. Pablo played the saxophone.
23. Tridiuum is period of three days of praying or mourning.

had her friends. She loved her pastimes, [among them] the dolls she always dressed up. In school she was a very applied student who never gave cause for punishment. As a young woman, she loved work and was [always] seen in the kitchen or living room preparing everything, giving it her very best. She went to Adelaida's house where she learned to be a seamstress, an activity that consumed her energies and her youth. Because there is never anything that is good that is also not coveted, from the most tender of ages Juanito loved her. If they did not get together early on it was in order not to contradict [our] weak opposition. Still, that love resurfaced later with an unstoppable resolution. The merits of her new life, who can say? Let Juanito, who is her breath of life, who feels the palpitations of her heart, who is one with her, who will die with her united in the Lord, [let him] speak on these matters.

Luz Moreno

March 7, 1951

A mis amados ausentes,

Beloved children, for as long as I am able I will look toward the place where I reckon my beloved absent ones are. My spirit will cross those blue distances [because] now more than ever [our] beloved beings need attention and incantations of love because you were not able to come as you desired. I think that you suffered more grief and I imagine you very sad and upset . . . If my voice could reach you, it would reach you like a beautiful bouquet of flowers in which you would see the magnificent panorama of your homeland with everything that is lovely and beautiful about it . . . You would see your parents, your brothers, your sisters, [and your] relatives and friends. You would see everything, but everything in spirit because the spirit is the essence of humans. Why do you get sad, daughter? Offer up your sweet and generous heart—[a heart] that must also be made of bronze to withstand that which is hard, that which is heavy—against these problems. If you are moved by the worries of your husband, parents, your family and friends, it is because your heart is so generous. But there must [also] be resignation. Let us ask God for peace and resignation. I do not want to even think that you are sad. It is true: we are not happy, but we are not complaining.

On the 5th we received your long-awaited letter. [You write] that you are all well, that there is a lot of work, [and] that Juan packs one thousand boxes per day and falls to bed very tired. That is why I advise him not to work so hard because his body is only meat and bones; all that work will sap his energy. As a worker ages he needs more rest.

War, even if it seems not to be, is like a wooden knife: it does not cut but it still bruises. This war has the world in great tension.

On the 3rd, Juana Padilla de Marquez Sr., Miguel Marquez's woman and wife, passed away. Because we had no cantor, he came from somewhere else; he sang really beautifully during the mass for 3 priests on the 6th. Religious instruction for the children began on the 5th. Only Hilario is still ill . . . My stomach problems continue . . . I am having really bad nightmares. I can hear one or two roosters; the town clock only works until 8 at night and then again at 6 in the morning when they call Mass. I spend most of the night tossing and turning. My heart palpitations occur only every 8 to 15 days. Receive our regards and thoughts. May God bless you and help you.

Luz Moreno

Beloved children,

It brought us much joy to receive the letters in which you tell us that you are well and in which you announce that you are coming during this month of November. May God grant you this blessed promise, and may it be easy to fulfill. [I hope that you are] happy throughout the entire trip and that you lament nothing. Just as when you left here to go to those far off lands, may no one rob you or ask for bribes. I want my little children to walk like the Israelites with that cloud that gave them shade by day and light by night. Really, what difference could there be between the [Israelites] and my children who are also members of that chosen people? Oh! My children, have faith in God. How could He allow you to be violated by sacrilegious hands, [you] who have done so much for thousands of benefactors?

Ay! Children! My spirit is dumfounded to learn that you were not able to find a way to leave the little dog—if you had a family, it would be more difficult. I understand that the love you feel for your little home is, without a doubt, what makes it difficult [for you] to leave that blessed place; that place [that is] showered with your love, your sweat, and your tears. It is there where you leave your soul. It is there where you leave your heart.

My beloved children, after considering your departure from your home, leaving it completely fixed and secure in every way, I imagine seeing you walk with much caution and worry. Behind you are leaving, further and further behind, that American land, full of memories and with the knowledge that soon you will return to it. At every moment something strange presents itself on the road. Once in a while you will think of the place you are headed to. Surely, there will be times when you will walk at night. What horror! The sun will rise and set many times. You will feel weariness [and] frustration, but you will by soothed by the thought that you are getting closer to your homeland. In regards to your parents, your brothers and sisters, and nieces and nephews, and all your friends, how to describe the joy and happiness that we will experience when we receive the telegram [that lets us know] you are on your way? We will wish to fly where you are and accompany you on your way back in order to defend you from all harm.[24] To comprehend—oh, my children!—the anxiety we feel to see you, you should recall the moments when you departed to that American land in search of better luck and our broken hearts because of your absence. We have passed

---

24. The first two trips that Pancha and Juan made were on buses. After that, they travelled in a station wagon Juan purchased around 1953. Obdulia Orozco, personal communication, October 22, 2013.

the hours, the days, and the years with the letters that came and went as our only consolation. Receive our memories.

Luz Moreno

～❧℥～

November 8, 1951

A mis amados ausentes,

Beloved children, on the 6th we received your letters in which you tell us that you are well, that you have communicated with Chilo, and that [he has] eaten the grapes you sent. We are filled with joy to see that communication has been established between San Miguel, Arizona, and San Francisco, California—the places where the beings of one blood live. We are filled with happiness because you tell us that on the 25th of this month of November you have resolved to visit your homeland. May God watch and support the resolution of my beloved children and may your guardian Angels give you shade and free you from all harm. I understand that you will not know how to leave your little house that has served you the way a mother hen does her chicks. You will embrace it and kiss it when you depart and you will tell God: "My God, you see with what worries we have commenced our outing, shield this house and its owners from all the dangers that the Devil, our common enemy, tries, in every way, to inflict on mortals. See how you are, and have always been, our defender. Because of you we came to this world, because of you we live like children, because of you [we live] like youngsters, because of you we are united by the unbreakable bonds of marriage, and [because of you] we left our homeland and committed ourselves to this America bringing in our chest nothing less than your sacred heart with your Name written [on it,] with faith and love and tenderness. In this we find happiness and glory. Because you are what we are made of and our God, we ask that you free [from evil] our little house and its owners wherever they may find themselves, and especially along that long road we have embarked upon. We are your children and you our Father."

On the sixth we set off on pilgrimage to the Cubilete. Lula, Josefina, Angeles, Román, Nacha the widow, and many others, [including] José and Jesús Orozco, came. 10 busses were needed. In the same paper that you wrapped my Dollar, I send you my appreciation. Because of the cramps that I get, I finish writing with much difficulty. I appreciate the advice that you, Pancha, give me for my health: eat 3 times a day and do not get angry.

The palpitations come more moderately; my stomach, too. I get headaches when not drinking milk. No more are ill, only Hilario. Receive our memories.

Luz Moreno

c. November 1951[25]

[A mis queridos ausentes,]

Like dawn announces the coming of the sun, we await the coming of our *Norteños*. In this way we see that as the days pass, our northern [horizon] shines with the white brilliance of [our] hope. Sing then, family, with joy; be gone the melancholy that has enveloped it for the past six months.

Poor are the prospects that we have to manifest, in a dignified manner, what these beings have meant to this family. But if we lack money, if we lack material things, we are not lacking in will, nor do we lack heart.

Come then my children, quicken your pace and if you think that you come alone [know that this is] impossible. You have never been alone. Divine Providence, our Guardian Angels, and all the Saints, always protect us. No, Christians are rich in protection. Since God founded His chosen people with Abraham, He has never stopped manifesting His protection. And surely, now that you travel on this road so full of dangers, the Virgin of Perpetual Help will assist you and liberate you from all evil. And even though we cannot do more, our spirit will always accompany you and neither the goods you left behind nor those you bring with you will suffer harm. You will arrive happy to your land, to your town, and to your family who waits for you with loving anxiety.

Luz Moreno

c. March 1, 1952[26]

My very beloved children, Juan and Pancha.

How short were the days you spent with us. How sublime they were; how quickly they passed, never to return. With what eyes will I see you leave?

25. Juan and Pancha stayed in San Miguel el Alto from November to March. The correspondence picks up in early March 1951.
26. Luz Moreno gave this letter to Pancha and Juan before they returned to Stockton, California.

With what heart will I feel the departure of my beloved children who are my life and hope? How will we repay you for all the favors that come from that benevolent heart of yours that is like a spring that never dries up and inundates [us] and erases our miseries. [You return] in good time to work in your *Norte*; may the blessings of [your] poor and old parents, united with the blessings of God, accompany you always [and may they] clear all spiritual and material danger from your path. May God's peace bring happiness to your house and may it give you eternal happiness. With [these lines] we give you our affectionate good-bye embrace. Goodbye, Goodbye, Goodbye.

Luz Moreno Memory

⤙❧⤚

March 9, 1952

Very Beloved Children, Juan and Pancha,

Once again we will begin our communications with the same interest in letting you know what happens with our family and in our town. It will not be possible to write to you as often and with as much precise detail as [I would like], but I will [write] with the goal of relaying [to you] the most important of our affairs.

I imagine that you have arrived, or are about to arrive, at your little house. What joy, what happiness your three-month visit brought [to this family] . . .[27]

Do not pity Lolo as he is well again after almost drowning in pure vomit. Ask God that he not drink so much alcohol again. He kills himself and he kills his family. All of them drink, but none like Lolo [who drinks] to kill himself.

We hope that you will let us know how your trip was. [Let us know] in what condition you found your house and the situation with your jobs; whether you got sick on the road, whether they robbed you, or if they lost your suitcases. [Let us know] if you found your little dog and whether the public order has been altered [by the war].

We were left saddened to see you leave, but [we are] hopeful that you will soon recuperate what you lost by coming to see and visit your land. Hopefully, the cold has lessened; let us know. [Let us know] if Korea is free, or at least whether it will soon be free and unified. Truman looks like he

---

27. Next section eaten by rodents.

wants peace, and the Russians mock the Americans. They [meet with the Americans] only to create difficulties. They do not open up a general offensive because they are afraid to lose. But there they go, little by little. The hate that the Russians have towards the Americans is so deeply rooted that they will never make peace. Receive our memories and our blessings.

Luz Moreno

March 19, 1952[28]

To my beloved children, Juan and Pancha.

Just when we thought that you had arrived at your home, we received the news that you were in Ciudad Juárez [stranded] because there was a transportation strike.

Later we got another piece of news [informing us] that you were in Santa Barbara, [California]. Now we hope that you arrive at your destination to put our minds at ease. We [also] found out that you were able to get all your belonging across [the border], that's good.

Here, we are as always: some sick, some well . . .[29]

My beloved children, Juan and Pancha, you may have thought it strange that I did not take advantage of your visit in order to converse [with you]. Instead, I was in my bed tossing and turning, day and night. You must have thought [that I did this] in order not to speak with you. No, I do not have any problems with anyone, neither with my family nor with Juan's. Since you left thinking that I would not speak to Francisca Romo, [let me tell you] that if on one occasion I did not answer her it was not because I was mad. It is because I am dying. People want to see me like before—the way I previously talked with Celso and the rest of the world.[30] Do not believe that I am mad with these people. If I have failed them in any way, may they forgive me; I do not want any falsities. While I live, I am willing to speak with anyone, depending on necessity. Assured of forgiveness, I send you my memories and the memories of everyone.

28. The next series of letters (March, April, May and June, 1951) have significant sections eaten away by rodents.
29. Next section eaten by rodents.
30. Francisca Romo was Juan Rivera's cousin. Celso was Juan's uncle.

August 21, 1952

My beloved children, Juan and Pancha.

As long as the mercy of God permits the beating of my heart, I will never cease to pronounce these sweet and dear names ... *Ausentes*, [your] departure has deprived us of our solace, causing us deep pain; [but] in that same absence you have showered us with generosity by the great ways that you come to our aid ... Your loving heart announces that you plan to pay us another visit. [We hope that this] visit is like the last one when you came and showered both old and young with many gifts. That is why we all wish that time would fly more quickly, so that the day would arrive when our beloved absent ones could give us consolation [and so that] you too will feel the satisfaction of being with your relatives, in your country, in your own town, [in] your HOME. What do you say, my beloved children? What hope do you give us? We nevertheless hope that by the end of November or beginning of December we will see you here. In the meantime, we should start thinking about what will become of your house and your little dog.

Here, we all know that life [in the United States] marches on with great order. [Certainly,] if you did not pay heed to this order you would not be over there ... I am sure that the government does not let any infraction pass without punishment. The immediate execution [of the law] is what is most important to the government of the United States—it wants obedience and submission. I do not understand why there are slaves and braceros that do not find good bosses. Instead [these braceros] get beaten, get paid whatever these bosses please, and in the end they get sent back to Mexico, sometimes without a shirt on their backs. Even still, people cannot stop talking about and praising the United States, filled [as it is] with all sorts of qualities. There are no lack of places where Communism, that black and horrible stain, enters and has entered [into the United States]. Very few [countries], neither large nor small, respect the United States. The United States cannot even look at lower class people, but [it has] Communists of every sort.

I think Pancha could come in September and Juan during the month of November. If not, both [of them] should just come together in November. The important thing is that you come. From this moment on, we await your arrival. We are confident that you will come. On the 19th of August, Luis the waterman passed away. From what I have been told, he was a very good friend of our Juan Rivera. Everyone here sends their regards.

Luz Moreno

CHAPTER 3

"Humanity Cries Tears of Blood"

On Religion, Epistles, and the End of the World

> Look, God is looking at you
> Look, He is looking at you
> Understand that you have to die
> Understand that you don't know when.
>
> popular memento mori in Los Altos[1]

A t the end of his life José Vasconcelos, the Mexican philosopher, writer, Nazi sympathizer, and former Minister of Education, eulogized the people of Los Altos as "the best racial contingent that our country has. [They] are of pure Spanish blood."[2] When he wrote this in 1959, the idea that Alteños were special because they had escaped the racial miscegenation that had tainted the Mexican gene pool with Indian and African blood was commonplace. Originally proposed in the decade after the Cristero Rebellion by Hispanophile intellectuals and artists who believed that Mexican racial and cultural identity was rooted in the country's Spanish past, this idea was popularized by the *ranchero*/cowboy movies of Mexico's golden era of filmmaking.[3] According to this myth of Alteño exceptionalism, Alteño men were light-skinned machos who loved tequila, horses, mariachi music, and private property. Alteña women were rosy-cheeked, fair-skinned beauties who remained aloof from the North American cultural influences that threatened traditional Mexican values. People from the region were thought to so prize their whiteness that, as a popular rhyme highlights, they preferred to marry first cousins rather than risk contaminating their racial purity: "Let's go to los Altos, where people are good Christians, who in order not to lose their blood, marry their first cousins."[4]

Central to this myth was the idea that the people of the region were the living repositories of a pure Catholicism that was free from Indian and African religious influence.[5] The proponents of Alteño exceptionalism lauded the region's Catholics not only because they purportedly spurned racial miscegenation and religious syncretism, but also because they had used their faith—a throwback to the militarized and zealous Catholicism of the Spanish Conquistadores of the sixteenth century—to fill the ranks of the Cristero armies with religious warriors.[6] This portrait of the Alteño as the fortuitous combination of geographic isolation, abstemious and heroic religiosity, and extreme racial pride was captured perfectly by the American journalist Jim Tuck, who wrote a book about Alteño participation in the Cristero Rebellion. Channeling the ideas of his local informants, Tuck enthused: "European, peasant, clannish, uncompromising about faith, tolerant about morals—these are the characteristics of *alteño* Catholicism and of the people who became standard bearers of the *Cristiada*. Nowhere else in Mexico is Catholicism so deeply and strongly rooted. Here is a community with ancestral roots in the most Catholic parts of Western Europe which has resisted all assimilative pressures and maintained itself intact on a red-clay plateau in upland Jalisco. Other Mexicans—assimilated Indians, mestizos, whites—may be devout, but they are still Catholics living in a secular society, while *alteños* belong to a culture which is distinctly Catholic."[7]

Academics have also argued that the Los Altos region is characterized by a religiosity that is more closely linked to the doctrines and institutional influence of the Catholic Church than other Mexican regions. They highlight the fact that Los Altos is at the heart of a geographical/cultural arc in the central-west part of Mexico that contains some of the country's most "highly clericalized, sacramental and parish-based" Catholic communities.[8] With a relatively high ratio of churches and priests per person and some of the most vigorous lay Church organizations in the country, it is not suprising, these scholars point out, that social Catholic resistance to Mexico's postrevolutionary agenda (especially its anticlerical laws and agrarian reforms) was so strong in the region.[9] These structural explanations help us move away from the tautology at the heart of Alteño exceptionalism: Alteños participated in the Cristiada (and Sinarquismo) because they were good Catholics, and their participation in these social movements proves that they embody an unsullied primitive/pure Catholicism. On the other hand, by placing religious activism firmly in the material world of men, structuralist academics define popular/local religiosity as merely the epiphenomena of politics or the reflection of base economic imperatives.[10] This attitude tends to obscure the important role that, as the historian Adrian Bantje argued, religion plays in providing the "discursive and practical matrix through which rural folk expressed themselves and made sense of the world."[11]

Luz Moreno did not ask for this engagement with the wider world. But when Pancha moved to the United States, a nation that he believed was defined by materialism, individualism, social and spiritual mobility, and a graceless and dangerous rationality, Luz felt it was his paternal responsibility to understand this world, to warn his daughter about the dangers she was facing living among the "godless" Americans, and to provide her with guidance about how to avoid losing her soul. He did this by writing letters that were the functional equivalents of the didactic epistles that the early leaders of the Catholic Church wrote to the Christian communities in the first decades after the death of Jesus Christ. Through these epistles Jesus's followers—most of whom believed that the Son of God would return within a generation of his death—taught the beleaguered communities of Christian faithful around the Roman empire the basic tenets of their faith. The Apostles also used their letters to warn early christians about false prophets, they encouraged them to retain their doctrinal purity in the face of false creeds and material temptation, and they consoled them as they faced persecution in a hostile world. Like the epistles of the New Testament, Luz's letters gave him both the space to figure out "an ethical critique" of the modern world he was certain was on the verge of being destroyed by its creator, and a platform to create a practical guide that instructed Pancha and Juan about how they should live with the bodily and spiritual dangers they were surrounded by.[12]

Luz saw the signs of this apocalypse everywhere. The Bible warned of God's wrath, newspaper headlines cried of war and social chaos, and, if that was not enough, the Virgin of Fátima had admonished three Portuguese shepherd children to pray for the conversion of Russia lest she drag the world toward an apocalyptic end.[13] While mere mortals could not ascertain the exact date of this calamity ("But the Day of the Lord will come like a thief in the night."), Luz was certain, as he constantly warned Pancha, that biblical time, the unfolding of a pessimistic universal temporal drama that revealed God's plans for his creation, was nearing its end.[14] "Clearly," he wrote to his ausente, "I see that you left on the eve of days of ominous misery. [Days] full of terror in which the dove of peace hides and the seven-headed dragon appears, filling the world with terror" (c. August 1950).[15]

Writing only five years after the United States used atomic weapons to destroy two Japanese cities, only months after the Soviet Union detonated its first atomic bomb on August 29, 1949, and during the beginning of the Korean War, Luz was living in an age of grand existential anxieties; a

moment when, maybe for the first time in history, millions of private apoca-
lypses formed a truly global zeitgeist of Armageddon.[16] Luz shared some
of the millenarian hopes, apocalyptic concerns, and eschatological idioms
of this transnational community, along with tropes that seem to transcend
time and space. Of these, the most important was the triad that "God is
terrible, that sins are punished, and the end is always imminent."[17] But his
end of the world narrative was also very much the creation of a poor, septuagenarian Mexican Catholic who was dying and writing at the end of an
era in the history of his country that was particularly fruitful for millenarian visionaries, utopian projects, and apocalyptic anxieties. From the dis-
senters of Tomochic, Chihuahua, who in "their magnificent anger" revolted
against the Mexican state in the 1890s declaring they would "obey no one
but God," to the Cristero faithful who shot the government infidels while
yelling "*Viva Cristo Rey!*" ("Long Live Christ the King!"), apocalyptic visions
and millenarian projects abound during Luz's lifetime.[18] Indeed, as recently
as 1941, Salvador Abascal, the most charismatic leader of the Sinarquistas,
had led eighty-five families into the desert of Baja California in an ill-fated
attempt to establish a Catholic colony based on the principles of social
Catholic doctrine.[19] The Morenos did not follow Abascal into the desert, but
Luz certainly shared the fiery Sinarquista's fears about the end of the world.

Luz Moreno was tired and seemed resigned to this end. But like many
people caught in the throes of apocalyptic anxiety, especially the poor
and socially marginalized, Moreno saw the looming cataclysm as a form
of spiritual Rebirth. A divine cleansing that, as he reported to Pancha,
would punish the wicked and ameliorate many of the problems he, and
other poor people like him, suffered in this life: "Our soul is what we feel,
what we want; [salvation is] like a complete pleasure to our senses and
our abilities. [Salvation is] not having to burn [in Hell], [not having] to be
hungry, thirsty, or sleepy, without ever being able to satisfy any of [these
needs]."[20] What Luz could not stomach was the idea that when the apocalypse occurred he and Pancha would die apart from each other.[21] Worse yet
was the possibility that by living in the United States, Pancha risked her
immortal soul and their chance for an afterlife together. His calculations
were simple, but in his mind unassailable: God wanted order in the world;
he wanted justice, and he wanted his creation to humble itself and praise
him as its creator. Like a good father, God offered his children a choice
between the materialism, moral decadence, and social chaos represented
by Protestantism and Communism and located in countries like the United
States and Russia, or the enlightened spirituality and social-moral order
embodied in the Church and located in Catholic countries like Mexico.[22]
Luz Moreno worried about his daughter because the society she lived in

had ignored the one "true God," embraced the Devil, and blindly committed itself to the pursuit of money and material things. By doing so, he warned Pancha, they were "raising crows that [would] one day turn on them and gouge their eyes out" (c. December, 1950).[23] He used his letters to warn her that though the Americans seemed happy and prosperous, they lived a life that was antithetical to God's wishes and that if she followed "those blind [men] who only love the Dollar," or if she gave in to the carnal desires that abound in her new country, she, like they, would "be damned" (April 8, 1950; October 20, 1952).

To avoid the fate of her neighbors, Luz instructed Pancha to remain steadfast in her religion, and encouraged her to profess her faith to the infidels around her, "if for nothing else than to compensate for the offense that these pagans are committing in not worshiping the true God" (October 20, 1952). Pancha's spiritual commitment to her religion mattered to Luz, because it would assure them a reunion in heaven. If Luz had believed that the materiality of the body was all there was to existence, then Pancha's life in Stockton would truly have made her absent. But Luz does not believe this; in fact, for him, their bodies, the fleeting nature of their existence, and their inevitable decline was not the paramount fact of life. His religion taught him that the soul was all that mattered; it was the only part of the human body that would live for eternity. If everything material, including the human body, was ephemeral then he and Pancha were not "mutually absent"; instead, if they could avoid the sins that came with living in a materialist world and prepare their souls for their eternal existence with God, they were only "incompletely present."[24] He makes this point in one of the first letters he penned: "Let us live in peace, communicating constantly, and let us make an effort to endure this cruel separation that is so harmful. Let us remember that even though our bodies are absent [from one another,] are souls together" (c. May 1950).[25]

Though he repeatedly returns to this notion, the dreamy vision of reuniting with Pancha in the afterlife brought Luz small comfort when what he wanted was to see her in this life. To escape the temptations that imperiled their reunion, Luz suggested that Pancha return to San Miguel. He acknowledged that living in Mexico would not protect her from the holy fire that God would soon use to incinerate the world; but, when the end came, he hoped that they would at least die together as a family, under the protection of the Catholic Church, and in the warmth of each other's company. If Pancha would not come home, if she insisted in living in the economic center of the world, but the spiritual fringe of Christendom, Luz committed himself to providing her with the spiritual guidance she needed to avoid losing her soul.[26] Central to this project was highlighting for his ausentes the forces, both terrestrial/material and heavenly/spiritual, whose interplay defined the drama of human existence and determined the fate of every individual. Luz inhabited a magical world managed by a vindictive God who was both Cartesian watchmaker and obsessive micromanager. This "Big God" had created the world, attended to its episodic and world-historic destruction, and was not above the fray of humanity's daily affairs.[27] In the Sermon on the Mount, Jesus informed his disciples that God, their Father, "makes his sun to rise on the evil and the good, and sends rain on the just and the unjust" (Mathew 5:45). But Luz Moreno, like the Israelites of the Old Testament, was not having any of that. His Father had a short temper, a long memory, the ability and desire to discriminate between the good and the wicked, and the weapons to punish the latter while protecting the former. God created the sun, the moon, and all the elements (air, fire, and water) and placed them "at the service of humanity." But when God willed it, Luz assured his daughter, rivers engorged themselves and flooded cities, clouds refused to shed their precious fluid on the parched lands of hungry farmers, and hurricanes destroyed the homes of unsuspecting victims (October 20, 1952). Did nature's elements, Luz asked Pancha rhetorically, behave "like mischievous children completely free to do as they please?" Or was their morally informed behavior—the fact that they act in "intelligent, fair, and just ways"—the reflection of God's judgment of humanity? The answer was obvious to Luz, and he assumed that it was just as apparent to his daughter. But just in case the logic of his rationale was lost to her, Luz spelled it out: "The fact that these elements have someone to guide them is precisely why they are so intelligent, so fair, and just. The Angels move the entire Universe, for and against us" (September 10, 1951).[28]

It is sometimes assumed that this magical understanding of cause and effect has faded into the past in the face of modernity and its scientific and rationalist discourses. For instance, the sociologist Anthony Giddens argues that human anxieties over vengeful and angry deities have given way to fears of a secular origin; fears of divine floods have been replaced by worries over environmental degradation caused by industrial pollution, the plagues of locusts, lice, and boils have been supplanted by the dread of epidemics originating in the jungles of Africa or First World laboratories, and the fire that God promised would melt the elements with "fervent heat," (2 Peter 3:10, 12) has become manifest in the threat of nuclear war. Giddens is certain that in this world there is "little place for divine influences, or indeed for the magical propitiation of cosmic forces or spirits."[29] Luz Moreno's understanding about how the cosmos worked, however, was defined by a transitional and capacious angst that was activated by both the modern machinery of death and by a premodern God of retributive justice. For Moreno there is no division between the material world of men and the spiritual world of the heavens.[30] His belief in divine forces did not imply a retreat from the material world of men, but rather a forceful participation in it, albeit with moral terms of engagement and heavenly allies that gave him, and poor people like him, a measure of control not readily available to them otherwise.

Luz Moreno lived in a universe that he believed was "ruled by will, not by laws: First the will of God, second the will of the saints, and last, by the will of man—when God gives him permission."[31] This devotion to an omnipotent and vengeful deity makes sense given that Luz feels that he, his Church, and his religion are engaged in a war not only with the Devil, but also with his materialist human allies who sin without remorse and refuse to acknowledge God as their creator. Still, it is a spiritual orientation that seemingly contradicts one of the assumed defining characteristics of Mexican Catholicism; that is, its spiritual and national orientation toward the maternal intervention of the Virgin of Guadalupe as humanity's primary intercessor with God.[32] As the letters reveal, the language and symbols of Mexican Marianism, anchored as it is in the image of the mixed-race Madonna and her nurturing, protective, and unconditional love, is not so much absent from Luz Moreno's religious discourse as it is redirected toward his daughter.[33] Panchita replaces Lupita as the maternal figure that Luz looks toward for comfort, for love, for mercy, and for the grace to believe "that he was worthy of love and capable of belonging, growing, transforming and having a reason to live with hope."[34] When Luz was not using his letters to console and provide guidance for his oldest daughter, he was using them to ask Pancha for consolation and to express his love for her and his appreciation of the material benefits she was providing for her family. In the first case, Luz was writing as a father trying to live up to his parental obligations; in the second, he was a supplicant composing a prayer. In both cases, like the prayers he recited before he went to bed, Luz's letters were efforts to "transcend absence"[35] that often only brought him around to thinking about death—his, his daughter's, and that of their world.[36]

We do not know for certain if Pancha organized and expressed her Catholicism using the ideas and symbols that we normally associate in Mexico with the Virgin of Guadalupe. We also do not know how Pancha received Luz Moreno millenarian epistles. Most likely she did consider herself a *Guadalupana*, and almost certainly her father's dark tidings were not news to her. Pancha was well aware of the risks she was facing living in the United States and was, if anything, more certain of her duties, more vigilant of the enemy, and more rigidly doctrinaire than her contemplative father. Pancha was a street fighter from a country where disagreements of many sorts were settled on the street. She was also a rebellious soul who had forged her militant faith in the crucible of a postrevolutionary activist Catholic milieu that, as Carlos Monsiváis wrote, "brought to the surface the bellicose will of traditionalist women capable of rashness, fury, sacrifice, and decisive extermination."[37] Luz, on the other hand, was a man of the book. Like the anticlerics he reviled, Moreno deferred to a deep and widely assimilated intellectual tradition passed on in social structures, rituals, and holy texts. But while the anticlerics were informed by the secular writings of the Enlightenment to see human time as progressing toward a better and grander future, Luz was nourished by the teachings of the Church, the Bible, and the Catholic press to believe that, like his weary body, a "geriatric" world was shuddering to its dark climax in spasms of violence.[38] Seeing him at church on Sunday, or sitting in San Miguel's plaza reading an issue of the Sinarquista newspaper, *Orden*, it would be impossible to imagine that he, this old ex-sharecropper, was waging an imaginative and rigorous engagement with the modern heirs of Voltaire and Rousseau. Yet this is precisely what Luz Moreno was doing. With his daughter living in the United States and with the world threatened by the hubris of man and the machinations of the Devil, Luz used his Catholicism to provide himself not only comfort at the end of his days, but also the matrix he used to make sense of his life and the death of his body, his society, and the world.[39]

This matrix, though, was not a neutral medium of information and stimuli, nor was it the product of a pure Hispanic Catholicism. It was, as the letters in this chapter highlight, a living, mutable organism encoded with the religious, class, and political ideologies, and affective sensibilities that Luz had absorbed and constructed from the newspapers he obsessively read, the social Catholic political movements that he and his family had participated in during the first half of the twentieth century, and the traditions of the region's particular form of Catholicism. While many observers view the religiosity of Alteños like Luz Moreno as the static product of their small world and their exceptional cultural and racial inheritance, his letters help us to understand how at least his religiosity was the ever-changing product of a myriad of entanglements with the material world he lived in. For Moreno religion was not a thing to be hidden away from the world of men and their wickedness or a blunt instrument meant to keep the modern world at bay.[40] Rather, his was a "kaleidoscopic" religiosity that pulsated with a messiness and a utilitarianism that highlight the hard, everyday labor of a belief system engaged with a wide world that he was both intrigued and repelled by, and by events, processes, bureaucracies, and technologies that constantly (sometimes fortuitously, sometimes dangerously) intruded into his life.[41]

Instead of marking him as a provincial man out of step with his time, Luz's dynamic Catholicism and his dedication to his correspondence with Pancha helped him keep his family intact (if not in physical contact) and define the conditions under which he hoped he and his family would become both citizens of the world that Pancha's departure had plunged them into, while remaining faithful servants of the god they had always served.

The easy possibility of writing letters—from a purely theoretical point of view—must have brought wrack and ruin to the souls of the world. Writing letters is actually an intercourse with ghosts and by no means just with the ghost of the addressee but also with one's own ghost, which secretly evolves inside the letter one is writing or even in a whole series of letters, where one letter corroborates another and can refer to it as witness.

Franz Kafka, Letters to Milena[1]

c. August, 1950

To my beloved ausentes,

My children, children of my soul, instruments of my life, [you are] moral and natural beings full of grace and the objects of my affection. You, along with all my children, form a beautiful scene that I admire [and] contemplate: a scene that calms the cruelest sorrows, as if by magic. To you, dear little children of mine, to you I direct my words, full of desire, hoping that upon reaching you they will find you in a calm state. Clearly, I see that you left on the eve of days of ominous misery. [Days] full of terror in which the dove of peace hides and the seven-headed dragon appears, filling the world with terror. But you, what were you to do? You had begun a new life; a life full of mysteries, a life that had to be tempered in experience.[2] What more appropriate time than now when good and evil dispute the Earth. Oh, my children, there will be so much to see all over the world because it is the place where mortals dwell, but it will not be the same everywhere. I must say that there have been pleasures and pains in this world; we do not know if in the future there will be peace, but we should be ready for whatever comes.

The 15th of August is upon us; we have to go to Jalos[titlán] or to San Juan and get robbed [because everything is so expensive over there].[3] They will do their best during those days. There will be three floats. In one, the Virgin Mary [will pose] as the universal protector for all needs. In another, the sacrifice of Noah [will be represented]. In another one, [it will be] Veronica. Also, in the month of July, the [church] organ was blessed and the Archbishop Don José Garive donated an expensive crown

1. Franz Kafka, *Letters to Milena*, trans. Philip Boem (New York: Schoken Books, 1990), 223.
2. Here Luz is referring to Juan and Pancha's marriage and their departure from San Miguel.
3. Virgin Mary's Day is an important religious celebration in many towns in Mexico.

that cost 6,000 pesos. On the 15th, Mnsr. Garive himself will bless it and will crown the Virgin. We are very saddened by the death of Chila, Chito's daughter; Mage is very weak. On August first, we received a very interesting letter in which we found out that Pancha did not find a job. Even when she did, Juan would not permit her to work because it was the graveyard shift and it would worsen her headaches. We received your gifts and contributions: some granted, some yet to be granted. It has rained a lot here. Many are finishing the last of their harvest, only Hilario is getting the short-end with his cornfield . . .[4] Around here there are many plagues, death abounds; some [people] have even been killed by lightning. A son of Jesús Lozano, along with another young man, died near the magueys.[5] In the [nearby] farms, some six or more have died from

[handwritten margin note: ? who is he writing to]

4. Hilario is Luz Moreno's brother-in-law, Secundina's (Cunda's) brother. The Morenos lived in his house.
5. Jesús Lozano was a family friend and baker in San Miguel. Chito Moreno worked in his bakery before he got married.

lightning strikes. Let us not even mention those who have died from other sicknesses.

Receive our regards,
Luz Moreno

❦

c. September 1950

My children,

I never tire of writing to you since I see that it is our only way of communicating. I send you regards in my name and in the name of my wife, your good and long-suffering mother, from your brothers, family members, and in the name of these children who all around us sing, scream, and cry [and whose] murmurings did not let you think when you lived here. [I send you regards] on behalf of all of those who found in your person a shadow, but who now sigh because they miss it.

We wish to know how you are. Whether have you gotten sick, [or] if the sounds of war have yet to disturbed your sleep. I do not know how it has been that someone would dare to wage war against such a rich country, a country that is so strong.[6] Not even the Americans themselves must have understood [why war was waged on them]. [Who would want] to die and leave such a rich country? [Who would want to] die and leave such a sweet and happy life? Oh, what a calamity! Because of God's just judgment they will they burn in Hell for dying outside the Christian religion?[7]

One only sees that which is material, that which has a body; one does not see [that which is] spiritual. One sees what happens to the body, but not the place where the soul goes as only God knows this. One almost loses one's mind thinking about God's judgments. United States, rich and powerful country, where do you now hide your joy, your wealth, and your power? Who has dared to put its hands on you? Was it not you who, not long ago, after having defeated the Germans, considered yourself owner of the world?[8] But oh, great country, powerful nation, can you not see that the religion you

6. Luz is referring to the Korean War.
7. Because Protestants were not baptized in the Catholic Church, Moreno believed they would all be denied access to heaven.
8. Luz is referring to World War II.

<u>profess is not the true one</u>? It is a pity that many [Catholic] missionaries have offered you the [real and only religion] and you have scorned it. And do you know what it means to scorn that religion? Now you are seeing.

[The true religion is the one] that you say is the opium of people, but it has power over life and death; outside of it there is no salvation. All the religions that imitate the Christian religion are false. For them there is no salvation. And what is salvation? Living eternally with God in Heaven? Our soul is what we feel, what we want; [salvation is] like a complete pleasure to our senses and our abilities. [Salvation is] not having to burn [in Hell], [not having] to be hungry, thirsty, or sleepy, without ever being able to satisfy any of [these needs] . . .

On the 12th, we received some letters in which, among other things, I found out that Juan had sent me 10 pesos. It had been a few days since you had sent them, but I did not know. When I read the letter that arrived on the 12th, I thought that the 10 pesos were included. Victorina, who was present, took the papers saying that they were sewing patterns.[9] Not having found my money, and believing someone had stolen it, I was very worried. When Victorina learned of the accusations I was hurling at those in El Paso[10] (and even against Victorina), Lula came and told me that she had had the money for several days and that they had not told me because that had been your wish . . . What a relief. Thank you dear Juan; thank you my Panchita. God bless you, my children. Receive my blessing and my sorrow because you are not coming to the Fiesta.

Luz Moreno

c. December 1950

[My children,]

Order is the basis of peace. As long as there is order, all things are guaranteed. Order belongs to God, and it is God who recommends it. No one is able to have order if they do not follow a law that is wise, prudent, and

---

9. Because her sisters were seamstresses, Pancha often sent them sewing patterns from the United States.

10. Luz Moreno assumed that American postal workers in El Paso, Texas had stolen the money.

just. Those who [believe themselves to be] wise and wish to straighten out the world without Christian teachings are very mistaken. They base their deeds on false premises. When God wrote His laws for His people, He knew man—He knew his inclinations [and] He knew his passions. He knew his weaknesses. That is why when He printed the Ten Commandments on those stone tablets—hard, firm tablets, as if He wanted to emphasize that His laws were not to be broken—[He narrated them] to conform to His honor and for the benefit of man.[11]

He presented the tablets in the middle of an enormous storm, [with] thunder and lightning. This is an eloquent [testimony] that is meant to tell us that this Divine Law should not be violated.

Those entrusted with the world do not recognize [God's] Law and are therefore very far from making world peace. The restraint that Christian law puts on individuals is no longer used. That is why lust, robbery, and hate are so common. Those who govern commit robbery [but] they do not want those they govern to commit robbery or murder. [In their] godless schools they are raising crows that will one day turn on them and gouge their eyes out.[12] God established order, and only in this order can one live. He who separates himself from order will only find death. That is why America looks for peace, but they look for peace by killing, by brusque and cruel methods. Blood seeks blood. When they stole half of Mexico, what were they asking for?[13] When they divided China, what did they expect? When they screwed Germany what did they expect? When they sent Protestant missionaries to Mexico, and to other nations, who was ultimately responsible? And now they cannot find their way out. Now they will see that mysterious hand that the infidel Baltasar saw write *mane tares pares.*[14] Now that nation will have to give a difficult account of its actions to God. His Kingdom will not be for you.

11. A version of this catechism is mentioned by William E. French: "Why did God write out his commandments? . . . to prevent men from forgetting or changing them." William E. French, *The Heart in the Glass: Love Letters, Bodies, and the Law in Mexico* (Lincoln: University of Nebraska, 2015), 174.

12. Here Moreno is referring to the secular schools that the revolutionary government established in Mexico. These schools and their "socialist doctrines" were reviled in the Los Altos region and were one of the sparks that initiated the Cristero Rebellion, *La Segunda,* and the Sinarquista movement.

13. Moreno is referring to the Mexican-American War and the Treaty of Guadalupe Hidalgo that cost Mexico half its territory in 1848.

14. "Mane tares pares" is Moreno's translation of the famous writing on the wall that Belshazzar (Balthazar) the last king of Babylon saw. Daniel interpreted the writing as predicting the end of the Babylonian empire. The citation from the book of Daniel

My children, Juan and Pancha, stay alert. God, through these words, advises you to stay alert and live every day as if though it were your last. As I have told you, the whole world is in danger, but more so Russia and North America. Receive our regards and do not believe that we do not wait for you. [We wait for you] but [we want you to come] not scared, not robbed. [We want you here] without any harm, and taken care of by your Guardian Angels. May God, with His unlimited protection, take care of you and, us. May the Virgin of Perpetual Help make you rich so you can help us, also.

Here I am very sad that on the holy day of the Virgin we will have no cantor—he went to his ranch. On the 12th, in Santa María, there will be 3 bullfights. Chuy Orozco "El Jitano" will enter the ring. We are well, despite my attacks. On the 3rd, there will be a ball game.[15]

Luz Moreno

c. January 1, 1951

[My children,]

Human beings live a life of constant struggle. No matter how adequate and anticipated our intelligence may be in organizing our lives, despite our moving away from harm, harm continues to cross our paths. We cannot be assured that our neighbor, or our friend, or the richest man in the world is [living] in peace; although money makes a man rich, it does not make him happy. Peace was not made for this world. The peace that the Angels heralded to the shepherds is not known in the modern world. Is there [peace] only for those with good will? And how will we recognize those men of good will so that we may take them as examples?

Only by testing him will we know a man's mettle. As long as our dignity is not challenged, we are passive and we are gentle. But if we were to be offended, we would want a thunderbolt in hand to take revenge on that offense. How do we make a crown that deserves an eternal prize? With kisses and caresses? No, that is for children. As Christians, we have promised to love God above everything and we should be pleased when the

(book 5 verses 24–28) reads: "This *is* the interpretation of *each* word. MENE: God has numbered your kingdom, and finished it; TEKEL: You have been weighed in the balances, and found wanting; PERES: Your kingdom has been divided, and given to the Medes and Persians." Moreno was predicting a similar fate for the United States.

15. Santa María is a town near San Miguel. Chuy Orozco is Jesús Orozco, Moreno's grandson, an amateur bullfighter who went by the moniker "*El Jitano*" (Gitano), the Gypsy.

occasion arises to suffer in the name of Christ, for it is then that we show ourselves to be proper Christians and men of good will.

The last day of the year has arrived. All the events that have happened to our family are evident. But the [event] that stands out is your marriage, your union. There is much to be said of this event, but why talk about something that you yourselves were a part of? I am astonished over [the difference] between what I first thought [about your union] and what I now see. I will never tire of thanking God for allowing me to see what I doubted I would ever witness. Even though Pancha and Juan were the main actors of the event they themselves were participating in, they could not be assured of the success of this unknown endeavor. It depended on God. And from us, what could be expected? Now you are well, you are employed, [and] you have your little savings. You only have one worry, and that is to visit your relatives as you promised when you left. I do not know if you will do it, or how much it will cost if you do, or if you do not. We regret that you must sacrifice in order to do it. But since you have performed miracles for us before, we are certain you will not leave us disappointed. Receive our regards, we are fine.

Luz Moreno

⁓ℯ℘⁓

c. January 1951

Beloved Children, Juan and Pancha

It is a great pleasure to speak with you and to admire that world that surrounds us with the grace that God bestowed upon it. Tell me my children, who can explain even the most minor of God's creation? The most learned, however hard they may try to explain, say nothing. And God chose to create all that is visible and even that which is invincible for man, His favorite creation. Both the visible and invisible world, our eternal mansion, has been promised to him.

At the very moment a child is born, an Angel comes to take care of him. How many Angels would we see if they had bodies? As many as there are people in the world. And why should there be so many Guardian Angels? Couldn't one Angel take care of all the world? Yes. But this is the way God wanted it, so that He could [more clearly] show us His mercy. Because God does not only love humanity in general: He also loves us as individuals.

Seeing all the precaution that God has put into protecting what He has created, [it is evident] that there must be a lot of danger. [There is so much danger] that if devils [who cause the danger] had bodies, they would cover the sun.[16]

How will we work to safeguard our soul when it is encased in a mortal body that experiments in attacking the Laws of God? Vision, taste, smell, touch, tongue are organs that are as necessary as they are harmful because sometimes in giving pleasure to one of these senses we lose God, and when we lose God, what is not lost? These 5 senses are the body's senses. But their functions are managed with the power of three faculties that belong to the soul: Memory, Insight, and Will. These faculties are an essential part of the human being. Human beings are composed of a soul and body. The soul is immortal. If man dies, his body dies. Death is the separation of the soul from the body. There are two places souls go when the body dies. Some, those that die in Grace, go to Heaven. Others, if they die in sin, go to Hell.

March 8, 1951

[My Beloved Children,]

Very soon, Coco, Lupe, Gloria, and who knows who else will arrive. Let us thank God who has helped us so much, and who has relieved so many of our illnesses, like Coco's, Lolo's, and Hilario's, if not entirely then at least partially. [We should also thank Him] for healing our children and our adults. When we are not careful we give all credit to the medicine. God and medicine can [cure] anything.

We owe all of our gratitude to the benefactors who helped out with the treatments.

Everyone from Lupe's family contributed to treat Coco. We are ashamed because we, her grandparents, did not even contribute 5 cents. See how they are coming to our town to free Coco from an illness that if not treated in the way it was would have killed her?

Praised be God and then those who know how to heal. God will bless their hands so that they can continue making happy those who are wretched. God will provide their hearts with the sweetest of pleasures.

How ironic that the opulently rich, who are supposedly happy, can only be so by surrounding themselves with material comforts. But what happens? They appear angry, irritable, envious, arrogant, wrathful, and quarrelsome. In their homes they keep some people in servitude, dedicated and subject to forced labor. They pay them whatever they feel like paying them. Instead

---

16. "Es tanto que si los diablos tuvierna cuerpo, no dava el sol al mediodia."

of carrying a Crucifix as a reliquary they carry a gun, a sword, or a shotgun as if to show that instead of having God in their hearts like Christians, they have the Devil, whom they love and serve.

My very beloved children Juan and Pancha, we would like to please you by giving you a picture of how everything is here in your land so that you would feel as if you lived here. I would like to present to you an [image] of our economic and moral life, of our religious and social life, and all the workings of our town. Instead receive the small offering of our intimate friendship and our gratitude for all the benefits that we have received from your hands. Receive our memories.

Luz Moreno

꧁꧂

c. June 1951

My Children,

I have already spoken to you a lot about the war. In the newspaper of the 30th they tell us the Communists have the Americans in retreat. The Chinese are the ones who have put the Americans into big trouble. [The Americans] are also at war in Germany. They are at war in Indochina. They will draft their young, from 18 to 20 years old ... and believe that they are the only ones that they [will need]. No, even the old [will] have to go [to war.] I see how worried the bosses are, the capitalists, and the lazy who only look at the poor and the hungry work. The day will come when they will be slaves in their own nation. Their flag, which is speckled with stars, will be replaced by the red flag of the sickle and the hammer. And all those who believed in the Monroe Doctrine [and] did not see that there is a [powerful] being, a God who made everything that we see and all that is invisible for his glory, [a God who made] the highest Seraphim and the smallest insect, both of whom await the end that He has [preordained], [do not see that] this God gave the United States great power, great riches, but He expects to be served. But no, the United States becomes arrogant, adores the dollar, and does not think [about the fact that] they are administrators [of God's gifts] and that when they die they have to account for themselves to God. Wicked is the man who confides in other men. Many say that nothing will harm the United States; that they will never lose [the war]. If they have a lot of power, it all comes from God and the day that God says "It ends here," [the United States] will cease to exist. Rome used to be the Mistress of the World—for 300 years it had the power, and the men who governed it believed that only they had power. They martyrized many Christians. And who ended up conquering them? A savage people, the barbarians who came down from the hills as a rabble, in mobs without order, like animals. They took those Romans who were comfortable in their wretched, materialist power and they tore up their tunics and broke their scepters. And if it had not been for Pope Pius V, not a trace would have been left of Rome.

As for the current combatants, is this lesson not clear? The Chinese are a nightmare created by the United States; but not just the Chinese: Mexico robbed, Korea divided, China and Germany also [divided], Puerto Rico oppressed. And that wealth so coveted by the rest of the world? That wealth: who will protect it? Who will take care of it? Who will care for its children, or those who emigrate there to live? They are dying in Korea and still cannot win. It has been a year and every day a thousand people die. How many young people can there be to replenish those demolished armies? But what does it matter? Even if they are our brothers, they are dying far away [from us]. Live alert, children! We live among ephemeral mortals that God created so that they would glorify Him in this world; in return He would glorify us in the next.

Receive our salutations and these historical notes as a gift. We are well, thanks to God. If you come soon, don't expect bad weather.

Luz Moreno

September 3, 1951

[Beloved ausentes,]

These moments are moments of great significance for me. They mark the beginning of the end. How many things would I have done in my life? How many things would I not have done? Oh, my children do not leave those things that compromise your conscience to the last minute. Many [people] desire honors, distinctions, and treasures as if in receiving these they would not have to be held accountable for them. I have received but one treasure, and it has been from God. It is not a material treasure: [it is] a living, spiritual treasure. What is this treasure? It is my sons and daughters. Are they not a treasure? They are more than a treasure. They are not like the treasures that materialists yearn for, nor are they like those treasures that are here today and gone tomorrow. They are not the kind of treasure that has brought Korea destruction and now threatens the rest of the world. No, the treasure that I and many other Christians possess is our children. But what a responsibility. If the children turn out good, great for the father;

if they are bad, poor parents. I am 73 years old and I never thought that I would make it to this age. It took me 10 years to begin to labor, 23 years to begin my real work, 50 years to reach the point in my life where I began to decline, and 73 to see the end of it.[17]

My dear children, you have already suffered enough with me so what good will it do you to hold me responsible [of all the wrong I have done]? It is better if you forgive me and that way God will forgive me more easily. I am going to leave you in a world full of calamities, and when the enemies of our Lord and the Christian religion ask you to prove your faith, do not fool around. What good will it have done you to have been poor and hungry all of your life, if for fear of bodily death you kill your soul?!

If in some parts it rains so hard that people are drowning, in other parts there is no water, not even for the cornfields. Here, the cornfields are drying up ... The Fiestas of September will be joyous for some, and sad for others. This all depends on the peace that they have in their heart and the health of their bodies and souls. The programs for the novena were ready on the second of the month and the Romans will come out on the 16th.[18] On the 19th there will be a fiesta at the Colonia de San José. The mass will be celebrated by three priests. Fireworks and music will accompany the procession from the parish all the way to the "Colonia." The old image of San José will also be displayed starting one day before [the procession].

Luz Moreno

September 10, 1951

Beloved children,

During these the happiest days of the year you are especially missed ... Even though we are here and you are there we should be intentional in uniting ourselves through our prayers to God ...

It is truly alarming to see the blows with which God is punishing the world. The war in Korea does not end. On the contrary, people are finding a reason to fight everywhere. Here in Mexico, the elections are hotly contested. Europe is on the verge of war. In Czechoslovakia [and] in

---

17. For a more detailed account see letter dated October 22, 1951.

18. By Romans, Luz is referring to children dressed as Romans who were paraded around town on horses to announce the high days of the September fiestas for Saint Michael.

communist China they are persecuting bishops, and those who are prisoners will die if no one speaks out for them. Nature's elements are plotting, and each is acting according to its character: either manifesting its strength or making itself scarce. Water, what has it done by flooding the rivers? By flooding the cities? And what about the drought that has damaged the cornfields? How pleasant is the air, the zephyr [that] calms our nerves? But what about that wicked wind that transports the plague? Or that imprudent hurricane that destroyed the homes of the poor inhabitants of Veracruz, Tampico, and San Luis Potosi? Do nature's elements not have anyone to govern them? Or are they perhaps like mischievous children completely free to do as they please? The fact that the elements do have someone to guide them is precisely why they are so intelligent, so fair, and just. The Angels move the entire Universe, for and against us.

My beloved children receive this gift. We are a little well, thanks be to God.

Luz Moreno

Beloved Children,

May God preserve you in peace. While we live in our land, without being able to compare our life to yours, we look at the horizon that saw us born, [and realize that] you are over there in a land threatened by a world full of enemies. Although many things are concealed, it is impossible to occult the horror of that war. The entire world is threatened. Some covet the resources of others, the strongest humiliate the weakest, [and] Russia . . . is always the world's nightmare. The people who govern [Russia] are the bad ones; the [Russian] people are not bad. We can always hope that the word of the Virgin of Fátima will come true and Russia will convert. [The Russians and Americans are negotiating a peace treaty in] Korea at the same time that they are killing each other. How will they resolve that contradiction? You cannot love and hate at the same time. It is evident that [each of them] would like to finish off their enemy with [military] might, but since they cannot, they pretend to want to stop killing each other. What is the truth? Beloved children, how do you believe you can live tranquilly in this confusion? Don't you see that as long as there is no understanding, [no] good will, and [no] forgiveness in the heart there can be no peace?

On the 12th we received a letter from Chilo from el Norte. He is working for 60 cents an hour. He is in Arizona in the company of Guadelio Pablo Trujillo and others from San Miguel. What do you think my beloved children? Moving to work in el Norte is so easy that soon Mexico will be empty. [The Bracero officials] go to each town, pick out a number of Braceros, and head out to el Norte. This way there are no problems or crowds [at the border]. The luck of the Mexican Braceros depends on the state of the agreement between the governments of the United States and Mexico. The important men from America are vigilant in all the work centers to [ensure] that the [Mexican Braceros] are paid the same as [American workers] and to [make sure] that they do not stop giving them food, dormitories, and to [guarantee] that they do not reproach or take advantage of the Mexican workers. What do you think my beloved children? Chilo has satisfied his desire to go to el Norte. Here we are well. Chilo says he is well. Me, your little old man, as always with his palpitations and the lack of hunger: [a] problem that is made worse by my lack of work and the sorrow of seeing Chilo go to el Norte. In the end, I console myself [with the thought] that while he is over there he will not get drunk. God give him strength to work such a difficult job and to endure the vigilance of his boss . . . Luz Moreno[19]

19. Pancha tempered Luz's enthusiasm for the calming effect that the United State might have on Chilo by telling her father that, as Luz wrote, "You tell me in your letter

October 2, 1951

[Beloved children,]

Here we walk more or less well with the help we receive from you. Our little ones were full of joy because we divided the money [you sent us] among everyone. I got $9.60. Many went to the bullfights; they were pretty good . . . the last bull was so fierce that they could not kill him, they could not even harpoon him with the *banderillas*.[20] A lot of people went to the Fiestas and because it did not rain and the sky was clear, the bus that goes between San Miguel and Jalos[titlán] was busy day and night. The plaza was full of cars and trucks and vendors. There were games only at the exit of the Hotel San Miguel. Damiana came by and found me on the 28th; she greeted me and kissed me. She came with one of her kids and asked when Pancha would be coming back. No one else from out of town came by.

On the 30th, three floats were paraded [around town]—one had San Miguel with six Angels playing trumpets. On another, the archangel Saint Rafael with [the] fish he used to cure Tobias who was blind . . . The San Miguel float was the responsibility of Estolia Alcalá, but Pancha Becerra composed it. The San Rafael float [was the responsibility of] Concha Alcalá. The last car was the responsibility of Domitila Jimenes, the mother of the Amayas. On this car, San Miguel was kicking out the bad Angels. [San Miguel] was bent over threatening the demons who were laid out on black [cloth], naked, except for some short underwear, but with horns. That float was very odd, though all of the [floats] looked very good. They came out at 1 o'clock, accompanied by music and fireworks. Chito rented some horses for the *piquete*, one of them got gored by a bull.[21] None of Lolo's family from Mexico [City] came. I have written to Chilo two times, but I do not know whether the letters have gotten to him or not. I know he is working; [but] it has been one month since he left, and nothing . . .

Receive our thanks for all the little gifts. You ought to know that we wait for you . . . please tell us, more or less, [when you are coming].

Luz Moreno

. . . that over there [Chilo] can also drink and party, that there are some very perverse women over there, that he can be tempted and lose his job, his time, his soul, and the grace of God." October 15, 1951, collected correspondence of Luz Moreno, 1950–1952.

20. *Banderillas* are colorful, small, harpoon-like sticks that are stuck into the neck of the bull to limit his ability to move his head and horns from side to side.

21. *Piquete*: Horses are used in bullfights to carry men who, using a long pike, stab the bull in the back of the neck and around the shoulders. This is supposed to weaken the bull and limit the range of motion in its neck and head.

c. September 1, 1952

[Queridos ausentes, Juan and Pancha,]

It seems that the Lord's Divine Providence does not abandon anyone. All events, even though they are different, somehow seem to guide virtue towards all of humanity. The difficulty of benefiting from these events comes because we ourselves destroy Providence's work and we end up hurting ourselves with our lack of wisdom. Events differ, as does the fate we make for ourselves. On the 31st of August, "El Chaparro," who used to haul meat, was killed by a truck that started up on its own; some swear it was started by some kid or other ... The poor guy was sweeping the streets when right then and there they ran over his head. The [municipal] president just could not decide what to do after listening to the many testimonies [given to him] by witnesses. The truth is that with all the traffic that this town has, and all the deaths that occur because of it, [it is only when someone dies] that people, the vehicle owners, the drivers, the government, and the people in general start to reflect [on the situation]. In the meantime, the victim's friends and family lament their loss. And all the while the number of trucks, cars, trains, and airplanes keeps growing.

On the 31st of August the programs for the Novena were published, we will do our best to send you a program. On the streets of the town there are many posts of about 12 meters in length. Rumor has it that the entrance to the bullfights will cost 30 pesos for the balcony and shade and 15 for seats in the sun. The priest is going to hold a bullfight on the 30th of September to benefit the Santuario de Guadalupe to raise money for the Fiestas Patrias, or the Fiestas de San Miguel as the Fiestas that start on the 14th and end on the 30th of September are known. He plans to hold a Requiem mass and a *Toros de aficionados*.[22] The interest of the town for this year's festivities manifests itself in the fact that there has not been any quarreling. In the plaza there is a wheel of fortune, [several merry-go-rounds,] and a game of *lotería*.[23] ...

Alas, my beloved CHILDREN, I wish I could transmit the vision of our town, all dressed up like a bride in her best attire. Those who reside in Heaven, Earth, and perhaps even those in Purgatory, unite to celebrate the festivities of their great patron [Saint Michael].

Luz Moreno

22. *Toros de aficionados* are bullfights where members of the audience were invited to fight a bull.
23. *Lotería* is a Mexican game resembling bingo.

My very beloved children.

We have lived apart for almost two years, and I see the patience with which you my long-suffering absent ones have suffered this feigned exile. I would like to have more life, for my limbs to be reenergized, and for my forehead to shine with more clarity the memories of this life that seem to fade away with the most minor disturbances of time ... [All of this I would like] so that we can continue this communication that so delights and relaxes me. It is the form of communication that is most replete with tranquility; it fills us and extends the pleasures that eat away at jealousy ...

This is the way it is, my beloved children Juan and Pancha: as if by a miracle God has kept me alive so I can manifestly see that [He] loves us a lot. We've seen it, we see it, and we will continue to see that God loves this family a lot. [It is a love] that has been especially evident in the compassion He has shown the family members whom He has cured during their grave drunken sprees. Ever since Juanito has become a member of our house, God's mercy has been admirable. For as long as Juanito is Juanito and Pancha is Pancha, we ... will live securely.

The 16th a letter came in which we found many things. For instance that Pancha is working. Well, Pancha, [because] your body is weak it must be a job that is easy and well-paid. Make sure that you do not hurt your backbone, or any other part [of your body]. In the same letter you let us know that [while] you had become aware that the boys had gotten drunk, [and] that Lolo had gotten very ill, you had not received news on whether Lolo had gotten well or had died. Oh, my cherished children, what a sorrow this must be. No, he was sick for about 8 days. He drank hard for 6 hours; during those hours the doctor came and gave him a saline solution while others gave him air with a hat. Father Hernandes went, but because [Lolo] was drowning in alcohol he could not give him confession. Now he is fine. This all happened during the Novenary. Some days he would go play [with his musical band] drunk. It was all a mess since he could not even play [his instrument] until the beginning of October. Next up was Chito who drank for 8 days until they healed him with a saline solution ... Chilo was the same, but now (October 17th) they are both fine. In my previous letters I gave you news about the *borrachitos* [little drunkards] but perhaps they have not arrived yet. Let's see if this letter arrives so that it may leave with no doubts [about their fate.] ...

Time passes with an order and harmony that highlights the protective care that God has towards humanity and the mastery and wisdom He has and under whose dominion corn is born in its furrow. It is the seed of the corn that died in the furrow and was reborn in the same furrow. Look how it grew and developed in the span of three months, to the point that it is a rich and abundant plant that adorns our fields and will fill our granaries and relieve our hunger. Oh, Men! Oh, Christians! What hymns of praise and gratitude should you sing to the Lord for the care with which He sees His creatures? There is nothing in creation that is not at the service of humanity: the sun, the moon, the air, fire, the animals, water. This, in terms of the material [world]. In terms of the spiritual [world], we have the Catholic Church that is rich in spiritual graces . . . Let us thank God for giving us seeds for 1953. [But] let us consider that although there is much to eat, it is under the control of the rich. The poor can only eat tortillas, beans, and the rest [of his sustenance] if they pay a high price [to the rich].

In the meantime, I look at the nation where you have chosen to permanently live, and we should all reflect on the fact that there is no place created by God from whom He doesn't expect the service that is due His glory. Or do you think that He is comforted by the fact that those Gringos have a religion other than the Catholic [religion?] What Creator is satisfied that each of His creations do as they please? Many praise the charitable conduct of the Gringos. [They say] that he even pays [people] to go listen to his doctrines, and that his doctrines copy Catholic doctrine. No, as long as the will of God, who is the author of everything created, is not done, nothing will turn out well [for the Gringos] . . . Who made the world? God. Why did He make it? For His glory. All things alive and dead must serve God and give Him glory. You, my children, Juan and Pancha, who have chosen to live in that pagan nation must profess your faith with double [intensity]; if for nothing else than to compensate for the offense that these pagans are committing in not worshiping the true God. Affirm your faith and do not [follow] those blind [men] who only love the Dollar [and those material things] that will remain when we die.

Luz Moreno

CHAPTER 4

"El Miserable Pueblo"

On Being Poor and Knowing It

Loneliness and the feeling of being unwanted is the most terrible poverty.
Mother Teresa

Luz Moreno and his family were poor; they worked really hard to be so.[1]
For six decades Luz labored as a peon and a sharecropper, and even in
his seventies he transported potting soil from the surrounding countryside
to sell in San Miguel. His wife Secundina worked as a midwife. His daughters Victorina and Ysabel made dresses, gave injections, and ran errands,
washed clothes, and cooked meals for some of the town's wealthiest families. His sons, while often given to drink, worked a myriad of jobs: Chito
made donkey jerky, transported fertilizer to the countryside and dead animals to the slaughter house, played music during cockfights, and raised
and sold pigs. Lolo was a mason and a violinist. Chilo made shoes in his
uncle Gregorio's shop in San Miguel and played music with his brothers all
over the municipality. Luz's grandchildren also worked. Jesús Orozco made
and sold popsicles at his father's *paleteria* (popsicle shop); his sister Lula
helped her aunts with domestic chores and with their dressmaking—she
hemmed dresses and sewed buttons. José, their youngest brother, went
to school and worked turning the crank that fixed caps on the bottles of a
locally produced soft drink. Their cousin, Sidonia, helped her father make
jerky by occasionally taking a hammer to the side of the head of donkeys
that were too old to be anything other than a delicious accompaniment to

a good mug of *pulque*.[2] Pancha, of course, worked in a cannery in Stockton and contributed to the Moreno economy through her remittances.

Together, the accumulated labor of over ten people across two countries earned the Morenos a penury that Luz, in a rare moment of understatement, summed up for Pancha in one of his letters: "Our lives are very simple and quiet and only as if by a miracle our family is able to obtain things to eat. Getting some clothes, forget it" (May 10, 1951). Luz Moreno's religion taught him to be resigned to this poverty, to tend to the matters of the soul, to ignore the temptations of materialism, and to be assured that God would punish the greedy in this world and the next. He preached this resignation to his daughter ("We lament [our poverty], but what we lack is the patience to [deal with the condition] that God or our misfortune has put us in" August 12, 1951), but as much as he tried to rationalize his poverty, as much as he wanted to be patient and wait for his just rewards in the next world, he could not fully stomach the injustice he saw in his town and that he read about in the newspaper. The world, as he complained to Pancha, was stacked against the meek and poor, and everywhere the rich and powerful seemed intent on extinguishing any ray of optimism that poor families like his had for attaining a better life. Whether it was local government functionaries making it more difficult for Chito to make donkey jerky, the federal bigwigs (and their foreign collaborators) who grafted money from every "revolutionary" social program they could get their hands on,[3] or the American farmers who abused the desperate braceros flocking to the United States, the world was full of examples that proved to Moreno that he, and people like him, lived, ate, worked, suffered, and died as they did because others were benefiting from their misery.[4] God promised they would inherit the Earth, but in an era characterized by high unemployment, inflation, low wages, and a political culture rife with corruption and greed it was, Luz asserted, the least talented and most violent members of Mexican society who got the lion's share of the country's wealth and power:[5] "As the world becomes more favorable to those who are the strongest, the most influential, [and] the most arrogant, the poor are the [ones who are] dispossessed. They are the ones who see government employees and their compadres become rich off the sweat of the people. They [see them] operate under the shadow of the government and receive thousands of pesos for doing almost nothing. They do not know how to make a furrow, but they are the representatives of the campesinos. They do not know what reason or justice is, but they do know how to turn black into white and white into black" (February 20, 1951).[6]

The knowledge that this society was not meant for them, and that no matter how hard they worked that the game was rigged, inspired hundreds of thousands of discontented Mexicans to join movement like the Cristiada and Sinarquismo. The activism of these Catholics, as well as that of indigenous peasants in the south, railroad workers in Mexico City, Catholic women in the central-west, and students all over Mexico indicate that the so-called Golden era (1938–1968) of Mexican authoritarian rule was not, as the historians Paul Gillingham and Benjamin T. Smith recently argued, an era "of static and uncontested domination over an apathetic people."[7] This popular disposition of discontent did not, though, have a place in the official version of the modernization project promoted by the Mexican government and its private sector boosters. In their eyes, by 1950 Mexicans had exchanged their chaotic and revolutionary past for a politically stable national community (guided by a benevolent one-party, patriarchal state), a common and inclusive national identity, and a seemingly endless supply of commodities and wealth generated by an industrializing economy whose gross domestic product between 1940 and 1980 grew at rate of over 6 percent a year.[8] While there is some truth to the booster version of the so-called Mexican Miracle, most Mexicans did not benefit from the economic transformations of the postwar era.[9] In spite of great advances made by the state to give Mexico's poor accessto land, health, education, and jobs during the 1950s and 1960s, Mexico had the second-highest level of social inequality in Latin America: in 1950 the bottom 50 percent of the population earned 19 percent of the income while the top 20 percent appropriated 60 percent. By 1978 the bottom half earned 13 percent while the top fifth 62 percent.[10]

Contemporary historians have not been the only ones to question the sunny optimism of mid-century modernization narratives.[11] While the myth of the Mexican Miracle effectively ended when the Mexican army massacred hundreds of protesting students in the capital's Tlatelolco Plaza weeks before the inauguration of the 1968 Olympics, Mexican intellectuals and artists had been publicly critiquing the economic, social, and political failures of the Revolutionary state since the 1940s.[12] The prominent historian, economist, and diplomat Daniel Cosío-Villegas wrote one of the first, and still most damning, critiques of the postrevolutionary project. His essay "Mexico's Crisis," published in 1947 in the influential magazine *Cuadernos Americanos,* was a broadside against the corrupt ruling class which, according to Cosío-Villegas, was "inferior" to the demands of the Revolution.[13] He called for the "purification" of this class and its rededication to achieving the goals of the populist liberal 1917 Constitution. While the political elite of Miguel Aleman's government scorned the essay, it stimulated a public discussion about the vitality of the Revolutionary agenda and the role Aleman's policies had in abandoning the "seductive power, the enchantment-like force, which it previously possessed."[14]

Yet for all the misgivings that Cosío-Villegas had about *Alemanismo* and its "neoporfirian" policies, he had faith that the modernization of schools and roads, the importation of technology, and the promotion of democracy and social egalitarianism by a less corrupt, more invigorated, and socially-conscious elite would help Mexico fulfill some of the promise of the Mexican Revolution. By the 1950s, even this optimism in modernity was no longer uncritically accepted by a growing number of Mexico's intelligentsia. Their dissatisfaction with various aspects of modernity was presented in a remarkable canon of works—movies, novels, and essays—that serve as dark counternarratives to the triumphalist narratives of the Mexican state. Among the most significant of these works were the writings of Juan Rulfo, especially his novel *Pedro Páramo* (1950), and Luis Buñuel's movie *Los Olvidados* (The Forgotten Ones, 1950). Both artists explored the physical, social, moral, and psychological fragmentation that provincial Mexicans experienced when they moved from their small towns and rural communities to urban centers in Mexico and the United States. For Rulfo, the outmigration of provincials turned Mexican small towns, like his fictional Comala, into desolate wastelands populated by the memories and murmurings of its dead inhabitants. Buñuel explored the condition of the nation's provincial population at the other end of their migration trek to Mexico City. In *Los Olvidados*, children living in the highly touted showcase of the country's modernity constantly reach out for each other attempting to remake the organic community they left behind. But like the ghosts of Comala, the forgotten ones of Mexico City only encounter solitude in a world filled with violence, immorality, and poverty.

For Rulfo and Buñuel, as well as for Octavio Paz, who published *The Labyrinth of Solitude* in 1950, this "permanent and constant orphanhood" stands as an indictment of an incomplete modernity that seemed better suited for destroying the old than it was at building the new.[15] Ironically, the work of these mid-century artists and philosophers can also be read as a middle-class reproach of Mexico's poor whose only response to the forces of the modern world seemed to be a self-defeating solitude. Nurtured by a dark transnational outlook and a deep millenarian mistrust in the notion of progress, Luz Moreno's letters bridge the religious oral culture of Mexico's province and the secular cultural products of cosmopolitan intellectuals like Buñuel, Rulfo, and Paz. The letters also reveal that Moreno had a wider range of emotional and imaginative responses to his loneliness and poverty than these intellectuals were willing to envision for him. Among the most powerful of these options was empathy. One of the most fascinating aspects about Luz Moreno's letters is how they highlight his desire and ability to see his life in San Miguel as intimately connected to the lives and fates of other poor people around the world. As an antidote to the dislocation and chaos of the modern world and as a salve against the losses and insults that he was experiencing in his old age, Luz sought comfort in the warmth that his immediate family gave him. He also expressed empathy for a transnational community of poor people he called *el miserable pueblo*. Luz was hardly provincial in his thinking and sympathies; he was a Catholic internationalist who believed that if it were not Christ who united humanity in life, it would be the atomic bomb and war that would bring everyone together in death (April 25, 1951; c. April 1951).[16] Worrying about his daughter, and her fate in the shadow of the bomb, or his son Chilo who went to pick cotton in Arizona as a bracero, enabled Moreno to imagine how his small corner of Mexico was connected to the wider world. It also nurtured in Luz a class-inflected "we-are-all-brothers-in-the-eyes-of-the-Lord" awareness about humanity's interconnectedness, in this world and the next. This transnational framework was informed by the newspapers Luz read, encouraged by the global religion which he was a part of, and inspired by his family's life in the United States during the height of the Cold War.[17] Indeed, while it may be true that many Mexicans thought of their country as the best place to watch the Cold War "from the ringside seats," Luz understood that the lives of all Mexicans were shaped by transnational phenomena and modern technologies that, whether they liked it or not, placed them in the ring with everyone else.[18]

Pancha was always more practical than her father, and less inclined to worry about things she could not control and people she did not know. She was not convinced that Luz should fret about the Korean War, the atomic bomb, or the fate of humanity. Her father's obsessions probably worried her more than any concern that his nuclear nightmares might come true. In San Miguel she would have talked to her father, and, in a way that was impossible to approximate using letters, calmed him down with reassurances that the world was not, in fact, at the precipice of the apocalypse. From Stockton all she could do was offer her distraught father paper and ink palliatives. Luz read his daughter's missives, but remained concerned. Sensing that Pancha was not as concerned about the Korean War and its consequences, Luz argues with her that even though the Korean War was happening far away, and among people who they were not related to, Pancha, as a good Christian, a conscious member of *el miserable pueblo*, and a "citizen of North America" who cooperates "materially and morally" with the war effort, should care about the well-being of her "brothers in Christ." Furthermore, it was wrong for her to neglect the "horrors of war" just because they were "happening far away and among strangers" (April 25, 1951; c. April 1951). If Pancha was unwilling or unable to empathize with the poor Chinese and Koreans who were dying in Asia, Luz begged her to see how the fate of these strangers was related to her life and work in Stockton, her brother Chilo's life as a bracero, and the poverty of her family in San Miguel:

It seems that as time goes by our life becomes worse. What good are the blunders of the powerful in fixing the world? Whether they fix it or not, is it not true that el miserable pueblo is still the tire of the car that carries most of the burdens of the world, including the price of peace? The powerful control the nation's wealth, invested with an authority that makes them owners not only of material goods but also of the humans who walk this earth. When there is peace, the poor are almost forgotten. When war arrives, "bring on the poor, his wife, and his children." The blood of the poor is spilled, maybe without justification or for a worthless cause, [but always] according to the caprice of the powerful. That the Americans do not want to share that wealth, not even with their allies? They refuse to allow Mexicans to freely go to work . . . [even] as braceros. But of course, during war all are welcomed (February 6, 1951).

Interspersed with Luz's commentary on the structural injustices that poor people around the world suffered at the hands of the rich and the powerful are his reflections on the misdeeds perpetuated by the Mexican government and its elite collaborators. Between 1940 and 1978 Mexico's ruling elite substituted the liberal activist agenda of the Cárdenas era (agrarian reform, worker's rights, state-funded industrialization) with an intensive and increasingly privatized program of capital accumulation, tourism, oil production, and public works. While many Mexicans benefited materially from this state-led modernization, the ones who gained the greatest advantage from the expansion of the industrializing economy were the elites themselves. This was the group that Luz writes cannot make a furrow yet consider themselves the leaders of the peasantry.[19]

Closer to home, the provincial elite, less connected to the centers of power in the nation's capital and less able to get their hands on the federal government's coffers, were nonetheless figuring out how to cash in at the expense of the poor.[20] While the pickings were more meager in small towns like San Miguel, the avarice of enterprising local government functionaries made it more difficult, in Luz's mind, for the poor to make a living.[21] One episode, involving Luz's oldest son Chito, highlights the frustration and anger that Luz felt toward the depredations and slights that the local elite perpetuated on him, his family, and the other members of el miserable pueblo. During the time Luz was corresponding with Pancha, Chito, the most entrepreneurial of the male Moreno siblings, slaughtered donkeys and turned their meat into jerky. He sold this jerky to local cantinas and *pulquerias*. Until about 1951 he had managed his business without paying taxes to the municipal government. Then around January 1951, a local functionary began to impose a one-peso tax for every donkey or horse slaughtered in the municipality. The officious meddler, Antonio Rábago, also required butchers like Chito to document that every animal they killed had been legally obtained (circa January 1951). One month later, Luz informed Pancha that someone from Guadalajara had filed a complaint with the local officials accusing Chito of slaughtering several stolen donkeys. Rábago was threatening to close Chito's business down. Luz was concerned about this intrusion because Chito was, next to Pancha, the person he most depended on for financial help. On another level—the toxic level at which material interests mix with moral indignation—Luz objected to how the local government hampered and profited from the (mostly) honest labors of his hard-working son.[22] It wasn't enough that the government limited the rights and privileges of the Church, now they were interfering with the God-given right of men to make their living and support their elderly parents.[23] Luz angrily lashes out against the government, their atheism, and their lack of culinary taste: "Men without conscience, without heart, the day will come when they will desire a piece of that meat and they will not find it. They think that each day is life and sweetness; but no, each one of those happy days is counted. God abhors the lack of charity. He sees the world filled with slavery and misery [and] the scarcity created by those who hoard products in order to resell them at higher prices. . . . The ignorance towards, or the abandonment of Christianity has sunken the world into a horrible chaos" (February 20, 1951).

Luz could hardly have been surprised by the disrespect and abuse that San Miguel's elite heaped on the town's poor; what more could be expected from people who had all but abandoned their religion for the material benefits of this world? He, however, expected more from San Miguel's clerics. They were God's servants and Luz thought that they should have respected and catered to the needs of the town's poor, if for no other reason than to recognize the fact that the poor had risen in armed rebellion twice in the previous twenty years to defend rights of the Church. But, as he recounted for Pancha, they too disrespected el miserable pueblo with a haughty and dismissive attitude that Luz found particularly offensive. One particularly evocative instance of this neglect concerns the clock in the parish church. Luz, who could not afford a timepiece, was upset because the Señor Cura would not fix the church clock. This was not important for the town's rich because, as Luz noted, they had watches and clocks to keep them company throughout the night. But, for Luz, the loss of the

church's clock meant that he spent his nights tossing and turning in his flea-infested bed, haunted by a "thousand ghosts," thinking about war, bombs, and God's judgment on humanity without knowing what time it was. In one of the most evocative passages of their correspondence, Luz writes to Pancha seething about indifference that the parish priest, the rich parishioners, and the municipal government exhibit to the needs of the town's poor:

> Nights become years as I toss and turn, unable to sleep [in] the silence of the night without knowing how many hours have gone by ... because the public clock does not function every other night, and even when it is working it only chimes on the hour or so quietly that it cannot be heard. How many times have I cursed the indifference of the Señor Cura, of the parishioners, of the municipal government, and of those who claim to have influence in society? They look at that clock with disdain and do not do anything to fix it ... The clock does not function when the clock is needed most: during the night. If we never had a working clock during the day, I would not mind; at night it is very necessary for all of us poor people who cannot afford a clock of our own. The rich have no need for a public clock (c. January, 1951; October 22, 1951).

In another letter, Luz writes to Pancha that the same Señor Cura had asked the rich people of San Miguel to donate a thousand pesos, or one of their cows, to renovate the church. Apparently the church had not been painted in almost fifty years and, according to the priest, did not have an adequate organ. Both of these deficiencies made San Miguel's parochial church (and in turn, its priests) look inferior to some of the surrounding towns whose churches were "beautifully decorated and ... adorned [with] very good organs." At the time Luz penned his letter, the priest was threatening to ask God to kill the cows of the rich because none had yet donated the money or an animal. Luz was not surprised by the tightfistedness of San Miguel's elite, but he was disappointed that the priest had not thought enough of the town's poor to ask them to contribute to the cause of beautifying the church. "The burden is heavier," he reports to Pancha, "but I think he should leave this task to us poor people. You would be amazed at how many thousands of pesos in eggs have been donated [to the church]" (July 23, 1952).[24]

While Moreno's private resentments against the Señor Cura did not amount to an outright rejection of the Catholic Church, his antipathy toward the local religious and secular elite does not align with popular images of the supposed deferential attitude that poor Catholics have toward their local priest. Luz's critique is also a bit jarring because it comes from a Catholic of such abiding faith, a man whose family had risked so much to protect their religion and the institutional privileges of the Church. A couple of factors may explain Luz's attitude. First, Luz's critical stance seems to reflect a central tenet of Sinarquista political doctrine. One of the party's more radical goals was to establish a nationalist Catholic theocracy in Mexico that was free from

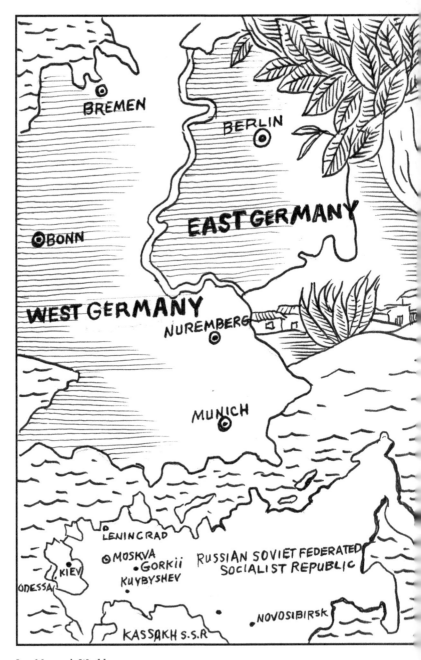

Luz Moreno's World.

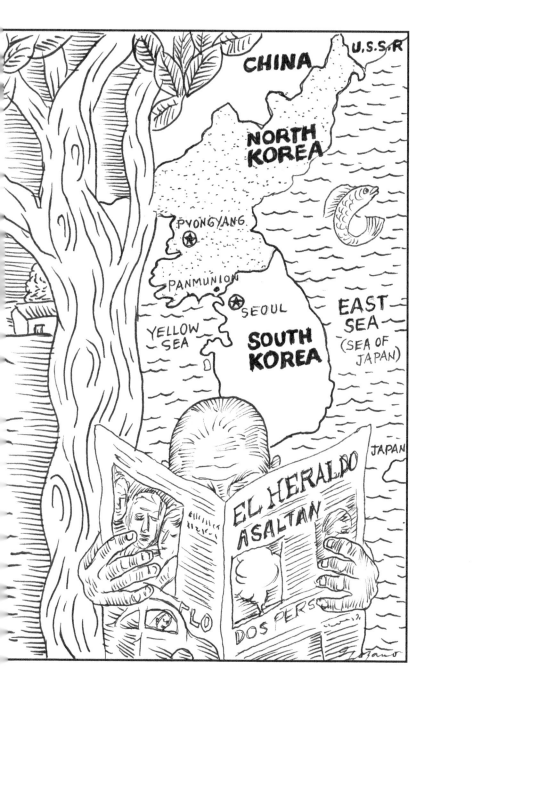

the control of foreign powers, especially the United States and the Soviet Union. Even though the Sinarquistas believed that this Catholic regeneration of Mexican society could only be achieved and maintained through personal sacrifice (martyrdom if need be) and an adherence to Catholic values, they emphasized that theirs was not a religious movement. Because they were regularly accused by their enemies on the left of being agents of the Vatican and puppets of the Mexican high clergy, the Sinarquista leadership was always careful to stress that they were not controlled by the Catholic clergy, who they believed were not always cognizant of or sympathetic to Mexico's authentic national interests. This attitude is exemplified by Salvador Abascal who when asked about the party and its affiliation with the Catholic Church hierarchy, responded, "We are proud to confess that we believe in God. We respect the clergy, but we are not controlled by the clergy."[25]

While Luz Moreno was very familiar with Sinarquista political doctrine, it is more likely that his critical stance toward the Church's local representatives came from more organic experiences. Indeed, the rift between Luz and the Señor Cura highlights the often hidden power struggle that occurs between common people, the local clergy, and their rich patrons over "ownership" of the Church. Luz's pious anticlericalism, his sense of entitlement to his contrarian opinions about the behavior of the local clergy, and his clear sympathies for, and identification with, el miserable pueblo, were products of his experiences in postrevolutionary Mexico.[26] He and his family had lived through four decades in which the persecution of the Catholic Church had resulted in moments when laypeople (mostly the region's poor) had not only fought and died for their religion, but had also performed many of the liturgical ritual activities that had normally been the exclusive purview of the clergy, such as baptism, weddings, and funerals. These experiences may have given Luz the sense that he had earned the right to express his disdain for a priest who disrespected the town's hard-working, poor parishioners.[27] Without foregoing his Catholicism or his allegiance to the Catholic Church as the institutional representative of God's will, Luz felt entitled to question the parish priest's competence, to chafe indignantly at how cozy he was with the town's elite, and to be vexed at his patronizing attitude toward the poor people who, in his mind, were the soul of the Church.[28]

Luz's epistolary laments about the injustices he sees and feels—in his family, in his town, in his Church, in his country, and in the world—also reveal the "hidden injuries of class"[29] that constantly and maddeningly reminded him that he was poor, alone, and insignificant. He complains about the stomach ailments that refused to allow him the peace to eat without vomiting the small portions of food his poor family gave him. He pens angry diatribes about the petty fights he had with his family over matters of money and respect. He bemoans the lack of deference that the young show him, and he complains about the humiliation of having to live in the house owned by an often angry and petty sister-in-law. Because these small aggressions and private humiliations occur in the most intimate of situations, the effects they have on the psyche of the poor and dispossessed are largely missing from the historical record. Luz's letters are important not only because they provide a first-hand accounts of the emotional pall and sense of social fragmentation that accompanied one poor person's encounter with a world in which economic opportunity was often predicated on nomadism, abandonment, and solitude. They are also important because they highlight Moreno's refusal to be crushed by the daily reminders that he was old and poor and that this world—the world of the rich, of the city, of the young, of the United States, of materialism—was not meant for him and people like him. Indeed, in rebuke of the plethora of midcentury portrayals of Mexico's forgotten ones as helpless pawns to the unrelenting and unforgiving forces of modern industrial capitalism, Luz's letters reveal a man with a rich set of coping strategies and empowering ideas. He had his religion that assured him that there was a better world than the material one he and his loved ones lived and suffered in. He had his empathy that reached out to the world and reminded him that even though he was poor, he was a member of a dignified, hardworking community that was loved by an angry and vindictive God who did not look kindly on the predations of the rich. He also had his family that reminded him that though they lacked material comforts, they did not have to be humiliated or unhappy (circa July, 1950). Lastly, Luz Moreno had his letters and his newspapers; missives from afar that regularly brought the outside world to his little corner of Mexico and guaranteed the old sharecropper that while he may have been lonely, he was not alone.

How did people ever get the idea they could communicate with one another by letter! One can think about someone far away and one can hold on to someone nearby; everything else is beyond human power.

Franz Kafka, Letters to Milena[1]

～ལྷ⹄～

c. July 1950

To my beloved ausentes,

My children, many are the causes that unite us and require our constant attention and communication. Both good and evil continually unfold. Many times the means to combat evil are not at our disposal ... Good sometimes becomes evil. The same with evil, which sometimes becomes a good. This confusion fills us with distrust to the point that often we refuse to do good, even when it is within our reach ...

Because sicknesses are a punishment imposed by God, we cannot avoid them. We are also often unable to avoid disagreements with others. Poverty is both good and bad. The same with wealth. It all depends on whether we do good or bad with [either condition.] If we are poor, and not humiliated by it, what do we need riches that could harm us? If by being poor we are obligated to work, what good would it be to be rich and lay around like a lizard in the sun, thinking about everything but God and our salvation? He who desires many things is not happy; rather, the happy person is the one who moderates his desires and conforms himself to his luck.

My infirmity has made me rather ill. I always [feel ill] during the rainy season beginning in July, [but this year it is worse] since Chila died.[2] I purged myself and I felt a little better. On the 7th I ate *carne asada* and *chile* with *atole* for lunch. A little later, I drank some milk; soon after that, Victorina gave me a [illegible]. Soon after, I felt a terrible nausea. I threw up three times: the lunch, the milk, the *atole,* and the remedy. After I had thrown up everything, I spewed out a salty spit. I did not eat until the evening, then I drank a *cal asentada.* ...[3] The rest of the people, like Mamá Cunda and the girls, are fine. Chuy[4] lost his job; I do not know why, maybe it's because he went to Guadalajara without permission ...

1. Franz Kafka, *Letters to Milena*, trans. Philip Boem (New York: Schoken Books, 1990), 223.
2. Chila was Chito Moreno's youngest daughter. As best as the surviving members of the family can remember, she died of dysentery.
3. *Cal asentada*: Because the water in the region was full of impurities, people added lime to their drinking water. Once the lime sank to the bottom of the container, the water was believed to be not only safe for drinking, but was also have curative powers.
4. Jesús (Chuy) Moreno: Luz Moreno's grandson.

The chief Ofelia Ramirez did not even come to San Miguel. She is touring Jalisco, Zacatecas and Tamaulipas, Ciudad Guzman, Jerez and Tula. Sunday the 23rd, she celebrated a public assembly in Tula, Tamaulipas; comrade David Contreras, the one from the National Committee, served as delegate. Comrade María de Jesús Ocampo, the one from the Jalisco Regional, accompanied Mrs. Ofelia on this tour. We expect a lot from her tour. The newspaper *Orden* is talking about war.[5]

Receive our salutations. Do not stop writing us, do not believe that [your letters] bore us. They are our only consolation. Luz Moreno, his wife, and his children, Congratulations!

December 24, 1950

[My children],

The reason I write is to tell you about what is happening in our home, our town, our nation, and even in the entire world. In our home, conflict does not stop. Presently, we do not know where my comadre Angelita is living.[6] She does not come home for any reason; she says everyone attacks her here. Pancha, you know how arrogant she is, with children and adults alike. She wants to get involved in every matter, and she wants her way in every situation. Even though she considers herself the ruler of the household, it is impossible for everyone to put up with her when she arrogantly expresses her poorly-understood whims. She has even scolded me for buying the newspaper. She should scold the drunkards instead of me. She says I do not live up to my obligations.

On the 13th, we were trying to wash the menudo ... but I was not allowed to help because I did not know how. Well, I lit the fire and I noticed how my comadre [Angelitas] was preparing [the cow's] feet; [because she was doing so,] I put a cow's foot in the water.[7] I should not have done that

5. *Orden:* the name of one of the Sinarquista newspapers. For details on the origin of the name and the schism in the Sinarquista Party that caused the name of the paper to be changed from *El Sinarquista* to *Orden* in 1946, see Hugh Gerald Campbell, "The Radical Right in Mexico, 1929–1949" (PhD diss., University of California, Los Angeles, 1968), 366.

6. Angelita Román was Cunda Moreno's sister. She never married and spent most of her adult life as the maid to one of the richest women in San Miguel. Through this connection, she accumulated enough wealth to purchase several rural properties and homes in San Miguel. One of the houses she owned was the house in which Luz Moreno and his family lived. The combination of her notorious bad temper and Luz Moreno's inability to pay for the use of the home caused many problems between Luz and Angelita and her brother Hilario.

7. *Menudo:* Tripe soup. The cow's feet were placed in boiling water to remove the hair before cooking.

because she said, "Why did you stick that foot in the water? The water is still cold." So I told her that I had seen her stick a foot in the water. She believed I was playing with words implying that she had "stuck her foot in it . . ." She got mad and said, "Well, so that I do not stick my foot in it again, I better leave." She thought I could not wash the menudo; but because I did, she got even angrier.

At night she cooked the menudo, [but] did not put the feet [that I had washed] into the kettle; [she said it was] because she could not find them, or because they would not fit. [This is what she said, but I think] it was just to spite me. She used to argue with Victorina, Ysabel, and Lula often. She could not stand the children and she always wanted [their parents] to hit them; she did not want anyone looking at her askance. We would not eat until sundown. Your poor Mamá would get so angry, but she would not let her see it. And now I do not know where she is, nor where she sleeps, nor where she eats; she does not come to the house. I know that she is sewing garments with María's daughters, but why she just does not return home is a great mystery.

I do not miss Hilario. He has never been fond of me; now it seems as if we are quarreling, but we are not. One day he told me not to put the cow chips near the laurel [tree], that I should put them in the backyard. I told him that the donkeys would tread all over them, and that [in that case] it would be better not to bring any. Then he said, "In all this time you have not been able to build a fence [to keep the donkeys corralled]?"[8] I told him, "I am not the owner to make such decisions." He answered me very angrily, "You are not the owner, yet you are here anyway." [I know] he meant that my family and I had no right to live in his house. Since then, we speak even less. He does not speak with me, nor I with him. It is not an ongoing issue. He does not talk to anyone about my comadre's absence. The mystery remains. You may assess the risks that these "cracks-in the-wall" pose to our moral household.

On the 22nd we received your letter where you let us know that work never ends. You wrote that you are filling many orders to be shipped, who knows where. It is good that there is a lot of work. What would you do if there were no work? You also write that you will visit when there is no work.

It hurts us not being able to see you, but we cannot ask for the impossible. Ever since you left we understood that it would not be easy for you to return. Do you think there is so much work because of the war? What other reason could there be? How else would the expenses of war be covered, if not by production? Each individual, native or foreign, is part of a collective [whose] cooperation is used to meet the needs of the individual and

---

8. Dried cow manure was used for fuel. If the donkeys step on the chips and break them into small pieces, they cease being useful as fuel.

the group ... Right now there is much trading with US Dollars, and that is because of the war. What a pity that this bounty of work will last such a short time and be filled with such sadness ...

My comadre Angeles [Angelita] is staying at Hilario's place, where she eats and sleeps. I do not know how much longer it will last. If she convinces Hilario to leave, we will lose this house. What justification would we have for living there? Who knows where we will end up. Our house is almost lost, is this not the case?

We are doing well. I have not had palpitations since the 15th of November; only once, but it lasted less than two minutes. I am not well. I am taking a purgative tonic and I eat some *menudo* soup. My dear children, you will see that if medicine is important for me, so is good nutrition. We send you our regards and our regret because you have not been able to come visit us. But it is better that you have work. You should pray to God for an end to the war and that He finds us worthy of His Compassion.

Luz Moreno

~~e&~~

c. January 1951

[My children,]

It does not matter how many letters come and go because they are not enough to satisfy our desires to know about the details of our lives. Juan complains about his corn, that he does not know if Chito has bought it, how much, and at what price. I have seen that he [Chito] bought good corn, more yellow than white. I am not sure how much, but around 10 *fanegas*, or more.[9] His letter might not have reached you yet, but he wrote to you around the middle of January. Chito was very busy during that time: someone brought in 30 donkeys for him to slaughter, and because he had to kill them he had no rest. His business is no longer free—he must now pay one peso for every jack or jenny donkey and for every horse or philly that he slaughters. He also has to prove that each animal was legally obtained. Antonio Rábago monitors this. Every day, Rábago goes to Chito and notes all the animals that are to be slaughtered in his logbook. Corn is at 55 cents per kilo retail, and I think your corn cost 35 pesos per fanega. What will you do with that corn? Because you are not coming [any time soon,] you can send word about what you want to do with it. If you keep it too long it will become infested and rotten and

---

9. 10 *fanegas* equals 16 bushels; 1 *fanega* equals about 1.6 US bushels.

cannot be sold at a good price. If he [Chito] mixes it with lime or something else, it will ruin it.[10] I am not the one who should decide on this matter, but if you can come up with something please tell us and we will gladly abide by whatever instructions you send. In Veracruz, they are offering jobs cutting sugarcane at 4.50 pesos per ton.

Your visit is certain, but we do not know when. Father will only be here if [your visit] is this year. You may ask yourselves, why so much doubt this year after so many years of life? If you only knew how difficult it is for me to walk with the heavy burdens we are facing now. Nights become years as I toss and turn, unable to sleep [in] the silence of the night without knowing how many hours have gone by . . . because the public clock does not function every other night, and even when it is working it only chimes on the hour or so quietly that it cannot be heard. How many times have I cursed the indifference of the Señor Cura, of the parishioners, of the municipal government, and of those who claim to have influence in society? They look at that clock with disdain and do not do anything to fix it. And if the bellman does not make the necessary repairs or, because of ignorance or laziness, does not look after the clock, it is only because the Señor Cura coddles him and lets him fall asleep. The clock does not function when the clock is needed most: during the night. If we never had a working clock during the day, I would not mind; at night it is very necessary for all of us poor people who cannot afford a clock of our own. The rich have no need for a public clock. It gives our town a bad image when compared to other nearby towns. Nowadays, we really do need a lot of strength to put up with our luck. God has Earth's days numbered. Humanity cries tears of blood. My children receive God's blessings and with it my blessings as well.

Your father,
Luz Moreno.

February 14, 1951

Beloved children,

May God keep you in His Grace. I send my regards. Tell me how you are doing? How has it been for you in this cold weather, and how is work is coming along? How do those gringos treat you? Have the Americans made peace, or

---

10. Lime was mixed into dry corn to keep bug infestation at bay.

have they killed all of the Chinese and North Koreans? I would like to know how many American [soldiers] have died because the newspapers here only say that Communists and Chinese have died, but not one single American. That is unbelievable; I know they do that to give the Americans an imaginary victory.

On the 9th [of this month], at 7pm, your sewing teacher Adelaida died. Her mass was on the 10th because there is no cantor. My *compadre* Jesús is at odds with the Señor Cura, and I do not know who will win.[11] The Cura

11. Jesús Delgado was Luz Moreno's friend and intellectual confidant. A man of many talents and interests, Delgado was the church's cantor, a painter, a musician, and the director of the town's brass band. He was also a Sinarquista who, among other things, painted the national and Sinarquista emblems on the flags that Pancha sewed for the party.

wants to give the girls the obligations of the cantor, such as singing the meditations of the third fall. Because Ysabel is the oldest, [he wants her] to teach the rest of the girls. Hilario, Ysabel, and Sidonia arrived on the 10th from Guadalajara. Only Chilo did not come because the herb business is getting difficult and people do not want to pay. My comadre [Angeles] is staying with us, [she] is having difficulties with Victorina— they hate each other. We had a turkey ready for your arrival, but the chickens came down with a disease; we were afraid that the turkey had caught it too, so we ate it—but in your honor. We still have the pig that Chito is fattening. Who knows what will become of it, it weighs around 8 *arrobas* [200 lbs].

What a shame it is that every [day] we lose hope of your visit. You tell us that right now it is not possible because Juan is not able to come . . .

If war is formally declared, we shall see both sides drag humanity [to its destruction] because of their whims. You tell me in your letters that they have invented a bomb so that people will not suffer the effects of the atomic [radiation]. I just cannot figure how this is so. The shards? Who will stop them from killing the poor people who find themselves around [the area where the bomb is dropped]? The contaminated air? Who will stop it from dispersing? That preference for work is slavery. Receive my regards.

Luz Moreno

February 20, 1951

[My beloved children,]

As the world becomes more favorable to those who are the strongest, the most influential, [and] the most arrogant, the poor are the [ones who are] dispossessed. They are the ones who see government employees and their *compadres* become rich off the sweat of the people. They [see them] operate under the shadow of the government and receive thousands of pesos for doing almost nothing. They do not know how to make a furrow, but they are the representatives of the *campesinos*. They do not know what reason or justice is, but they do know how to turn black into white and white into black.

There was a complaint in Guadalajara by someone whose donkeys were supposedly lost. [He was certain that] they were slaughtered here. Mr. Santiago Davalos also raised a complaint over the same issue, and that is why an order was issued in Guadalajara that donkeys could no longer be slaughtered here. Men without conscience, without heart, the day will come when they will desire a piece of that meat and they will not find it. They think that each day is life and sweetness; but no, each one of those happy days is counted. God abhors the lack of charity. He sees the world filled with slavery and misery [and] the scarcity created by those who hoard products in order to resell them at higher prices. We ourselves are the cause of all the disorder in the world. It starts in the homes, the towns, and the nations. The ignorance toward, or the abandonment of, Christianity has plunged the world into a horrible chaos.

Illness does not stop visiting us. On the 16th, I had palpitations again and they lasted 3 hours. At the same time, I had a horrible colic. My stomach hurt me like in the rainy season, so I drank lemon tea and rested. I even had a tick in my ear for over two months. On the 17th, I put water in my ear and lay down, because I had gotten rid of one like that before. As soon as I felt it start to tickle my ear as it walked out, I called somebody to come help me pull it out. It is much easier once it is visible. Victorina was the one who pulled it out. She is very squeamish and almost refused. Only you, Pancha, pulled them out without disgust. Ever since I was a child they have always grown in my left ear, never in the other ear. Hilario's doctor says that he seems to be doing better because of his bed rest. Everyone else is fine. We send our regards and I hope that you are not now suffering too much [from the] cold.

Luz Moreno

꧁꧂

singular / collective

February 26, 1951

My dear children,

It seems that as time goes by our life becomes worse. What good are the blunders of the powerful in fixing the world? Whether they fix it or not, is it not true that el _miserable pueblo_ is still the tire of the car that carries most of the burdens of the world, including the price of peace? The powerful control the nation's wealth, invested with an authority that makes them owners not only of material goods but also of the humans who walk this earth. When there is peace, the poor are almost forgotten. When war arrives, "bring on the poor, his wife, and his children." The blood of the poor is spilled, maybe without justification or for a worthless cause, [but always] according to the caprice of the powerful. That the Americans do not want to share that wealth, not even with their allies? They refuse to allow

Mexicans to freely go to work ... [even] as braceros. But of course, during war all are welcomed. If they refuse to help others, it is good that now they will fight alone. Who would they complain to?[12]

It has been a year since I watched you prepare your things to leave. My first words to Juan were, "Do not forget to keep up with the war." Juan responded, "No, there is no war. The Russians are broke and there will be no war for at least 10 years." You had just arrived at your destiny in April ... when war broke out in July. Then you told me that the war was far away and that nobody was worried. I reminded you to stay aware, to look out for yourselves because war is like the flailing legs of a drowning man, only the water can endure them. You know that the place most affected by war is North America. Therefore, you should look to live somewhere else; small towns are the least affected [by war.] Would it not be better to live in a small place, instead of those larger towns where there is more [trouble]? ... On the 24th we received the photograph of both of you. Thank you for this gesture. May God repay you for so much goodness, but we are sad because we do not know when you will come visit us. On the 3rd of March they will inaugurate the monument to the Niños Heroes in Guadalajara.[13] The President of the Republic will be there. I would also like to go. We send our regards.

March 10, 1951

To my absent children,

Beloved children, spring has arrived and by now you must have felt a little warmth in those cold lands. How do you rest? You are not likely to feel as warm as if you were here, but at least it should be less cold. Here, the rain clouds have moved in. Perhaps each month will bring us closer to the rainy season.

How are you doing in terms of health and employment? What do you think of the crowds of people that surround you? You, who are closer to the areas that are fighting for their freedom, would know better which matters require more attention. Here the newspapers more or less inform us that the Russians will not wage war for the time being; [but] the Koreans

---

12. Moreno is directing his ire against the United States and the Bracero Program that was siphoning off many of the region's working age men to the Unites States during the Korean War.

13. *Niños Heroes*: Cadets from the military academy based in the Chapultepec Castle (Mexico City) who supposedly flung themselves down the side of the castle rather than give up the Mexican flag to the American troops that invaded Mexico in 1847.

do not stop killing each other. If that question goes beyond the limits of provability, what then is really happening? The conditions of an undeclared war, together with the conditions that the people are subjected to, make the situation unbearable. *El miserable pueblo* finds itself as if on a tumultuous sea: they come and they go. The government gives hope of employing [the braceros], and there go [the men] guessing where they should go to get permission so as to be allowed to go to the Promised Land.[14] And while half the world makes plans for their lives, the other half resists the attacks [of the world] and gives [us] an example of patience. Man is the enemy of man. The modern world is admirable for its science, but there are people who are very ignorant. People's ignorance varies in many ways. Some people only have superficial knowledge of some things. They do not know how to read or write, but they are of good will. Others know nothing and are of bad will. Other people are half rich and half wise, partly good and partly bad. These [people] are neither for God nor for the Devil. Other people are very smart in material matters, but mean spirited. They are only good for losing themselves and losing others ... The world is made up of all these types of people. Good people come from this mixture. In the end, only God will know who will win. My dearest children, in some way I would like to give you a gift. Please receive these letters that are inspired by the love I have for you. I hope they are of some help to you. I send our regards. We are well, thanks be to God.

Luz Moreno

c. April 1951

Dearest children,

Even if it is only once in a while, I would like to direct [my attention] to you, greet you, and have you tell me about the luck you have had in those war-torn lands that are nevertheless coveted by the rest of the world. We are not satisfied with our situation—we want Dollars ... We want to obtain them at any cost. Take a look at the Russians, if [the United States]

---

14. Candidates for the Bracero Program were chosen through a complicated process that involved a lot of luck, persistence, and not a little corruption, bribery, and access to patronage. It is described in Timothy J. Henderson, *Beyond Borders: A History of Mexican Migration to the United States*, (Malden, MA: Wiley-Blackwell, 2011), 73–74; Michael Snodgrass, "Patronage and Progress: The Bracero Program from the Perspective of Mexico," in *Workers Across the Americas: The Transnational Turn in Labor History*, ed. Leon Fink (New York: Oxford University Press, 2011), 245–266.

is not careful their nation will be taken from them. We the poor, who suffer miserably, want work in order to see those Dollars in our possession. War, as terrible as it is, would not matter [to the poor] if the Dollars would come. That the Mexican government has promised thousands of Mexican [braceros to the United States]? If the situation in Korea does not end, there will be no remedy: we will go to drink from the bitter chalice of death in war. What will it feel like to die against our will, some here and some there? I would like for us to die together; but no, we will die as God wishes. For the last time I send you my writings. I have no money. My world has turned upside down. The world will remain behind. Please pray for everyone, even if I do not write again.

I received the photographs from Korea. We saw the Chinese; it is sad to see that those poor people are not respected, even in their own nation. They were pulled from their land and they were split open like watermelon. They were taken from their nation to fight in Korea. Now they

are being bombed in their own country. No, to be poor and dark-skinned is a great shortcoming. In <u>the past, the dark ones were beasts of burden</u>; <u>and if it were not for the Catholic Church, those poor races would still</u> <u>[live] like slaves</u>. To this day there are Indians in some countries who are steeped in paganism. If Christian civilization does not come to them, those people will be lost. You ask me not to write "Don Juan" or "Doña Francisca" on the envelopes? Well, I do it because in the [post] office I speak with the employees, and inside the envelopes I speak with my children.

Maximino is in bed with an intestinal fever; he doesn't even have money to cure himself . . . The Church cantor has already arrived. My poor compadre [Jesús Delgado] is making flowerpots and sad faces. The [cantor] sings very well, even though he is old. We are going to have a Novena for Saint Joseph, it starts on the 3rd and ends on the 11th [of April]. We send our thoughts; we are well. The Feast of the Señor de la Misericordia will be held.[15]

Luz Moreno

April 25, 1951

Beloved children,

My desires to see you grows at the same rate as my hope that you will visit diminishes. I see how your circumstances grow with difficulties. And though I wish these difficulties would end, they continue to grow. The war has made the world a different place . . . and although it seems that there are more jobs, these jobs are more strenuous. We <u>all have the same predisposition to oppress</u>; that is why in the North there are many oppressors and many oppressed. The oppressors are some opportunistic and unjust American farmers who take advantage of the hunger of those who cross over without the protection of any authority. They give them a job, but do not to pay them what is just. [They pay them] whatever they feel like paying. And the oppressed receive these wages that instead of mitigating their hunger only increases it. And yet, no matter how harsh and inhuman the treatment that they receive is, they do not learn.[16]

15. *El Señor de la Misericordia*: is the Christ that is the patron of Tepatitlán, Jalisco. The fiestas in Tepatitlán to honor *El Señor* are held during April and culminate on the 30th of that month. Tepatitlán is about 60 kilometers away from San Miguel.
16. Luz is referring to the Bracero Program.

Regarding Juan's work: he might not be subjected to such humiliations, but he is not absolutely free from them given that he does not have the same freedom he had before the conflict started. He was expecting to have vacation time this year, and was denied. If the ones that control public policy could get away with it, they would use other people's hands to handle the matters of war since these [matters] burn their hands like fire . . . Work is as necessary as rest, sleep, healthy and nutritious food, and meals [eaten] on a regular schedule . . .

I have written that I am not able to write you often or without some effort because I cannot afford the postage. I do not exaggerate anything, nor do I tell you this to seek pity. I tell you, if you choose to believe it, because when you are 73 you will see [how it feels]. In the letters we have received, you give us hope that you will visit. You say that you will visit as soon as your home is finished [and] rented. That you work on the house for two hours every day and are very tired every night. May God give you the strength to continue the tasks that you have imposed on yourselves.

I am very happy that you, Pancha, are not afflicted by the war. That you both live tranquilly, as if you lived in Mexico. This is good; I hope you continue this way. No, if we do not pay attention to its consequences, war does not seem so bad. [It is only bad for those] who have family members who go to war. Even if they are dying by the thousands, if they are not our relatives, it does not affect us too much. Scarcity concerns us only when we do not have the money to buy what we need. If we lived in those places, witnessing the carnage up close, then we would be deeply affected by the war: hearing the screams of the soldiers, the wailing of the orphaned children who search for their parents, [seeing] people sleep in the open, cold and filled with terror. And not for one or two days, the war in Korea has already lasted almost a year and there are no signs that it will stop.

Does this scene cease to be moving because it is happening far away and among strangers? If we are beings who call God our Father and the source of our existence, then these tormented strangers are our brothers in Christ and we cannot be [insensitive] toward their suffering. Now you live in that nation and you form an integral part of it. As citizens of North America [you are] obligated to cooperate materially and morally [with the war effort]. How far are those who are dying from those who might just as easily die? It is good to have serenity and not to worry about much; that, however, is very different from neglecting the horrors of war, or not having compassion for those who are dying for a worthless cause.

Receive our regards and our news, as rude as they may be. Here, everyone is fine. I hope to go to Tepa[titlán]. May God bless you.

Luz Moreno

～∾e∾～

May 10, 1951

To my unforgettable ausentes,

Beloved children, the events of the day have us very worried. It looks like misfortune is at our door: vices, jealousy, pride, ignorance, misery, the lack of charity, the lack of respect for adults, parents, and the old, [as well as] to those who guide [our] souls, scarcity, the lack of jobs, the loss of crops, the lack of security in the countryside and in the workshops, and the lack of unity to achieve good (people only unite to achieve ill). All of Hell is loose; that is why there is no peace, that is why the world burns in flames. War, plague, and hunger threaten to finish off humanity, and we are so resigned that we all walk in unison to Death's cart. We drink vices up like water and we sin against God as if He were a wooden stick . . .

Our lives are very simple and quiet and only as if by a miracle our family is able to obtain things to eat. Getting some clothes, forget it. As soon as Mamá Cunda saw herself cured of the burn [on her foot] she [went] to visit homes.[17] The girls, Victorina, make one or two dresses, work as cooks, give injections, [and] wash [other people's clothes.] Isabel runs errands, helps with the dressmaking, attends to our kitchen, and is the authentic, severe, and energetic voice of our home—she never speaks softly, always loudly and heatedly, and no one escapes [her wrath], not even the oldest [among us], not even her father. Lula, the tame one, the harmless one, the obedient one, suffers the scoldings with calm. She is, after all, an orphan.[18] Since her mom died I thought that they would see her with compassion, but instead they come down on her even harder; she works all day and even then they are not happy with her.[19] Jesús [Lula's brother] is making popsicles; he may not make much, but he no longer

17. "Visit homes" refers to Secundina's job as a midwife. Secundina had hurt her foot and had gone to get it cured by the "Brujas de la Cantera." The so-called Witches of the Quarry were women who lived by the town's stone quarry and who served as midwives, nurses, and doctors to the town's poor. Their cure for Secundina's ailing foot was to burn it, which only, according to Luz, exacerbated her problem.

18. Her mother was Pancha's sister, Micaela.

19. "They come down on her even harder" is a translation of *les save aser leña el palo caido*; "and even then they are not happy with her" is a translation of *ni por eso queda vien*.

thinks about *el Norte*. José [their youngest brother] is in school. Chilo goes to Guadalajara and sells his essence and returns to his town with the blessings of God and his parents. Chito is killing [his donkeys] without the knowledge of his father or the government; his butt will rue the day when they catch up with him. He brings dead pigs on his donkeys and he transports fertilizer, he plays music during the cockfights, and he raises [his own] pigs. He is the hardest worker. Lolo is a master mason [and] violinist, too bad that he likes to drink; right now he is skinny [illegible].

Receive our offerings and our memories,
Luz Moreno

July 3, 1951

Beloved children

On the 25th, we received some letters and a Dollar that surely must be for Mamá Cunda on this the day of days, the 60th anniversary of her birth. In this, my letter, I send my most sincere appreciation because you decided to honor the Being who has created you and has adopted a silent but laborious attitude in and out of the home. She is the center around which all the interests of the home are concentrated. It is known, and seen as a general rule, that the Mother is [the person] through whom love is made manifest. You do very well, my Children, in honoring your Mother; and now more than ever that she finds herself in a weak state because of her age. She is finishing her mission on earth, and these manifestations [of love] give her breath and vigor. You give an example worthy of imitation, and you sow a seed that in time will give its fruits.

On the 29th, Chuy Orozco left for Matamoros with the intent of finding work. We are not lacking in troubles and worries. It afflicts me to see people from my family leave. Here, he was working with Chilo [making] shoes but he is very inconsistent and gets tired of it and leaves his work. You will see that soon enough he will return. Lula was sick, her throat hurt and she had a cold on the 28th. To top it off, she saw her brother [Chuy leave], it makes me sad to see her.

Lolo was very drunk on the 24th, 25th, 26th, 27th, 28th, and 29th, and now he cannot cure himself. He is very unbalanced. He had been well for a long time. On the 24th of June he and his musical group played at a house; all the drinks were free and they all got drunk. Since that day, Lolo, with the pretext of getting better, has continued to get drunk. Chito and Chilo are working very honorably. Chito killing donkeys here and there and Chilo making shoes. It has rained a lot; they can't even work for the mud.

It seems that the war wants to end, that is what the newspapers are saying. The communists do not know what to do with the world. They proposed a cease-fire—let us see what their conditions are, they are probably very harsh. Each side wants to end [the war] in a better position [than when they started]. This is not possible. Beginning the war was easy, the settlement is difficult. I believe that when the war ends, the need for labor will diminish. That is why you can work now with more ease and you can plan your return with more liberty.

The world asks for peace. But we want peace among vice. The way the world is going nowadays we are forcing God to punish us. We see how the elements are against us: the seasonal rains are very irregular; it either doesn't rain or it rains too much. Sicknesses like infantile paralysis are epidemic. Famine, lack of jobs, are vices that tempt us like demons. If we ignore the virtues, how are we going to face the enemy without weapons? We lack religious instruction.

You will see how much the world's luck will change. War is like a plague because it obstructs peace. Without peace there is no liberty, and without liberty there is no progress. The seasonal rains began on the 24th and have continued in abundance until the 1st of July. If they continue this way, they will not be able to sow.

1st of July, onomastic day [name day] of Cunda. Thou art fortunate, my children, because your purpose is to honor your MOTHER. She feels happy because she sees that her children love her. The children feel proud because God has preserved their treasure, their Mamásita. Children of mine, your absence has cost your mother tears. In these past days Chuy Orozco left to see if he could get to that coveted land, but he got to San Luis [Potosí] and returned because that American Government is very harsh. If there were not people so well-established over there, as if they were from over there, there would not be so much interest [in going] from those here who are in great need. Till next time.

Luz Moreno

July 23, 1951

Juan and Pancha, our unforgettable ausentes and much-loved children,

There are many things that worry us, and as long as we do not communicate them our pain does not ease. When you split something it decreases in size; likewise, when you share a pain it decreases in intensity. This is the reason for having friends, for having relatives, and for having people

of our own blood who will watch over our family. But some may say that this is only so when there exists an equal opportunity to reciprocate, which is not the case here because you are rich and we are poor. [You are] generous and we lack goodness, and are perhaps ingrates. With what voices, with what reasons, are we to speak about virtues when we do not even know virtue? We question ourselves, we make a thousand efforts to reciprocate [your] generous acts; still, we find it impossible to equal your generosity. This may well cause dismay in the people to whom we owe many favors. But do not think that way, do not think that your favors are left [hanging] in thin air; we will be faithful and will be at your orders, send us what you will. We the wretched, who are not worth anything, offer ourselves up to your wishes. We appreciate your favors, and in these times of trial there is nothing left than to depend on generous hearts. In these times of calamity and misery, our union and our fine friendship is a necessity.

What do you think of the Korean War: will it be resolved or will it continue? You can bet that if it resolves itself that peace will not be true peace; [it will not be a peace] that is based on the principles of Christian charity. It is a peace based on the demands of the Reds, who [ask] that North American troops be removed from South Korea, that Red China take part in the United Nations, [and] that Formosa belong to China. In the end, [what they want] is for Korea to become part of Russia; or at least for everyone [the United States and Russia] to have their own piece. The 38th Parallel is nothing but a fiction created by the Russians and North Americans during the last war. Last year on the 25th of June so much distrust was generated [between the Russians and the Americans] that over the course of 1951 there have been more than 1 million deaths, only to remain in the same situation.

On the 22nd I had strong palpitations; [they] lasted a long time, [about] 5 hours. Ask God to not make it so. Receive our remembrances. Do not forget this poor family!!

Luz Moreno

c. July 14, 1951

Beloved Children,

We received your letters on the 13th of July. . . . Along with the letter we received some photographs that we took great pleasure in contemplating [because they showed us] the faithful reproduction of the human figures of our beloved, generous, and absent children in those majestic mountains. We are very happy that you chose such a nice day to spend climbing those hills. I looked at each and every one of those photographs and I was struck at how plump and pleasant Pancha looked with her white dress and Juanito stylishly dressed ala Americano. Here, we deal with our cruel destiny and our great desire to find ourselves in your presence. Thanking you for your generosities, we send a hug.

All over the republic rural workers are complaining about the torrential rains and the hailstorms. I have yet to be caught outside by a hailstorm. Because they no longer ask me for soil, it has been a month since I bring any. Many people are bringing soil.[20]

The temptation that grips those who want to enter the United States as braceros does not end. If from one side [of the border] they threaten them, from the other side they give them hope. It would be better if they would just prohibit their entrance and give them no false hopes. Or they should just let everyone enter—[either everyone,] or no one. Both governments play innocent of the causes that obligate Mexicans to go over illegally. Even a blind person can see these causes: How, and with what peace, can one cultivate the land in Mexico without guarantees? The usurpers are just waiting for the harvest in order to steal it. The American government does not want to give any rights to some; yet these Mexicans see thousands [of their compatriots] who [have lived in the United States] for so long that they are just like [American] nationals. No, this is wrong, very unequal, [and] very unjust. The work is very heavy because they do not hire enough workers. . . . If we all lived in unity, you would see how different things could be. There would be no borders, and if there were any they would be there merely as a convenient way to divide the 5 maps.

Luz Moreno

August 12, 1951

Beloved children,

On the first days of August we received letters saying that you are well. [These letters] console us and . . . give us strength to go on dealing with our separation. How we would like to show you the luck that we have had here. Sorrows do not leave us in peace, vices, and illnesses. Conflicts are provoked for reasons just and unjust, with cause or without it, fights happen. Some are long, some short, some are customary, others are not.

There are no solutions to our miseries, and we have problems because we were born poor, and poverty is what causes conflicts between people.

20. Moreno is referring to his job selling potting soil.

Perhaps when you see our letters you will think that we are holding you responsible. No. You may judge as you like, but the truth is that our condition is what it is. We lament the [lack of] necessities [we need to] live, but what we lack is the patience to [deal with the condition] that God or our misfortune has put us in. Let us not blame such and such a person [for our condition].

The buses of the *Alteño* [bus cooperative] are beginning to be a force to be reckoned with. [They are going to construct] a road that begins, or is projected to begin, from El Valle [Jalisco], through San Miguel, to León [Guanajuato].[21] On the 4th some new buses were blessed with music, the pealing of bells, and food. The [office] of the Cooperative of the "*Alteña*" is located in the portal of the [municipal] court....

The situation in Korea is of global concern. They are pushing and pulling, giving hope and then taking it away. In the year that they have been fighting they have not fixed anything. The goal of the Reds is to finish off the Americans. They have set an infinite numbers of traps all over the world, it is just that nothing has worked out for them yet. Why do the Americans play dumb? The difficulty in attaining peace is that the Reds do not want it ... They have been negotiating peace for over 15 days while [they continue to] kill each other in cold blood. How many soldiers have already died in these days hoping for peace [while] their stubborn leaders [are] insistent on shooting bullets? How many will moan in the horrors of hell for having died in Korea to [the] caprices [of their leaders]?[22]

In America itself there are communists willing to prepare an attack on the American public. They have jailed many [communists], [but] how can they relax having enemies in the very foundations of their home? ... Only one thing holds back the bad, and that is that the nation is very big. But 200,000 have gone [to war] and even more Americans will go ... and without justification. Each is blaming the other. The Russians say they want peace and are always fighting. [The Americans] kill Chinese as if they were killing bugs, [but the Russians] have not learned their lesson. Well, when is

21. The first bus companies in the region were founded in the 1930s and were organized as cooperatives where all the workers owned a piece of the company and worked as associates, rather than as employees.

22. Luz is writing about the negotiations that begun in the village of Kaesong on July 10, 1951. The negotiations started after the Chinese entered the war on the North Korean's side and brought the struggle to an essential stalemate along the 38th parallel. The negotiations continued for another two years, while, as Luz points out, both armies continued to massacre each other. Armistice was called on July 27, 1953.

Stalin going to give in? Not until someone kills him, but he does not allow it. You will see, my children, that not until they finish off with all the bad nations will this war end. . . . My children, receive this poor letter and our blessing and the blessing of God. Live very carefully and with much caution. We are somewhat fine, thank God. Awaiting your arrival, do not forget all of your relatives.

Luz Moreno

September 15, 1951

My beloved children,

We felt both happy and sad when we found out that Pancha was going to come to the fiesta but then did not come because Juan nearly broke his leg. In all this time nothing had happened to him, and surely Pancha did not feel right leaving him alone by coming knowing that the doctor would not cure him well. God forbid something else should happen to him, who else but she could care for him? All of us, your family, felt bad about the hardship that Juan suffered and the pain that Pancha felt to see her own husband like that. We pray that God give you strength . . .

Chilo has gone to *el Norte*. We do not know if he will cross the border [even though], he has all of the required [documents] from both governments. In Calexico, California they are granting very short legal entries, from 40 to 27 days. They are paying 75 cents an hour and 6 dollars a day. I think it is to determine who the most qualified braceros are. [We are hearing] that at the US border, in the American states that border our national territory, there are many [Mexicans immigrants] who yearn for the American Dollar. Many go illegally to that Promised Land in search of the Dollar, and they give more importance to it than to tending the corn in their own country. Compared to the Dollar, everything seems to be stacked against corn. Corn needs a lot of water, while the Dollar does not need to be watered. Well, it does, but in an indirect way. In order for an individual to go and do what is needed, they must first eat. And everything that he eats, grows with the help of water. The political instability [in Mexico] makes the best workers leave in search of something better. What will we do? Shall we only eat Dollars?

Ysabel wants Juan to bring her two deep bowls to accommodate a lot of food and two flat plates. She [also] wants Pancha to send her some cutlery. And she says to make sure to come to the fiesta together because we have several plump chickens for you. Just pretend that you are free. . . . I told you about a year ago that I was seeing you for the last time; and although I did not see you, I still might be able to see you this time. I don't know.

Luz Moreno

❧

October 10, 1951

[Beloved Children,]

It is as if Chuy Orozco cannot find himself unless he goes to *el Norte*. He wants to know if it would be possible for you to arrange a long visit, although a short one [would do]. [He wants to go] in order to work and get some Dollars. For a long time now he has believed that you would arrange his passage, and he has made a great effort to go. Lately, they told him he was not old enough [for the Bracero Program]. But even then he has not desisted. What could he gain by going as a tourist? . . . Send him your best opinion on the matter. I tell you that *el Norte* leaves us with no time to rest, even Ysidoro wants to go. From the newspapers we learned that American farmers no longer want Mexican braceros, that it is better to hire American workers. But who is going to stop the more than a million unemployed Mexicans that we currently have [from going]? . . .

The new temple for our lady of Guadalupe that is being built over by the quarry . . . has three covered vaults that cost 3,000 pesos. They need three more and the cupola. The priest says that he likes to finish what he starts because this is what men do. [He says] that he does not care if the people say that he asks for too much [money].

We await your arrival with great joy, but we ask God that he allow us to see your visit not as something extraordinary, something out of the range of our possibilities but as something that is simple and natural. It will bring us joy to see each other. But this joy should be prudent, indulgent, and judicious. There should be calm and serenity. For you who are traveling among many dangers, be very cautious, there could be clashes and thievery . . .

Luz Moreno

❧

October 22, 1951

Juan and Pancha,

Just as you send us regards, honors, and kindness at the beginning of your esteemed letters, I hope to relay to you that our hearts, although shriveled because of our current trouble and more so because we cannot see our absent ones, nonetheless seek to gain your approval. We tell you that we are resigned not only with your decision to [go to the United States], but also with Chilo's [decision to leave] and with any one else from this family who may wish to leave. Why would we want to see you here, but hungry? . . .

Lolo was unable to get his papers, but he hopes there will be a lottery for the selection of Mexican braceros. It is said that there are over one million unemployed Mexicans, let us see how they find employment for all of them. Although they also say that they do not want Mexican braceros; that they want to save the jobs for natural born Americans. In reality, there is much confusion—the party continues, everyone does what they want, and the Dollars drive us crazy.

Oh, my children, I write you this letter so that you know that I am very ill with diarrhea. It began on the 14th. Like every day, I went to the bathroom twice without cramps; on the 19th I could not stand it any longer. I went to go see Senovia, and she gave me some powders that I had to drink every two hours. As of this moment, I have drunk two. I do not know if they are going to work. Meat is bad for me, chile, pork, mole, birria.[23] Above all, though, worries and anger [are bad for me]. Let us wait a couple of days to see what happens. I write to you because I am really messed up.[24] I have had palpitations for 8 days now. Today, I feel so ill I cannot stand the sharp pains. Do not become alarmed, my children, God will cure me. I tell you that I lose my sleep mainly in the darkest [hours] of night when the horrors of the same night awaken a thousand ghosts. It is not until the morning that I get some really good sleep; this, of course, when I am well. But when the bedbugs and the fleas keep me up, there is no clock to tell me what time it is . . .

I fear, my children, that you will become alarmed by my news. Ask God for calm, for me and for this family. Receive our thanks for the Dollar you sent Mamá [Cunda], she received it on the 14th.

Luz Moreno

October 25, 1951

Beloved children,

I well understand the pain that you feel at not receiving any news from Cecilio or Lolo. We let you know that Chilo left on September 12. When we received

23. *Birria:* spicy goat meat.
24. *"Me lleva la trampa."*

news that he had arrived at his destination, we also let you know. Now what is happening is that Chilo is not writing anywhere. I am not sure that the letters from San Miguel will arrive to where Chilo is. We also send [you his] address; I do not know if it is correct. We live in confusion. You also tell us that you have written to Chilo and that he has not responded. I think that it is because he does not have time; if it is for another reason, I do not know. What do you want to know about Ysidoro? Well, he was not able [to get contracted as a bracero], so he is calm until there is another selection of braceros. That you are not coming until you hear from Chilo and Lolo? Well that is for you to decide. Chilo is our concern and you do not even know if Lolo has crossed over. [We don't know] whether Chilo is in Arizona, or they have moved him. [In either case] I think that it is laziness that keeps him from writing. Let us hope in God that it is not because of [a more] serious matter. In the letters that you have sent us you say that [you will be visiting us] in early December. Well, it seems late to us, but better late than never.

The distance that separates us provides for us and takes away from us. It provides us with the means to arrive at and find ourselves in a place where it is easier to find a job. [This job] may be troublesome, [but] it pays better than in Mexico. It takes away from us because it deprives us of communication that is timely. If there was something we wanted you to know right away, it would take 15 days. If something serious should happen to someone, it would take 15 days [for you to learn about it]. Only with a telegram, but if there is no [money] to pay for it, oh well. On Sunday the 21st there was a *jugarrera tumbando* for the benefit of the temple that is under construction.[25] They brought in a bull that they rode on. A young guy named Elias fought the bull; [but], because he was quite drunk, the bull . . . took him in his horns and injured him badly in the right leg—[the bull] picked him up many times. Jesús Orozco was there, luckily he was not gored. Tell me how cold has it been over there, because here it has rained and it has been very cold. Receive our memories and the longing we have for the day to arrive when we can see you here. Here there are no more ill except Hilario and Papá Luz, but one day [he is] ill then [he is] well.

Luz Moreno

25. *Jugarrera tumbando*: bulls were let loose in the bullring and the public was allowed to run among them.

July 23, 1952

To our beloved and absent children: Juan and Pancha,

Each day our longing and desire to see our *ausentes* grows. Three months have gone by since you returned to your jobs, distancing yourselves from us and your fatherland, leaving our hearts and our souls with an emptiness that time cannot fill nor anyone can console. And although we see that there is no other way for you to make a living, we see that the good [that comes with living and working in the United States] comes with sweat and tears. This makes us beneficiaries of the fruits of your labor, sacred fruits that make us wish we had words of thanks worthy of your deeds. But if we are not capable [of paying you back], we pray that God repays you all of your favors, and that he console you my CHILDREN in such a way so that you may feel as if you live in paradise. Remember, my CHILDREN, that to suffer with patience and in the name of God is to make a treasure [that is redeemable in] heaven and will make your hard work tolerable.

My beloved children, now that I have sent you my regards, I would like to know if you have received the letters that I send more or less about every eight days with no other objective than to maintain constant communication with you and to keep you up to date on the latest news. I know that some of this news does not get to you in a timely fashion and with incomplete information since I really do not have anyone here who can keep me informed on nothing and because I fear causing fights or sorrows [in the family].

On the 29th, the priest proposed that the parochial church should be repainted. He asked how old the [current] paint job was and they told him about 48 or 50 years. "Well, surely this paint was not meant to last a lifetime." He said that in Santa María, a mere ranch, the church was beautifully decorated and that the church in Jalos[titlán] and San Juan were also beautifully adorned and had very good organs. Here [in San Miguel] there was nothing. "There are rich people here who own cows and oxen worth 1,000 pesos," he said. He wanted to gather 80 people who could donate 1,000 pesos each for the painting, and 40,000 more to buy an organ. Until now, no one has come forth to make such donations. He said that if they did not want to donate the 1,000 pesos, or their cows or oxen, he was going to tell God to kill them.[26] The burden is heavier, but I think he should leave this task to us poor people. You would be amazed at how

26. " . . . to kill them.": I presume the cows and bulls, not their owners.

many thousands of pesos in eggs have been donated [to the church]. The Father said that he had to suspend the project of the Sanctuary of Our Lady of Guadalupe.

We are all fine. Only Hilario and your Papá Luz [are ill]. Papá Luz asks that you send us money for our milk.

Luz Moreno

～e9e～

August 26, 1952

Beloved Ausentes,

The cornstalks are so worn away that, even though they have already begun to sprout their hair, they do not make noise in wind. When cornstalks are young and get damaged they are able to get better because new leaves grow to replace the torn ones ... but every night the storms come and bring with them thunder and hail. [The rain is so strong] that the water goes in between the roof-tiles and leaks right on top of me, so cold. I do not understand why the cornfields are not growing, and those that have, are growing but are not blooming. Pure stalk.

On the road to Jalos[titlán], one can see one or two tiny *mogotitos*.[27] Chito's cornfields are pretty big, only the final output is in doubt. The small plot of land that Lolo planted grew large, but it choked up and there are parts that are turning yellow.[28] In general, the crop season is bad here in San Miguel ...

Victorina has a little white pig that she keeps in Hilario's shed. It must weigh about 8 arrobas.[29] If she wanted, she could leave her until November, when you come, so that she [the pig] can give us a taco ... Try your best to make it for the corn harvest, if not, at least by the end of November.

We would like to know how it has been for you up North? Here, we hear contradictory versions of the news. ... They say that it is going well for some and bad for others. [It is] as if the law, the law that should govern the most remote corners of the nation, does not affect some people: some are screwed

27. *Mogotito*: the piling up of corn in the open field used to protect corn from the elements when a barn is not available.

28. *Pero se encaño*: when a farmer plants too many seeds in one area, the resulting clutter of corn does not allow any of them to grow sufficiently strong enough to sustain the growth of corn.

29. One *arroba* equals about 25 lbs. The pig weighed about 200 pounds.

and others are not. The ones who are at fault are the disobedient landowners ... [who] behave toward their Mexican brothers as if they have lost all reason. They should treat [Mexicans] like what they are, brothers from Latin America. They are not physically blind, but they are spiritually blind. They are nothing but a bunch of ignoramuses who sooner or later will get what they deserve from Russia. Do not forget your father, who keeps you updated with the news.

Luz Moreno.

CHAPTER 5

"Newspapers Are Liars"

On the Importance of Reading and Writing

There is a national narrative that is written daily, and daily erased.
Elena Poniatowska, *Fuerte es el Silencio* (1980)

This is how Elena Poniatowska, the most renowned chronicler of the lives of Mexico's marginalized populations, expressed both the ephemeral nature of their existence and the impermanence of their stories. Poniatowska has dedicated much of her career to using oral histories to preserve these stories. Other chroniclers, in Mexico and Latin America, have used court documents, material objects, and statistics to provide insights into the lives and thoughts of the "people without history," but to date there exist precious few published first-person accounts of a Latin American poor person's life. The most famous, if not the only, of these is Carolina Maria de Jesus's *Quarto de Despejo* (*The Garbage Room*, 1960).[1] *Child of the Dark* (the English-language title) is the edited version of a diary that Carolina María de Jesus (1914–1977), a single Afro-Brazilian mother, started to write in 1955 when she lived in Canindé, a *favela* (shantytown) of about fifty-thousand poor rural migrants located around the city of São Paulo, Brazil.[2] Discovered, edited, and then championed by the journalist Audálio Dantes, de Jesus's diary became a national best seller in Brazil and a worldwide phenomenon.[3] *Child of the Dark* was published in the United States in 1962 during the turmoil of the civil rights movement. Its American audience, who bought over 300,000 copies of the book in 1960s, clearly saw part of their country's tortured history reflected in de Jesus's life and her struggle against racial, class, and gender discrimination.[4]

Born into extreme poverty, in the poorest region of Brazil, de Jesus, the granddaughter of slaves, received only two years of schooling.[5] Yet despite her lack of formal education, Carolina loved reading and writing ("The book is man's best invention so far"[6]), and seemed to live most intentionally and fully when she was immersed in the life of the mind: "Everyone has an ideal in life. Mine is to be able to read."[7] Indeed, Carolina referred to herself as a poetess ("The politicians know that I am a poetess. And that a poet will even face death when he sees people oppressed"),[8] and spent most of the time she was not picking trash to make money to feed and clothe her children, reading novels and the newspapers, writing fantasy stories about princesses and dragons, and chronicling her life in a diary.[9] Luz Moreno also had an ideal life, and like his Brazilian contemporary it involved an intimate and heartfelt relationship with reading and writing. A sharecropper with the soul of a poet, Luz loved to read newspapers, became an obsessive letter-writer, and believed, as he wrote Pancha, that God had given him the "erudition to have followed a literary career" (c. September 1950).

It is difficult to imagine that people who led lives of such severe material constraint could harbor visions of literary grandeur. But both de Jesus and Moreno were persistent, enthusiastic, and confident chroniclers of their lives who skillfully and movingly wrote about their inner longings, the personal humiliations they endured, the material deprivations they (and others like them) suffered, and the rich people and larger structures that imposed such conditions on them. These qualities make de Jesus and Moreno's literary output extremely attractive to outsiders. But no one is a prophet in their own land, or, apparently, in their own time. While international progressives embraced Carolina María de Jesus because her story reflected the struggle of poor and black people around the world as well as the ruthless immorality of the capitalist system, most Brazilian intellectuals viewed her with suspicion. Liberal Brazilians wanted de Jesus to think more programmatically and structurally about inequality in their country. They believed that she was an aspiring bourgeois who was overly fixated on attaining material comfort for her family and herself. Conservative Brazilians, on the other hand, were embarrassed by her exposé. They, along with many liberal Brazilians, thought de Jesus should not have aired Brazil's dirty laundry to the world and believed that she was too opinionated and uppity for a woman of her class and race.[10] This criticism was echoed by Carolina's neighbors in Canindé. They were embarrassed by her portrayal of their community and saw her literacy (then her fame and money) as yet another affectation by a woman who thought entirely too much of herself.

Their anger was often directed at de Jesus in racial terms: "I sat in the sun to write. Silvia's daughter, a girl of six passed by and said: 'You're writing again, stinking nigger!'"[11] While their racism is indefensible, their guarded often hostile attitude toward de Jesus's literacy was partially engendered by de Jesus's frequent declarations that she was going to write a book in which she would chronicle all of their misdeeds: "You are ignorant . . . I am going to write a book about the favela, and I am going to tell everything that happened here. And everything that you do to me. I want to write a book, and you with these disgusting scenes are furnishing me with material."[12]

While not subjected to the public scrutiny or the racialized animosity that Carolina Maria de Jesus's literacy inspired, Luz Moreno's dedication to reading newspapers and writing letters did arouse suspicion, if not outright hostility, from his daughters Victorina and Ysabel.[13] Victorina and Ysabel were astounded at the dedication and frequency with which Luz wrote to Pancha, and they were concerned that his constant griping about the condition of the world, his body, and his emotions were unduly worrying their sister.[14] According to Luz, every time his daughters saw him writing a letter they would exclaim, "You're going to go write?" "What are you going to say?" "Where do you come up with so much to write to them?" (May 23, 1951).[15] Victorina and Ysabel also suspected that Luz was painting them in a bad light, telling Pancha how they were supposedly mistreating or disrespecting him. These accusations worried the siblings because they feared that Luz's complaints would influence how much money Pancha would send, and who she would send it to.[16] Although Pancha often included a dollar or two in her letters for her parents and siblings, it is clear that the emotional significance of the monetary remittance was sometimes more important than its actual economic value.[17] Every letter from Pancha carried the potential to enchant some, but not all, members of her family. Because Pancha did not have unlimited resources, nor unlimited time to write back to everyone who wrote to her, someone was bound to be disappointed by the contents of the fat envelopes that everyone in the Moreno household knew contained gifts, money, and some of the "wonderful things" that Luz imagined the United States was full of (September 6, 1951).[18] In this atmosphere of desire and scarcity it is no wonder that Victorina and Ysabel, the sisters who were left with the responsibility for maintaining and providing for the fractious Moreno household, were wary of Luz's seemingly secret communications with Pancha. The animus and suspicion generated by Luz's correspondence with Pancha also highlights just how emotionally and financially dependent the Morenos were becoming on Pancha's remittances, and provide a small measure of understanding about the weight of the burden that migrants like Pancha carried as they shouldered the emotional and fiscal well being of their extended families in Mexico.[19]

Luz Moreno did not understand why his daughters were so hostile, and he was angry at what he thought were their naked attempts to sow discord within their family. He saw his letters as expressions of love, and the natural extensions of his parental duty to inform his daughter about the world and the dangers that they all faced: "I just write about what happens here, how we relate to one another. I write whatever happens in town, good or bad, sad or happy, past or present, events in general or in particular. The pulse of the world, such as it is" (December 4, 1950). Moreno was also disappointed that his daughters were not as enamored with the epistolary culture he had so fully embraced. Their narrow vision, their refusal to see writing for the important and beautiful activity he believed it was, frustrated him, and he let Pancha know about it: "These myopic, inexperienced children try to gain advantage from even the most sacred of things. Do they think that my heart's [allegiance] can be divided so as to cause trouble in the very center of my home?" (May 23, 1951).

In spite of their suspicions (or maybe because of them), the Moreno family waited with great anticipation to hear the mailman's train whistle that announced the arrival of the day's mail.[20] Upon hearing the whistle, or seeing the mailman ride his bicycle down their street, adults and children would gather in Luz's house. There they "anxiously" listened to Pancha's words as Luz read her letters out aloud (c. February 6, 1951). The public reading was expected and welcomed by the Moreno family because some of them (mostly the young children) were illiterate and reading the letters was the most efficient and democratic way of circulating Pancha's salutations and the best way of reanimating Pancha's text/speech hybrids.[21] Luz welcomed the chance to read Pancha's letters to his family because he believed that this performance, full of the bodily and aural cues that make speech such an intimate mode of conversation, had, as he wrote in one of his letters, the magical effect of transporting their ausente to San Miguel:[22] "And as your letter is being read, he who wrote the letter appears to be in the room and a healing balm seems to wash over our hearts and bodies" (c. February 6, 1951).[23] In addition, Luz hoped that if he opened Pancha's letters and packages with the whole family assembled, he would diminish their suspicion that he was misrepresenting Pancha's wishes or misappropriating the gifts and money she was sending—it was the functional equivalent of a magician pulling up his sleeves in front of a cynical audience. He also anticipated that by reading the letters out loud he would garner from his family a bit of good will and understanding to allow him to continue the activity that he loved so much.[24]

Meanwhile, in Stockton, the personal politics of who was privy to the information contained in the correspondence between father and daughter was no less fraught. While Luz's letters were intended for Pancha, some letters also included salutations, queries, and information that were intended for her husband Juan. This did not mean that Pancha wanted to share all her correspondence with her husband. Indeed, one day when Pancha was writing a letter to her sister Ysabel, Juan asked to see the correspondence. Pancha felt that the letter was private and refused to show it to her increasingly irate husband. When Juan angrily insisted, Pancha tore up the letter in an act of defiance that nearly drove him to violence.[25]

It is clear that Luz had appreciated the written word as a key to understanding the nature and sources of knowledge in the world and as the only way he had to maintain contact with his beloved Pancha. But his daughters' query, "Where do you come up with so much to write to them?" is also valid. Where did he come up with so much to write about? What was the source of Luz's abiding faith in the written word? Why, given his minimal formal education, his own conservative sensibilities, and his rootedness to his birthplace, do Luz Moreno's letters sound so worldly and modern? To answer these questions, it would be helpful to compare Luz's letters to the ones his wife, Secundina, wrote to Pancha. Written with a barely sharpened pencil, Secundina's letters are curt, awkward missives aimed at sending salutations, conveying endearments, asking for favors, expressing appreciation for favors rendered, and transmitting blessings and goodwill. Secundina tells (she repeatedly uses the verb *decir*) Pancha many things, but her letters implicitly recognize that without Pancha's physical presence any form of "real" human communication (in other words face-to-face oral communication) would have to wait until they were reunited in San Miguel. Her letters were, as the following excerpt highlights, essentially versions of oral conversations, uncomfortably and reluctantly committed to paper:

> To my beloved children, Juan and Pancha. With this letter I greet you and hope that you are well. These are my hopes because our health is fine, thank God. After greeting you . . . I tell you that the whole town sends its greetings and that I am very grateful to all the people because they remember you. Pancha, Lucia asked me to tell you to do her the favor of bringing her an american dress, make sure you don't forget, wear the dress so you can get it past [customs], because she really wants an american dress. She won't tell you what color because you know what she likes. Receive many greetings from your mother and all your family, we will ask God that nothing happens to you here or on the road. Pancha, I appreciate the cards you sent and even more the dollar, which was very useful. Pancha,

the money you sent your father arrived ... and everything you have sent has arrived from the first dollar to the last handkerchief, ribbons ... the socks, the ribbons for María, all of it has arrived, nothing was lost (March 25,1951).

In comparing Luz's letters and Secundina's, I do not want to imply that one form of correspondence was better than another. While Secundina could write, she had not made writing an indispensible part of her affective life, and her correspondence does not pretend to recreate the intimacy she and Pancha had when they both lived in San Miguel. The shy and introspective Luz, on the other hand, had internalized his literacy.[26] His letters contain some aspects of Secundina's grudging functionality, but they also betray an enthusiasm for and a self-assured comfort with the technology (he mixed his own ink and seems to have taken pride in the aesthetics of his hand-writing), the institutions (the postal services of two countries), and the logic of transforming human emotions, ideas, and utterances into scripts that is generally absent from Secundina's letters. Luz was not willing to let the distance that separated him from his daughter become an obstacle to the warm conversations he craved. If Pancha was physically absent, she was always on Luz's mind and never more so than when he wrote to her, imaginatively anticipating her joy and sorrow at what he was inscribing on paper. It was an intimacy that was hard earned; and, for the old and lonely Luz his correspondence with Pancha was, as he repeatedly tells her, a life affirming activity he could not live without. "What would we do," he writes to Pancha, "if we knew nothing, neither from here to there nor from there to here? More or less it would be as if we would have died already."[27]

In person, Luz Moreno was a quiet and socially reticent man who spoke in hushed tones and conversed with averted his eyes so as to rarely look at anyone directly.[28] These qualities may have predisposed him to embrace an activity and a habit of mind that is done, by and large, but not exclusively, in isolation.[29] But the Luz that appeared in Pancha's mailbox was not the retiring soul he was in person; the epistolary Papá Luz was voluble and engaging, eager for conversation, and self-assured in his views. This literary and idealized version of her father moved easily from the intimacies of daily life (sickness, bad weather, the grinding life of poverty, the absence of his beloved daughter, gratitude for money sent from the United States), to religious and philosophical reflections (the treasure of the Catholic faith, the stages of human life, the materialism of American culture), to trenchant political observations (the mutual destructiveness of the Cold War and the cynical self-interests of nations), to a brooding apocalyptic vision of the end of time, his and the world's.[30] This dexterity allowed Luz to simultaneously imagine how his world looked like from many viewpoints, including the

Secundina Román Moreno (sitting) with Francisca Moreno, Bonifacio (Chito) Moreno and his son, Luis, c. 1953. Courtesy of Obdulia Orozco.

perspectives of his daughter who was working in a California cannery, the poor Chinese peasant dying on the Korean peninsula in a war not of his making, and an angry God tiring of his creation and readying himself to destroy it.[31] Luz's ability to split his consciousness, to see the world from multiple perspectives, and feel history flowing through time that was both earth-bound and divinely determined is a curious sensibility that is mostly absent from Secundina's letters, and, as his frustrated daughters under-stood, requires some explanation.[32]

Luz Moreno's poverty, his Catholic internationalism, the development of mass immigration from Los Altos to the United States, and the opportunity to write letters to his beloved ausentes—never before presented to him when all his family and friends lived within walking distance—helped lift Luz out of "conventional time-space" and render "physical and political borders powerless." These factors, though, do not sufficiently explain the modern quality of his epistolary voice.[33] What seems to differentiate Luz Moreno from his family, and his letters from most other texts produced in and about San Miguel during this period, was his critical engagement with newspapers.[34] Looking at his letters from the distance of almost seventy years it is clear that beyond personal talent, Luz's literacy and his desire to write with aesthetic intent was nurtured by the narrative logic, vocabulary, and world perspective that newspapers exposed him to. It may well be that many Mexicans, especially those living in the so-called *provincias*, received their first and most important images about the modern world via forms of mass communication such as the radio, the cinema, and the personal communications of returning immigrants. But it would be wrong to overlook the importance of the written word as a conduit of information for people who could not otherwise learn about the wider world. As other writers have argued, small towns and rural areas were not, at least not since the end of the nineteenth century, literacy deserts. Many Mexicans, of all classes, were exposed to opportunities that enticed or required them to read and write. These provincial *letrados* (men and women of letters) read newspapers, wrote letters, deciphered commercial advertising, responded in writing to the bureaucratic requirements of an expanding state, formalized business transactions with contracts, and read, wrote—or at the very least, signed—political petitions. Luz Moreno was one of these nonelite, nonurbanized, though not rural, *letrados*.[35] As is evident in many passages from his correspondence with Pancha, Luz was familiar with the Bible, read the political missives of the Sinarquista party, and considered secular newspapers sacred texts that not only nourished his soul and mentally transported him to a world that had suddenly become his to worry over, but also gave him the practical information he and his family needed to negotiate all of its dangers and take advantage of some of its opportunities.[36]

Ysabel and Victorina thought their father was foolish for putting so much stock in the unreliable written utterances of people he did not know and whose trustworthiness could not be verified by experience, reputation, or physical contact.[37] They could not understand why he would waste what little life he had left pouring over the dailies for information about wars that were very far from San Miguel and among people who were strangers.

Luz Moreno reading a newspaper in the courtyard of his home, c. 1950.

Nor could they abide his penchant for complaining to Pancha that they were not caring for him and that he could not sleep because he could not stop thinking about the Korean War and the looming nuclear holocaust. In their eyes the newspapers he read were filling his mind with the ideas and scenarios of doom that were driving him crazy. Ysabel and Victorina argued that if he really wanted to sleep at night, if he really wanted to stop obsessing about the end of the world, it would be better, as Luz reported to Pancha, for him to use the money he spent on newspapers "to buy food" (September 21, 1951).

While Pancha's sisters could not understand their father's fascination with newspapers and believed that his correspondence was unnecessarily worrying Pancha, Luz conceived of his letters as personalized newspapers, and himself as a news correspondent who provided his daughter an essential service: "Do not forget your father, who keeps you updated with the news" (August 26, 1952). Having internalized the technology and the mental logic of literacy, Luz refuted his daughter's charge that newspapers spread misinformation, and by implication that he was foolish to believe what he read in them, by writing: "Many say, 'No, the newspapers are liars.' And I say that by reading we discern truth from lies because there is no rule without exceptions. Just as there are people who are liars, there are people who are sincere and speak the truth; not everyone is the same. The spoken word is the same as the written word. Why such hate towards newspapers? Who else brings you news from around the world for fifteen cents?" (December 4, 1950). Moreno, however, applied his critical pessimism unevenly. For example, even though he believed that *Orden*, the official newspaper of the Sinarquista Party, was "a beacon of light in the midst of the ignorant darkness" (August 30, 1952), he was sure that secular newspapers were politically biased, and/or willfully incomplete. This was especially true when they covered topics related to the interests of the rich and powerful, like the Korean War: "Have the Americans made peace, or have they killed all of the Chinese and North Koreans? I would like to know how many American [soldiers] have died because the newspapers here only say that Communists and Chinese have died, but not one single American. That is unbelievable; but I know they do that to give the Americans an imaginary victory" (February 14, 1951).[38] In addition, while newspapers provided useful, but sometimes misleading information about the "visible world," Moreno thought that they contained "very little about the interior life of the individual," and not a thing about what God was thinking (August 30, 1952; May 23, 1951).

The philosopher G.W.F. Hegel, who was as addicted to reading his dailies as Luz Moreno, once wrote that, "Reading the morning newspaper is the realist's morning prayer. One orients one's attitude toward the world either by God or by what the world is. The former gives as much security as the latter, in that one knows how one stands."[39] While Hegel described reading the daily newspaper as a lonely exercise akin to prayer, Moreno's experience tended to the more Catholic communal. Indeed, while he read the paper by himself, on a bench in the plaza or in the courtyard of his house, the experience of immersing himself in the affairs of the world, was also an activity that was facilitated by and enabled conversations with other Sanmiguelenses who, like him, read the dailies, were involved in the Church, had been social Catholic activists, and believed that newspapers were conveyors of a certain (never absolute) truth. The most important of these small town "men of bookish bent" was Luz Moreno's *compadre*, Jesús Delgado Román.[40] Delgado was an organic intellectual, an artist of local renown, and a Catholic revolutionary. In 1917 Delgado and Father Abraham Andrade, inspired by the encyclical *Rerum Novarum*, founded a Catholic worker's union for poor people in San Miguel who did not want to join secular, socialist-leaning unions.[41] During the Cristiada Delgado was arrested by the government for running a rebel printing press and for serving as the personal secretary to two of the most important Cristero leaders of the region, Victorianio (*el Catore*) Ramírez and the insurgent priest, José Reyes Vega.[42] In the 1940s Delgado, along with Pancha's uncle, Gregorio Román, organized the Sinarquista Party in San Miguel. While Gregorio Román was the party's political rabble-rouser and militant organizer, Delgado was its intellectual, philosophic, moral, and aesthetic heart. It was Delgado who understood and appreciated the political and philosophical tenets of social Catholicism, and it was he who led the weekly meetings that Sinarquista men, women, and children held to plan political actions and to discuss politics and religion.

Jesús Delgado was also an artist. He was an oil painter who decorated the Mexican and Sinarquista Party flags that Party members held aloft during their frequent public marches; the director of the town's municipal orchestra; the cantor and director of the church choir that Pancha and her sisters were a part of; a song writer, a poet, a historian; and a self-taught architect who designed the catacombs and shrine for San Miguel's temple of the Virgin of Guadalupe.[43] He was also a photography enthusiast who took it upon himself to chronicle the Sinarquista movement in the region. Later in life, as the Sinarquista movement lost its political vigor, Delgado opened a music and art school in his home for the town's children. So well established was Jesús Delgado's status as the keeper and creator of San Miguel's history and culture that when Stanley L. Robe, a professor from the University of California, Los Angeles, went to Los Altos to collect folktales

Jesús Delgado and Children's Music School, 1933. Courtesy of Obdulia Orozco.

and legends in the 1940s and 1960s, he turned to Delgado when he visited San Miguel. Robe, as he wrote in his description of his "Informant," was clearly impressed by Delgado: "This informant was of more interest for the personal reminiscences and local history that he narrated than for his tales and legends. He was much more articulate and aware of intellectual matters than are most small-town informants. He had serious interest in music and had been director of the town band."[44]

While the rest of the family wondered about Luz Moreno's love of newspapers and his dedication to writing, Delgado, as he was fond of telling Pancha, considered him his intellectual peer: "My *compadre* Luz is the only one I can talk to about important matters."[45] Luz Moreno, normally not a conversationalist, spent hours speaking with his *compadre* Jesús, communing over the day's events, and analyzing them in light of their religious and political convictions. While Pancha was off with her uncle Gregorio canvassing the countryside and trying to convince their neighbors to join the Sinarquista Party, Luz Moreno and Jesús Delgado sat in Delgado's house and talked about religion, life, and the condition of the *miserable pueblo* around the world.

Carolina Maria de Jesus was not fortunate enough to have a person in her life with whom she could converse about the issues that swirled in her head. Isolated, but never alone in the teeming favela, when she needed to vent her frustrations about the world, de Jesus wrote in her diary or penned letters to politicians complaining about her poverty and the miserable conditions of her life. Carolina, like Luz, thought of herself as an altruistic reporter who documented the miseries of the *favela* for the public good ("Here in the favela almost everyone has a difficult fight to live. But I am the only one who writes of what suffering is. I do this for the good of others").[46] The "others" in de Jesus's imagination were, like Moreno's *miserable pueblo*, an imagined transnational community of poor people that was deprived of the same basic necessities and buffeted by the same injustices and prejudices that made her life so difficult. Physically confined to her favela, de Jesus wondered whether she was alone: "I am not going to eat because there is very little bread. I wonder if I'm the only one who leads this kind of life. What can I hope for in the future? I wonder if the poor of other countries suffer like the poor of Brazil?"[47] Three years earlier, five thousand miles away, and in another language, Luz Moreno was wondering the same thing. Literacy allowed Luz and Carolina to imagine, among other wonderful and terrifying things, the world outside of the small and impoverished spaces they occupied. Each was convinced that the written word had a special relationship with truth. They read the newspapers to receive this truth,[48] and they wrote to impart this truth to others.[49] Both these acts opened them to withering criticism from their peers, but also, and improbably, allowed them to imagine the possibility of each other's existence.

Writing letters, on the other hand, means exposing oneself to the ghosts, who are greedily waiting precisely for that. Written kisses never arrive at their destination; the ghosts drink them up along the way. It is ample nourishment which enables them to multiply so enormously.

Franz Kafka, *Letters to Milena*[1]

❧

c. September 1950

My children,

It seems incredible that such a natural thing would get to the point that it would seem marked by the laws of conflict.

Paternal love: we see that in modern times, parents suffer from a lack of respect to their authority. Children are subject to their parents as long as they are like birdies in the nest; as they grow older, they also grow more ungrateful. I do not want to say that there are no exceptions—there are children so good that they are the ballast, the sustenance, and consolation of their parents. But [just as some children are good, others are not]. Some pull one way, others pull the other, and at every step there is conflict, there are fights, and the consequences are so difficult that many times there is not enough Holy Water for so many devils. In our family, there is a difference between sons and daughters . . . The boys have made a fool of me, but the girls have not. I do not want to make generalizations of this sort, [I only want] to see how true this generalization is to our situation.

When Juan wanted to be part of this family, who knows what he thought of us . . . [If he reads any of my letters,] it is only out of politeness. Who is Juan? And from whom are the letters? Juan is an experienced man, an incomparable man, a man with a heart, and with charity. He is a man of valor and energy who knows what to do, and who knows how to command. [He is] a man who has lived a long time on American soil; he has command of the English language, which is a great advantage.

The qualities of his personality have been tested by the very people who most doubted his sincerity.[2] It is rare for people who are united through marriage to [truly] care for each other, [yet] Juan is loved by most of this family. And the letters that Papá sends, what are they about? Papá is a poor old man who sins more out of ignorance than out of malice. His intention

1. Franz Kafka, *Letters to Milena*, trans. Philip Boem (New York: Schoken Books, 1990), 223.
2. "The very people who doubted his sincerity . . .": Luz is referring to his family and their initial rejection of Juan.

is as pure as the sky is blue, but that he is sometimes as obstinate as a donkey cannot be denied. God gave him more patience than a donkey. He gave him the erudition to have followed a literary career, but as a youngster one does not think the way one does as an old man. When I settled down, I had 25 years of life experience, 10 years of work in the country without receiving more than food and clothing. I had 12 children; the first one I do not want to even mention her name.[3] Why do they disrespect me now? Because I'm old! Well, from this old man come these letters. Juan and Pancha receive this gift. We are sorry that you did not come to the party.

Luz Moreno

December 4, 1950

My children,

We have spoken much through our letters and that is how we have relieved our desires to see each other. Perhaps many of the letters that Papá Luz has sent you from San Miguel might not have been very pleasant for you; they might not have satisfied your taste, and they might not have conformed to your sensibilities. Maybe some [letters] have lacked the respect or refinement that your position deserves? This is due to my ignorance and not to malice of any sort; that is why I beg your forgiveness and understanding. Around here, as soon as they see that I am about to write a letter, they tell me, "Papá, do not write to them any more, you just worry Juan and Pancha. You are very rude." And I tell them that I just write about what happens here, how we relate to one another. I write whatever happens in town, good or bad, sad or happy, past or present, events in general or in particular. I write about the pulse of the world, such as it is. Many say, "No, the newspapers are liars." And I say that by reading we discern truth from lies because there is no rule without exceptions. Just as there are people who are liars, there are people who are sincere and speak the truth; not everyone is the same. The spoken word is the same as the written word. Why such hate towards newspapers? Who else brings you news from around the world for fifteen cents?

The situation in which our people currently find themselves in is very sad. There is very little work. Wages are terrible. Everything is very expensive; only our labor is worthless. Cunda is working at the Cornejo Hotel. Papá Luz takes occasional trips with the donkeys to get wood, but only for

---

3. Luz is referring to Pancha.

use in the kitchen. Victorina has sewing jobs every now and then and takes care of her chickens. Ysabel helps Victorina run errands—she helps in the kitchen, and cares for her brothers and nephews. Lula does whatever is asked of her; she gets money from Papá Mino [Maximino], although he is screwed right now.[4] With the cold weather, his ice cream bars are not selling well, and he has many debts and a wife to care for. Chilo doesn't know what to do with himself and he has kept on drinking. Lolo [Isidoro] is not doing well; he was working during the rainy season with Chito, but now has no work; [he only works] when he is asked to play his music. Chito continues to slaughter the donkeys and horses and cows they sell him at half price or the ones they bring him that are already dead. This son helps me out by lending me donkeys to work with. Whatever I earn, I keep. I do not even reimburse him for the donkey's feed. Hay is so expensive ... the most I do is bring bagasse, but only when I feel like it.[5] I do give my grandchildren whatever money I can. I wish that this one son [Chito] would always have plenty of money because he is the most giving and he takes care of me.

Luz Moreno

c. February 6, 1951

My dear children,

Many things happen without your knowledge, or if [this knowledge] reaches you it is late. News arrives late from here to there and from there to here. As soon as something occurs here we want to communicate it to you, and I am sure you want to do the same. Illnesses and sorrows come and go without comment because the distance that separates us is so great. The intensity of our affection becomes lost in this desperation and, at times, we attribute this to the fact that we have not received a reply. The advantage of written communication seems so small. Yet if days go by without receiving a letter from you, we are filled with anxiety and desperation. When it is time for the mailman to deliver the mail, and he blows his whistle, all who are home get excited; those who were absent, arrive anxiously asking, "Did a letter arrive?"[6] And as your letter is being read, he who wrote the letter appears to be in the room and a healing balm seems to wash over

---

4. Maximino Orozco: Lula's father and widower of Micaela Moreno, Luz's daughter.

5. Bagasse: the dried residue left after the liquid has been removed from sugar cane or grapes. It is used as animal feed and sometimes to make paper.

6. "He blows his whistle": Mail carriers in San Miguel, as in other parts of Mexico, rode around town on bikes. They would blow a whistle in front of the homes of families who had mail.

our hearts and bodies. Some of the letters I have sent may not accurately reflect the respect that you deserve, but they do reflect the well-earned confidence that we all have in you. This [confidence] is inspired, and becomes every time more evident, by the acts of love and compassion that you have extended [to us], like during Ysidoro's illness. I have never seen this kind of benevolence in my life. Now that we are separated, the only thing that serves as a consolation is the epistolary correspondence.

The parish priest is building a chapel in honor of Saint Joseph on Don Antonio's lot, where Minerva Street ends. On Sunday, February 4, there was a large bazaar that extended two blocks from the chapel. Ysabel made tamales and Chito's girls made other foods, but I cannot tell you who made what because I did not know about the bazaar until Lula brought me some tamales to my bed. She told me that the foundation, which I had seen but could not figure out who was starting to build there, was for St. Joseph's Chapel.

Why, my children, am I so full of grief? It is because I could not go to the [festivities of] *La Candelaria*.[7] I had a palpitation when I went to get wood, and it was so strong that I blacked out while riding the donkey. I stepped down from the donkey and continued on foot; half an hour later the palpitation was gone. The first of the month arrived and I could not go [to the festivities of *La Candelaria*]; the second of the month arrived . . . and I was afraid that I would get another attack on the way there. I went to Jalos[titlán] on Tuesday, the 6th of February, but it was a short trip. I left at 9 and only stayed an hour and a half before I came back. It is because I am crazy, don't pay me any mind. On February 6, at 5:15, Hilario, Ysabel, Sidonia, and Cecilio [left] for Guadalajara to look after Hilario's health. Pray to God for Hilario's health and that He may not forget us during this difficult time. Everyone else is doing well. Let us know how you are getting by with this cold weather. We wonder how you are putting up with it up there; we can barely stand it down here . . .

[Luz Moreno]

May 23, 1951

To my beloved Ausentes,

Beloved children, every time I sit down to write to you my desire to see you is eased. Here, whenever the girls [Isabel and Victorina] see that I am about

7. The festivities for the *Candelaria* (candles) are held on February 2nd and commemorate the presentation of Jesus in the temple. In Mexico, it is tradition to serve tamales.

to write, they tell me: "You're going to go write?" "What are you going to say?" "Where do you come up with so much to write to them?" These myopic, inexperienced children try to gain advantage from even the most sacred of things. Do they think that my heart's [allegiance] can be divided so as to cause trouble in the very center of my home? The ordeals that I am seeing I have never experienced before. My luck has changed. Even if my children would all turn their backs on me, I would be resigned to such a fate. But [the only ones who have turned on me] are the daughters who are still with me. They are tired of work and tell me that I am the cause of their misfortune. If I brought into existence my children and grandchildren, then I should provide and clothe them so that their needs would not cause the slightest trouble for my daughters. The little ones are a nuisance, but how am I to prevent them from showing up at our house? Victorina, Ysabel, and my comadre Angeles cannot stand to see the children. But I know that not all my children are against me. I am comforted that you, Juan and Pancha, as well as all my male children are with me.

I make these observations with the utmost clarity so that all those who come to understand what is happening to me . . . can tell whomever they wish. Not even when I was strong enough to work and to receive insults did I see myself in such a fix, nor so vulnerable that the slightest trouble causes me so much harm. They ask me: "Papá, what can we do to relieve your palpitations?" And I tell them that I find it hard to believe that they are concerned about my health when [they] are the very ones who anger me by being disrespectful. Are you not obligated to give me what I need? What I eat, I buy with what I earn. Does this not help you?'

The 17th at 11 at night Anita Becerra died.[8] I did not go see her. I only went to the mass that was [presided over] by 3 priests. My compadre Ysabel came, but I did not speak with him because he cannot stand to see me. The Festival of Mirandilla is over and I did not attend because I had very strong palpitations. Chito continues killing donkeys, but without a license. Lolo is well. Chilo with his shoemaking business . . . Mamá Cunda is well, but a little hobbled by rheumatism. It is cloudy with some rain. Corn is 70 [pesos] a kilo.

Dearest children, the whole world should understand what is happening in the places most affected by the war. At the very least so that we can figure out exactly what we should expect, because we are in the same circumstances [as those unfortunate souls] and should expect sooner or later to suffer the same difficulties. What we get from the newspapers

8. Anita Becerra was María Moreno's (Ysidoro Moreno's wife's) grandmother.

reveals very little about the interior life of the individual. As to what God is thinking: who would know? President Truman has on his hands a great nation that is rich, powerful, coveted, but it is becoming divided. That issue between Truman and MacArthur over his [Truman's] determination to dismiss [MacArthur] from [the position] he has held in Japan for 14 years has opened up great fissures in the heart of the political [system in the United States] . . . MacArthur will be, and is, the cause of many disturbances that will culminate in many advantages for the Russians. This, even the kitchen maids know.[9]

It is difficult to rule when one's power is not founded on the most sane or true principles. The Supreme Pontiff Pius XII continues to teach the world how to govern, how to avoid wars. It is not difficult for us to forgive. Yet [we prefer] vengeance; we prefer to kill our brothers, as if killing insects. That is why [we have] the bomb, the machine gun, and the rest of the facilities that exist to kill and be killed. The weeping of the orphan nor the tears of the widow move us. All of this is in the visible [world]. Who knows how God is judging all the thousands of men who die every day in that [long suffering] injured Korea. Will they be saved? Will they be ready to go to Heaven as soon as they die on the front? Who will have the courage to witness all those souls—their fathers, their brothers, their children—entombed in Hell . . . Oh, Saintly Father, Oh, Beloved Pastor do not tire of calling these fools to reason; for even as Your Paternal Voice resounds, these jackals, like the savages they are, and in the light of day, relish the blood of their brothers. No one knows, nor do they want to know, the commandment of love. Luz Moreno

Beloved children Juan and Pancha. The first matter that we direct your way is that we hope you are well because we learned from some letters that we received before the 15th that our Juanito had received a blow to his leg. Full of pain, we want to know if he is well. In the same letters came many small gifts. I am not able to tell you what kind of objects came because they came wrapped really well. I only tell you that all the children went crazy, as well as the adults. May God give you more and reward such a large and fine benevolence. The children see the adults write and they want to write also. Cuca begged me to write a letter for her because she does not know how to write. Oh, my children, what is this movement? Where is this effort

---

9. On April 11, 1951 US President Harry S. Truman relieved General Douglas MacArthur as commander of the United Nations forces in Korea. This act was precipitated by a growing rift between the men over how to prosecute the military conflict in the Korean Peninsula and MacArthur's increasingly aggressive tone towards China. Truman did not appreciate that General MacArthur made pronouncements and military decisions without first consulting or getting permission from the president, and he feared that MacArthur's aggression would escalate and widen the conflict.

headed? Isn't it true that these children have hearts, and that with these same hearts they give God glory and learn the gratitude that they owe their elders, loving them and recognizing that the blood that runs through their veins is the blood of their kin . . .

Receive our memories,
[Luz Moreno]

~e9e~

September 6, 1951

My dear children,

I admire the effort you make to attend to your family from such a distant land. Every so often we get small gifts, [some days] for some, [other days] for others. Everyone, especially the little ones, touch and feel your letters to see if they are fat and contain some of the wonderful things that that Nation is full of. This restlessness, this waiting, this is what mitigates our sadness and melancholy. Do not doubt, though, that this interest in your gifts [has created] envy. [Indeed], because I write to you often and ask you about things I want to know, they accuse me of being indiscreet. Like when I asked you what you were going to do with the corn. In other instances, they have accused me of writing thing that put Ysabel, Victorina, and Cunda in a bad light. They have come to hate me since about six months ago. Even though, now, they are respecting me more.

On the 4th, at about 5 o'clock, Papá Luz gladly received the Dollar bill that you generously sent me. I do not know how to express my gratitude towards such kindness; kindness that I did not find even amongst my closest [relatives] when I was growing up. I served my family as a very young boy and I never received any sign of affection, or justice. Since they would leave me to tend to the animals, they would not even take me to mass. I was dressed in rags during the rainy season when I worked as a planter or with the team of oxen. I worked 23 years as a single man and 30 as a married one, and I never saw a sign of justice, much less affection, from my father, not even at the time of his death. Today, my dear children, I see the great affection and care that you have not only for me, but also for all your family. Why, you are even charitable towards strangers! With God on your side, you shall be happy. May you receive our gratitude as well as these few words, and we will be waiting for your response. The more the better. We will also send you one or two [letters].

Luz Moreno

~e9e~

For my absent children,

. . . In the name of everyone, I give [you], Juan and Pancha, our most humble thanks [for the money you have sent us] . . . We ask God to provide you with more, to keep all bad away from you, and shower you, my beloved absent ones, with many goods.

My beloved Juan, do not punish your body—let it rest by coming to your homeland. You are not a wooden stick; allow yourselves, my beloved children, a small repose and you will see the advantages.

As for the sicknesses, only Hilario continues to suffer. My stomach continues to be upset, with vomit and the palpitations. The girls, Victorina and Ysabel, say that [I get sick] because of what I eat. Yes, it is true that after I eat I feel a weight in my stomach that is only relieved when I vomit. But what about the palpitations? I tell them that it is bile brought on by the anger [they cause with their complaints]: "Do not ask for money," "Do not write so much," "Do not buy those newspapers. The newspapers are driving you crazy," "It would better to use that money to buy food." Everyone should be allowed to do what brings him or her pleasure. When Prospero Padilla lived, he gave me many newspapers, and I became accustomed to reading them.[10] Now I buy them when I can, but I did not think that it would be such a grave offense. The rabbit leaps when one least expects it.

[We must] move forward, my absent children. Move forward or we will die before all these difficulties. Difficulties that are common enough, but do not cease to be a bother. They are like wooden knives, they do not cut but they bruise.[11] Though they are family, Victorina and Ysabel, Cunda and Angeles do not understand. The men [Chito, Lolo, and Chilo] are my friends. Lula [is] the most docile and kindest [of them all], but they heap on the abuse "*como a palo caido*."[12] Absent Children, do not forget Lula. Receive our complaints and our gratitude. May God give us patience.

Luz Moreno

July 29, 1952

My very beloved children, Juan and Pancha,

[Because] it takes a great deal of effort for me to write to you, I regret that my letters are of little interest and make such a small impression on you. I am well aware that everyone else receives as many letters as they send. Around here, as soon as they see that I am going to write you a letter, and without really knowing what I am going to write, they tell me, "Where do you come up with so much to write? All you write is nonsense. You are going to tell them we do not give you enough to eat, [when in fact] you stopped eating [to avoid becoming ill] and that when you do have money you buy things that are harmful to you."

I think that it is better if I do not write to you anymore. Let me know whether you want me to keep writing or not. Like I say, [I am willing to write to you] even though it takes a lot of effort to do so and I do not have money for postage. I always feel sad when I do not write to you so, even if the whole world around here makes such a big fuss about it, [I will continue] to write. I was with Hilario the other day and he told me that he could only sleep face down, not on his side, because of his cough. In addition to my rheumatism, I sometimes feel dizzy. With rest my heart palpitations come less often and [when they do come] they are milder. The 15th [of August] is drawing near, and I do not have a way of securing my ticket [to Jalostitlán].[13] I told them, for a whole two weeks, that I would like to go to Jalos, and they promised

10. Prospero Padilla was a friend of the Moreno family.
11. "*Son como cuchillos de palo, no cortan pero mayugan.*"
12. "*Como a palo caido*": "As if on a fallen stick." Luz is alluding to Lula's condition as an orphan who gets more abuse because she is the least able to protect herself.
13. The 15th of August is the festival in Jalostitlán. The town celebrates the assumption of Virgin Mary.

me that they would help me. They are all good to me; I am the only bad one. Receive our best wishes and excuse me for everything.

Luz Moreno

⚜

August 30, 1952

To my beloved ausentes, Juan and Pancha,

Desiring that you be up to date on the latest news, I send you some newspapers that will give you some good information. This newspaper[14] swears to publish only the truth, just as any individual who joins Sinarquismo swears before God to defend the Christian faith, even if it costs them their life. It is the newspaper that speaks frankly without beating around the bush or [inspiring] fear. It publishes the good things the government does, as well as the bad. It is the defender of the rights and justice of Mexican people. It is like a beacon of light in the midst of the dense and dark ignorance of most of its children. I am sure that no other group has exhibited as much heroism, valor, and personal sacrifice as [the Sinarquistas]. The 127 martyred [Sinarquistas] are an example that impresses even its most demanding admirers. Since the beginning, nothing but hatred has been directed towards the Sinarquista Movement . . . Sinarquismo does not conquer with brute force. It does not speak with ignorance, because in Mexico, as in all parts of the world, there is ignorance. Nonetheless, there is always a guiding light that destroys ignorance. Their [the Sinarquistas'] advice for us is to be united as one, so that we may do good, not bad, because it is well known that individually the only thing one can achieve is wasting one's time. One's sole purpose in life should be to right that which is wrong . . . The moth that eats away at good intentions is envy. The independence of Mexico from Spain, and the wars of reform, the wars against France, and the modern [struggles] of the Union Popular, the Cristeros, and all the efforts of the Sinarquistas have been lost, and will continue to be lost, because of jealousy, [a jealousy] that sometimes comes from the movements own participants. Everywhere we seek our own glory and not the glory of God. They were jealous of *"el Catorce"* and that was the end of the Cristero Movement.[15] Write back if you receive this newspaper.

Luz Moreno.

14. Moreno is referring to *Orden*, the official newspaper of the Sinarquista party.
15. Victoriano Ramírez, *"El Catorce,"* was a Cristero hero born in municipality of San Miguel el Alto. He was betrayed and killed by one of the factions of the Cristero movement in 1927. He is called El Catorce (the 14) because he had supposedly killed fourteen men in a gun battle.

CHAPTER 6

"The Anxieties of an Old Man Are Very Sad"

On Being Old and Preparing to Die

Once again this life hobbling before me, what am I saying this life, *this death*, this death without sense or pity, this death that so pathetically falls short of greatness, the dazzling pettiness of this death, this death hobbling from pettiness to pettiness.

Aimé Césaire, Notebook of a Return to the Native Land (1947)

In spite of his nickname (Papá Luz: Father Light), Luz Moreno (literally: Dark Light) spent much of his life in silence and in the shadows of his much more voluble family. Luz was a sharecropper who was considered an enigma, even by the socially awkward sharecroppers and taciturn peasants with whom he often associated. But now he was dying. After seven decades of life, the lonely Moreno looked at his world and saw that both it and he were hobbling toward what seemed like an inglorious, and at times undignified, end.[1] The old Sinarquista was not destined to die the heroic death of a religious martyr. Instead, his passing felt like a long, slow, forced march through a seemingly interminable series of indignities, losses, and separations: the loss of the centrality of his religion to the external threats of the modern world; the loss of his ability to be physically self-sufficient; the loss of his family to immigration and alcoholism; and the loss of his position as a man in his community and as the head of his family. These losses, and the premonition that death was not far off, pained Moreno but also freed him to sit down and attempt to anchor his life and to give it, and his death, meaning in a thoroughly modern way. At the end of his life Luz took pen to ink to paper and, among other things, attempted to evoke the social, spiritual, and emotional conditions that would allow him to understand himself not only as an elderly person who had lived a life worthy of dignity and respect, but also as a dying man and a faithful Christian who was entitled to a good death.

The concept of the good death is a set of Christian precepts that instructs believers on the proper way of dying in a state of Christian grace. Originally composed by Jean Gerson in the fifteenth century, the treatise that became the published manual called *Ars Moriendi*, or *The Art of Dying*, was presented at the Council of Constance (1414–1418) as an essay titled *De arte moriendi*. Many scholars believe that the codification and publication of the manual was prompted by the social, physical, and spiritual insecurities generated in the fourteenth century by the Black Death and The Hundred Year's War (1337–1453). In the wake of these cataclysmic events the Church wanted to systematize and popularize the pathway to Christian salvation for a community of faithful who worried about God's judgment and who were eager for instructions about how to secure their access to heaven. The manual included six chapters that detailed a rich set of rites and prayers that helped Christians imitate Christ's life and achieve the spiritual equanimity he had found as he accepted his fate prior to his crucifixion. To achieve this state of grace, individuals were instructed to embrace the central precepts of their religion, to accept death, and to reject the temptations of the Devil, especially infidelity, material temptation, despair, impatience, vanity, and avarice. The manual also encouraged the dying person to set their worldly affairs, most critically with their family, in order. This last requirement was essential because it was the dying person's family and close friends who were expected to accompany the infirmed as he or she lay dying. Their demeanor and state of mind served as a litmus test as to whether the person had achieved a good death. While domestic unity indicated that the deceased had left their affairs in order, rancor, jealousy, and acrimony between family members indicated otherwise. Domestic discord signaled both a life that was not well lived and a death that would be less than peaceful.

In practice the Christian ideal and the actual achievement of a good death varied over time and between social classes. For elites in both Europe and Mexico, a good death in the early modern period required that they set aside money to pay for an elaborate funeral procession, a burial inside the grounds of the church, and the dedication of multiple masses to be orated for their soul. After the eighteenth century, these often-exorbitant public displays of devotion among the elite gave way to more private and somber rituals of piety.[2] But what about the poor? If we know little about what they yearned for in life, we know less about how they approached death and how they defined a good death. Beyond the quantitative facts of their deaths (how many, when, why), a qualitative understanding of what the Mexican historian Juan Pedro Viqueira calls "*El sentimiento de la muerte*" (what the poor yearned for in a good death, what they feared, and how they worked to achieve the former while avoiding the latter) is almost absent from the historical record.[3]

While Luz may never have read the *Ars Moriendi*, he was the inheritor of the religious cultural attitudes and spiritual hopes that it had generalized in the Christian world in the previous five hundred years. Like his Christian counterparts around the world, Luz wanted to be respected by his family and wanted them to absolve him of his shortcomings as a father and husband before he died. Luz imagined a death tableau in which he and his family were together in his final moments, full of love and purged of the rancor that sometimes characterized their relationships. As he approached his end, Luz realized that it would be difficult to achieve this death scene. He worried that death would come to him or his loved ones in a sudden and terrible manner that could leave them either separated from each other in this world or spiritually unprepared for the afterlife in heaven. As noted in previous chapters, Luz feared that Pancha would succumb to the temptation of the materialism of her new country and die outside the grace of the one true Church. He was also discomforted by the thought that if he died first (almost a certainty given his age), or if a nuclear war broke out between the Soviet Union and the United States, his whole family would not be able to complete the domestic scene of death he yearned for. The desperation that Luz felt at the possibility that world events would keep him and his family from achieving the confident, even exuberant emotional state that a good death required permeates his correspondence to Pancha. Luz was particularly worried about the Korean War, the event that Luz believed would trigger a nuclear holocaust: "If the situation in Korea does not end, there will be no remedy: we will go to drink from the bitter chalice of death in war. What will it feel like to die against our will, some here and some there? I would like for us to die together; but no, we will die as God wishes. For the last time I send you my writings. I have no money. My world has turned upside down. The world will remain behind. Please pray for everyone, even if I do not write again" (circa April 1951).[4]

This gloomy, lonely, and claustrophobic tone—one that is absent the playful, ironic familiarity that supposedly defines Mexican attitudes toward death[5]—is so suffused with despair that it makes it difficult to avoid the conclusion that in spite of his best efforts to live a dignified old age and die a good death, Luz was experiencing his last years of life as a series of painful physical, mental, and social losses (September 11, 1951; February 15, 1951). While it is evident that death, decay, and loss colored most of Luz's meditations, it is also important to remember that there is great danger in conceiving of the aging and dying process, his and other's, as only a "pathetic series of losses."[6] This stance often obscures a whole range of positive actions that people take to come to terms with old age and the efforts they make to live and die with a dignity and purpose they hope will, in the phrase made famous by the French historian Philippe Ariès, tame death. The narrative of aging and the specter of death as a series of losses also ignores the strong impulse that motivates people to create stories about their lives that are full of meaning, passion, and originality.[7] So while Luz's obsessive letter-writing may have seemed irrational to his family and unremittingly dark to readers now, the examples collected in this chapter also highlight how writing his correspondence allowed Moreno to create a personal narrative that attenuated the fears he had about growing old, of being ignored, of being erased—of dying alone.

The biographical offerings that Luz Moreno penned in his correspondence to Pancha helped him fight the erasure that many old people fear (October 22, 1951). Writing about his life, his town, his memories of his daughter, and their time together helped Luz create a narrative that linked him not only to his ghostly ausentes in the United States, but also tethered him (and them) to the time, space, ideas, and traditions that gave meaning not only to his life, but also to his impending death.[8] This explains why Pancha's life in the United States, the question of where she would die, and the matter of her continued religious orthodoxy mattered so much to Luz: If in migrating and living among Protestant Americans Pancha disowned her family, abandoned her faith, forgot her town, and forsook her culture, she not only forfeited her place in heaven—as Luz constantly reminds her—but also the moral and historical context that gave meaning to her father's life, his death, and his legacy. To mitigate the threat of this erasure, Luz implored Pancha to "receive our memories." He wanted Pancha to remember him, a still-living ancestor, to not forget where she came from, and to not forsake the religion that united them as a family.[9] While most of his letters are characterized by a pathos of "nostalgia laced with sighs," Luz also wrote Pancha poetic letters full of hope and a marked lightness of spirit that showed how much he loved life and how important it was for Pancha to know that in spite of his age and the distance that separated them, he still existed.[10] In one letter Luz, employing a rhetorical strategy found elsewhere in his correspondence, creates an imaginary conversation to share his thoughts about aging and dying with Pancha: "We ask a young man: 'What do you make of life?' [He answers,] 'Very beautiful.' If we were to ask an old man if, after having suffered many years of maladies, he wanted to die, he would respond, 'I want to live.' How sweet it is to eat, to sleep, to travel, to listen to the birds chirp, to contemplate the flowers, to see the forests, the lakes, and seas. To receive the rays of the sun that warm and animate creation" (c. January 1951).

Luz Moreno's correspondence allowed him to appear to the person he most loved. It also gave him hope that if Pancha recognized his presence,[11] if she valued his memories as worth remembering, and she if wrote back, he could exist and die as a human nobler than the sum of all his anxieties, the poverty of his material circumstances, and the diminishing abilities of his decaying mind and body. Existing through other people's perceptions, though, is a treacherous strategy for older people, who, in addition to inhabiting a fragile body, increasingly become physically and emotionally isolated from the sensations and the social world that gave their existence and, they hope, their death meaning.[12] While they hope that people will see a sympathetic image when they see them, often, as was the case with Luz, others see is a pale, misshapen version of the elder's imagined best self. Obdulia Orozco, Luz Moreno's granddaughter, often tells the story of boarding a bus in Guadalajara during the morning rush when she was seventy years old. Jostling with her fellow commuters to reach the door of the bus, she suddenly heard the driver ask the riders to move out of the way to "let the *viejita* (old lady) on board." Obdulia, shocked not only by the callousness of her fellow commuters, but also by her own insensitivity to the needs of a vulnerable old woman, stopped, moved to the side, and looked back to see if she could be of assistance to the poor viejita. It was at that moment that she noticed that everyone was looking in her direction, that her fellow passengers had parted for her, that she was the viejita.[13]

Obdulia recalls this incident with a healthy measure of amusement and self-deprecation. She finds humor in the gap between her sense of self and the image that her seventy-year-old body projected to a crowd of kind strangers.[14] What Obdulia experienced as comedy, Luz endured as tragedy. As he writes to Pancha, the net effect of his palpitations, his rheumatism, his volatile stomach, his diminishing eyesight, his shaky hands, and his increasingly unreliable mind was not yet death. Rather, it was a debilitating and chronic physical impotence that slowly and cumulatively prevented him from carrying out the activities and responsibilities that for most of his life had publicly and privately defined him as a man, as a father, and as a poor but hard-working and respected member of his community. Luz wanted to continue living and he wanted his limbs and his mind, his physical strength and his mental acuity, to be reenergized.[15] But as he hobbled along the sunny side of the uneven, rose-colored sandstone sidewalks of San Miguel, the septuagenarian caught fleeting glimpses of how others saw him, and he could not help but despair. Young people snickered, and former employers, seeing how "time ha[d] destroyed the body that once caused admiration at work," refused to hire him.[16] Most people, given that they were neighbors, friends, or family, greeted him warmly and moved aside when they saw the *viejito* shuffling down the street. Luz accepted their formal signs of respect, but in his mind, and as he wrote to Pancha, he could not but help intuit and feel sad by the finality of their judgment: "What is that old man going to do if he is not even able to carry his own bones?" (September 11, 1951). Even in the sanctuary of the confessional, the portal to the afterlife he had faith would redeem the misery of his corporeal existence, Luz was reminded of his liminal status: "I confessed myself with Father Bergara; when he asked me how long it had been since my last confession, I told him that it had been a year. 'Oh, old man' he told me 'why so distant from God? You are at death's door and at the end of your life. For penance I want you to confess every 3 months.' Me, in the condition that I was in; well, that just made me very sick."[17]

Luz did not believe that everyone in San Miguel thought of him with such disregard. Some of his neighbors took genuine pity on him and extended unsolicited kindnesses that he was sincerely grateful for: "It may be because they see me so old that they say that that man is history. Many people, of course those who have charity, give me ten or twenty cents. Or when I buy something they give me more than what I purchased; this brings me joy and sadness" (August 30, 1951). While he appreciated their kindness, it was a cutting compassion that reminded Luz of his poverty, his old age, and how both of these contribute to a dependent status and a sense of being useless that seemed worse than death. From what little is known about what it feels like to grow old in Latin America, we can speculate that despite the myth that Latin Americans love and respect their elderly more than those of other cultures, Luz was not alone in feeling unappreciated and vulnerable in his old age. The American anthropologist Oscar Lewis found echoes of the scorn Luz was feeling among his elderly contemporaries in the southern town of Tepoztlán, Morelos. Lewis reports that older members of this mostly indigenous community feared dependency more than they feared death because, as he wrote, "a 'useless' old age is considered a sad thing."[18] Echoing Lewis's work, the anthropologist Nancy Scheper-Hughes has found that among the poor residents of the Northeast of Brazil old age was a condition akin to—or a precipitating factor in creating—wrenching poverty. She contends that while individuals who still have the physical strength to work can "get by" and live a life of "self-respecting" poverty, the old and the infirm, "the truly wretched [,] are those who must beg to eat and who are too sick to work."[19]

Luz's condition was not as dire as the Brazilian poor that Scheper-Hughes studies. In spite of the fact that he often described himself as part of the miserable pueblo (the wretched of the earth), he got by, and with his children's help he lived a self-respecting poverty. But, as his letters show, his poverty was a condition earned at the expense of familial peace and exacerbated by his age. This concerned and embarrassed Luz because he knew that his only chance for redemption in this life, and hence his only opportunity to achieve a good death, came from his hope that at least his family respected him; that if in public he was darkness, in his home he was light;[20] that if on the streets and in the eyes of the young and his social betters he was but a bag of bones indistinguishable from the rest of the miserable pueblo they held in contempt, that in his home he was ceded the social status he expected as the patriarch of the family.

This sense of masculine entitlement was centered on a soft hierarchy and a religiously ordained organic order that was based on clearly delineated but complementary roles and reciprocal responsibilities. Luz believed that while a man was the king of his house, he shared this kingdom with his wife, the queen, and their children, who were their vassals.[21] But as he grew older and less able to meet the expectations that his wife and children had of him, even this more-or-less egalitarian (but idealized) role as *paterfamilias* was denied to him. When Luz had been physically able to work and earn money, and while Pancha lived in San Miguel and was willing to tend to his physical and emotional needs (April 23, 1951), Moreno had been shielded from seeing how little power he actually had in the family. But once he was at the "doors of his tomb" and was physically unable to perform the duties of a man, his relationship with his wife and daughters was altered.[22] Without Pancha to shield him from the full ramifications of his dependency, Luz saw his situation as it truly was: he could no longer work; his sister-in-law, Angela, owned the house he and his family lived in; his wife Secundina and his daughters, Victorina and Isabel, cooked and cleaned for him and earned the money that purchased the clothes he wore and the food he ate. Luz may have still worn the crown that his religion and gender entitled him to, but because of the duties they performed, the money they earned, the decisions they made, and the attitudes they displayed, Cunda, Victorina, and Isabel were, in everything but name, the "men" of the Moreno home.[23] Luz may have reigned, but he did not rule.

Immigration has tended to decrease women's influence in Mexican society as men's mobility increased their access to information and economic opportunities and women's work and social networks were devalued, the relative economic power and youth of the Moreno women (plus the fact that it was Pancha who had migrated and was the source of "*los Dolares*") solidified their hold over the household.[24] Their position and responsibilities also, at least from Luz's perspective, embittered them and freed them to make audible accusations that they had once only been whispered: Luz does not meet his paternal obligations, he cannot keep his sons sober, he does not provide for the expenditures of the household, he spends what little money he has on newspapers and postage stamps, and instead of helping with the household chores he writes letters and spreads rumors that make them look bad.[25]

Luz denied spreading rumors, but he accepted most of their other criticisms because he knew that they were right.[26] He could not meet his culturally and personally defined responsibilities as the male head of the Moreno household. The only thing that kept him from total dependence was the money that his son Chito gave him from the profits of his donkey jerky business and the dollars Pancha periodically sent him via mail. These gifts mitigated Luz's financial "wretchedness," but they also emphasized just how radically his old age and its accompanying physical impotence had transformed his relationship with his children. In spite of his desire for a good death, Luz was dependent on the kindness and material support of his impoverished, hardworking, and somewhat embittered children.

Luz Moreno's situation reaffirms the Jewish saying: "When the father gives to the son, both are happy. When the son gives to the father, both weep."[27] It also makes it difficult to see how the aging and self-aware Luz was experiencing his last years of life as anything other than a wholesale disassembling of both his body and his social world. There is, though, another way of understanding his despairing letters, the painful maladies he suffered, and the relationship between the two. While pain, illness, injury, and old age "unmake" the physical body and "deconstruct" the social world of the afflicted—the very arenas and relationships that ground our understanding of self over time[28]—they also provide individuals with the chance to creatively remake themselves.[29] Seen from this perspective, Luz's discussions of his maladies, his old age, his loneliness, and his dread of dying a bad death are impassioned, creative, purposeful requests to his daughter for an intimate and wide-ranging conversation about the dissolute condition of not only his body but of the world around him. As Luz saw it, his decay was mirrored and related to the decay and disorder of the world around him: his poverty was part of larger social injustices, his familial conflicts were inseparable from the political/military conflicts of the Cold War, his sickness was part of a cosmic illness that was going to extinguish his life and (via the atomic bomb) bring an end to all of God's creation. The letters in which he bemoans these disorders are laments, but they are also a testament to his desire to transcend the dazzling pettiness of his death and his yearning for justice, order, and good health—for himself, his family, and the world. In a world increasingly defined by absences, ephemerality, individualism, loneliness, and disjuncture, Luz wanted real things, things that were solid, and things that were eternal: He wanted to see his daughter, he wanted not to be alone, he wanted to be healthy, he wanted to be useful, and like Dostoevsky, he wanted to be worthy of his suffering and of his death.

Luz Moreno wanted a good death, but he was not in a hurry to die.[30] In spite of all the suffering and pain he wanted to live; and he hoped that by telling his story to Pancha he could forestall, or at least tame, his death.[31] It was not enough. On December 2, 1953, after seven decades of life, and three years of writing letters to his ausentes in Stockton, Luz Moreno's body stopped functioning. This could not have come as a surprise to Luz. He saw his body decaying and death approaching, and his letters are full of meditations on the subject. In some letters he was full of hope about the time he had left and the prospects of an afterlife in heaven. In other letters, he was depressed about the realities that defined his life and his death as a series of losses. Both are part of the dialogue that Luz created for and with Pancha. Reading and responding to these letters must have been emotionally wrenching for Pancha. For Luz, a man whose feet treaded lightly on this earth and whose soul was barely able to wrestle with the demons that threatened it, his correspondence was an exercise in redemption. The letters he wrote afforded this mortal and imperfect father one last chance to transcend the pettiness of his death, one last chance to make himself worthy of his suffering, and one last chance to proffer both his pain and his death to his daughter as an infinitely loving act.[32]

In order to eliminate as much of the ghosts' power as possible and to attain a natural intercourse, a tranquility of soul, they have invented trains, cars, aeroplanes—but nothing helps anymore: These are evidently inventions devised at the moment of crashing. The opposing side is so much calmer and stronger; after the postal system, the ghosts invented the telegraph, the telephone, the wireless. They will not starve, but we will perish.

Franz Kafka, Letters to Milena[1]

━❧❦━

c. February 1951

Beloved and never forgotten children,

For all of us here knowing that you are doing well has been a motive to praise God because He is the One who takes care of His children. I marvel that after one year in those American lands you find yourself well and healthy. I am also amazed that . . . you have made us beneficiaries of what, with such hard work, you have earned.

I imagine you like buzzing little bees, making the honey that providence has placed in your hands, defying the rigors of time without forgetting that you have a part of [your family here in San Miguel]. [A family] that during the day implores our sun to go and warm the limbs of our children who hope to see, if only intermittently, the face of that beautiful star . . . Who has suffered more in soul and body than you? [You have suffered] in your soul because of the separation: where can one live better than in one's own land? The [Americans], some will see you in a good light some in a bad one. I wish that the affliction that one suffers when there is no one to ask for consolation had not happened to you because those pains and sorrows cause more anguish than when one is [physically] beat.

On the 20th, we received some letters in which you tell us that you will be able to come to spend three months in order to rest, although you don't know when. Hopefully, when you know more or less when you are coming, you will tell us with enough time so that we will not be surprised by your visit . . . You tell us that you are no longer that cold; this is good. On the 20th, at 5 in the morning, I had palpitations that lasted 4 hours. I had administered myself a purgative because I had been sick from my stomach, [I think this is because] they now make food with sugar and this has hurt me. [I] cannot reconcile my conscience to the exigencies of the Church, because it is not

---

1. Franz Kafka, *Letters to Milena*, trans. Philip Boem (New York: Schoken Books, 1990), 223.

within my abilities to do so. I confessed myself with Father Bergara; when he asked me how long it had been since my last confession, I told him that it had been a year. "Oh, old man" he told me, "why so distant from God? You are at death's door and at the end of your life. For penance I want you to confess every 3 months." Me, in the condition that I was in; well, that just made me very sick. I wouldn't want you to be saddened by this, that's why I want you to ask God for my health and the health of everyone.

[Luz Moreno]

~∗∾

October 22, 1951

Juan and Pancha, my beloved ausentes.

I want to greet you. I want my heart to unburden and alleviate itself of my heavy worries. As long as I remember your pure and generous actions, I can only but express my gratitude for your goodness. Finding myself experiencing many difficulties, I have no other option than finding in death the peace I never found in life.

God granted me 74 years of life. My first years I spent wailing. They said I was afflicted with a donkey sickness.[2] When I was 7 years old, I was responsible for taking food to my father and Zenon [out in the fields]. At the age of 9, they put me at the yoke of the oxen to clear the fields, to gather the feed, to take care of the animals, and to do all the chores at home. During the rainy season I had to care for the animals and was rarely able to attend Mass. Between myself and Zenón, we would plow 5 or 6 *yuntas*; we would harvest the hay, and carry our bundles back to the corral. [There] we would cut beans and beat them clean.[3] This went on for 25 years. In the year 1899 I thought about marrying. My father, realizing that my labor would be needed, thought about leaving his ranch and going to *la Tinaja*. By the year 1900 we had settled at *la Tinaja*, and that was the year [Secundina and I] were married. And what was my father's determination at seeing my new independence? "You no longer fit in *La Tinaja*—you must find somewhere else to farm." How could I stay? But when my brother Panchillo married, father Magdaleno said, "This one will not leave from here. As long as there is one plant to be sowed, he will sow it."[4] I swear!

2. "*Los primeros años los pase llorando Decian que tenia enfermedad de burro.*" Supposedly, Luz coughed so much as a child he sounded like a donkey.
3. *Yunta*: a parcel of land or a team of oxen.
4. See chapter 1 for elaboration on the dynamics of rural inheritance in Los Altos and the concept of *desconocimiento*.

I continued on with my life accepting the children God gave me. [I had] a job so miserable that I was barely to procure our daily corn. When I would plant on borrowed (and not so good) land, [I could scarcely] grow 6 bushels of corn and a few beans. I was employed at [my father's] house as if I was a peon and was paid only 37 cents per day. That is how I lived for 26 years, until my parents died. I was given a 300 peso inheritance. (From the 10,000 pesos saved from harvesting during 26 years only 2000 remained at my parent's death, the rest having been spent by my parents and brothers.) After the death of my parents, now about 22 years past, I am on the brink of death under the protection of my children. It is not until now, after 60 years of continuous labor, that I have stopped working because I cannot do it anymore. Only God knows how I will spend the days I have left. My sons are very kind. Of my daughters, Pancha is kind; Victorina and Ysabel are kind only when they want to be.

Luz Moreno

c. January 1951

[My children,]

What will ever turn out according to our desires? Desires are not granted. If at any time we assume that one of our desires has been granted, it is only because we changed our desire to fit the outcome.

They say that even the best cook leaves a whole tomato uncooked.[5] We live under laws, constraints, and advice. We cannot make a move without asking permission . . . Perhaps our interests square with our desires because we live under laws. We cry without being injured. We complain about the many things we need, and also about the things we have too much of. We are not in need of peace to live tranquilly. What we need is somewhere to establish this peace. We are not in need of money because one cannot forge peace with money. Peace cannot be offered to everyone because not everyone wants peace. Nor should we fight with everyone because there are many who would rather pay than fight. Our wants and needs are in constant movement, some are leaving and some are coming. When we ask for pleasure or sorrow, for something good or something bad, we actually do not need to ask for them as they will come on their own.

---

5. "*Dicen que a la mejor gisandera se le ba un tomate entero.*" To *guisar* is to stew food, usually with tomatoes and onions. Luz used this aphorism to convey to Pancha that everyone makes mistakes.

They say that hope is the last to die. We all hope so. They also say that he who hopes [and waits] also despairs.[6] They say that time is money. Time passes and does not return. How beautiful time is. Better yet, how beautiful life is for however saturated it may be with sorrows, we embrace it and do not want the moment to arrive when we have to let it go. We ask a young man: "What do you make of life?" [He answers,] "Very beautiful." If we were to ask an old man if, after having suffered many years of maladies, he wanted to die, he would respond, "I want to live." How sweet it is to eat, to sleep, to travel, to listen to the birds chirp, to contemplate the flowers, to see the forests, the lakes, and seas. To receive the rays of the sun that warm and animate creation. To feel the gentle breeze that invigorates our body. To lift our eyes on a peaceful night and take delight in the infinity of planets that travel above our heads. Oh life, beautiful life, do not end and I will live happy. To war, to death, those who are bored with life. Those who are not, that they not even think of [war and death]. My children Juan and Pancha, receive my thoughts as a gift to you. Here, we are fine. May God and Virgin Mary bless you and protect the ones in this household.

Luz Moreno

February 15, 1951

To my beloved children,

Time goes by bringing consolation and sadness, but lately it seems that there is more bad than good. Time made us children some 73 years ago. He who writes was once a child, now he can barely write these lines. On his head you see a thin veil of clouds, like those that cover the tops of mountains, it bears witness to the effects of time. Walking feebly is nothing but [testimony to how] time has destroyed that body that once caused admiration at work. The scorn that an old man suffers should be attributed to the passage of time. The old man sees the specter of death approaching him, and although both young and old await death, it is more imminent for the old man. The sacred scripture says, "Rise before a bedridden person and give honor to the old and dying."[7] Currently the young take pleasure in laughing at the old. Those

---

6. "*El que espera desespera.*"

7. "Thou shalt rise up before the hoary head, and honour the face of the old man, and fear thy God: I *am* the LORD": Leviticus 121:32. *King James Bible* Authorized Version, Cambridge Edition.

we loved disappear because time has determined the end of their life. For 50 years now, you, my children, have seen this world; now that it is burning in flames: What do you think?

Poor Chito! They no longer allow him to slaughter donkeys. It was his only business. This President is very stupid.[8] How can he prohibit something so necessary for those who enjoy eating donkey meat? He [would] need to prohibit it in all areas, or [declare that] donkey meat should no longer be considered food. There is no lack of sorrows. This misfortune bothers me because I see that currently Chito has no other way of making money. He plays music only now and then. Truckloads of pigs, well, very few.[9] Since he was the one who lent me donkeys to bring soil, soon there [will be] none for him or me.

In one letter I received from Juan he tells me, among other things, that he will take me as contraband to live with you. Well, [I would do it] for the pleasure of seeing you since you are not able to visit. But I would remain sad seeing that so many here would also like to see you. That is how we will pass our lives, between dreams and disappointments, until the day arrives for us to go to Heaven . . . We are all doing well, only Hilario is still ill and is bedridden. We send our regards. The [religious] exercises for men started on the 12th.

Luz Moreno

April 23, 1951

My beloved children,

A piece of paper is not enough on which to tell you my sorrows. But I will not speak of another thing since presently I feel a great despair over what my daughters—those who stayed with me—have done. [I speak not of] the daughter [Pancha], who for a long time carried the financial burdens of the house and the problems created by brothers and nephews, and parents. [The daughter] to whom God presented a life, not altogether of her own choosing, but certainly better than the life she had before. [No,] I speak of the daughters [Isabel and Victorina] who stayed [home] complaining about nuisances; who, without finding whom to blame, have made (me) the author of these conditions. About 20 years ago they had good will towards their brothers. They would tell others about it: "We

---

8. The president of the Municipality of San Miguel el Alto, Jesús Cornejo.
9. Chito also slaughtered pigs.

never forsake our brothers, we help them where we can." Now that they are angry, they object to everything: that I have not fulfilled my [fatherly] obligations, that they are not the ones who are married [to their brothers], that their wives should take care of them, that whatever [money] they obtain is for themselves and not for their [brother's] drunken binges, that I should provide for the expenditures of the household. Now that I am at the doors of my tomb, they accuse me of these things. I think they have a point. But the only thing they accomplish [with their complaints] is to make me sick with bile. [It is only after] I throw up and spew yellow, bitter bile [that I feel better] . . . I [do] not know what to do . . . All that I ask is that they do not burden me with these charges now that I am nearly upon my death. Punish me here (on Earth) as you like, I deserve it; but at least when the fair judge asks me about this particular case I can reply, "Sir, my children forgave me, forgive me also." My beloved children, Juan and Pancha, do not be scandalized by these sentiments as you are beyond reproach . . . I make you aware of these things to lighten my responsibility and to soften my conscience. What else can I do in my impotent [state]?

The ground [upon which you stand] is shaken by current events. The decomposition of social order does not stop, every day it grows. All social classes are moved. Man rebels against man. It seems that the authorities do not derive [their legitimacy] from God. They believe that man fixes all. [They believe] that [all they need] is to be feared by inventing weapons [and by] enlarging their armies with the very people who should be working the land and increasing production. They use the youth—18-year-olds who are the hope for the future—and let them die. Be it with reason or without, all that matters is that the millionaires are happy. Those who are comfortable in this life do not want others to enjoy [their riches]. They change militaries, they make meetings, kill thousands, and the situation does not get better. [Why?] Because they do it without God, without charity.

Sports have become very popular. Do they believe that these people [athletes] are not a burden on production? Only if they did not eat, or dress, or anything. On the contrary, the blind government spends thousands on rewarding something that has no merit. It would be better to reward puppeteers.

The illnesses neither kill us nor leave us alone. The palpitations come every 8 days; [when they do come] they hit me three straight times. The rheumatism on my right knee does not let me walk; [my knee feels] as if it is dislocated. Occasionally, the ticks punish me. Every year I get 2 in my left ear, and in my right ear, where I never had one before, I now have one. Because they are all disgusted by them, there is no one to take [the ticks] out and they stay [in my ear] until they decide to leave. Only you, Pancha, would take them out when I wanted you to. Hilario seems to be doing well, and no one else is sick. . . . I am waiting for the Fiesta del Señor de Misericordia, without knowing if I will go, due to my palpitations and lack of money. Receive our memories.

Luz Moreno.

～٤9٤～

July 1, 1951

My beloved children,

I would not want to lose touch, even though I have many difficulties. I am impotent in so many ways: I cannot see, I get cramps in the hand that I write with, my brain gets tired, I forget what I write . . . and what I write is an inadequate reflection of what I should write. I have this feeling that drowns me and drives me crazy. I would just like to show you my sorrows and the troubles that we have in the family, but you are probably tired of hearing and seeing the same things in my letters. I do not need to write or talk [about these things] for you to figure out that Father is a poor old man. Still, I raise my voice and direct my gaze toward the far-off land where I know my beloved children live. I greet you with my deepest affection. I offer my gratitude, and I beg that you do not forget your poor family who, though distressed by your absence and battered in many ways, is still consoled because you are like a balm that fortifies us.

Chito bought a piece of land from Hilario Román for five thousand pesos. By September, he will give him what he can and the rest he will pay later . . . It is sad, the water does not want to rain evenly. All you hear are laments [about] scarcity. What will happen to us if it does not rain? The hay costs three pesos, and Chito does not know what to feed the donkeys. [The rich] do not even want to sell alfalfa. They have everything and they deny everything. . . .

The first of July is Mamá Cunda's day, a day to rejoice for this family's children. Receive our regards and our feelings printed in this letter. They lack importance, but contain our wishes that we live in peace, that God not abandon us, and that our pleas may unite to ask God for a good rainy season.

[Luz Moreno]

～٤9٤～

July 12, 1951

To my beloved absentees,

Beloved children, even though it may be late, even though it may be with much sacrifice, I send you my writings. They are poor, they are simple, humble, and maybe the ones you least look forward to because they are pure laments. What else could I write about if not what makes me suffer? The time of my life has passed me by. Death, with all its horrors, approaches. You my children, I see you as the only relief I have, if not to avoid death and its causes, at least as a small refuge [from them]. I see you dedicated to the work of your time and my sad sentiments will serve only as a nuisance. In the year since you left, we have sustained ourselves by exchanging our feelings. [But] the Devil has created so much jealousy [in the family] about what I write that I no longer find a way to write to you. I could never have imagined how divisive one's love for his children could be. Receive through our humble writings, our great love.

Luz Moreno.

August 1, 1951

Juan and Pancha, my beloved children,

Time and its effects continue manifesting themselves in all of Creation. Time itself creates new things and new beings who join the beings that already exist. Humans are subject to the same changes that occur to things of every class and condition. All moments are formed by time, and these go into forming seconds, minutes, hours, days, months, years, and centuries. What thing does not exist in time? What thing does not demand time? And what cannot be achieved with time? The worker sows his seed into the ground and waits 8 days to begin to see the effects of time. After 60 days that seed will flower. 30 days after flowering the plant will have a nice corn. This is the effect of time. Experience [teaches us] that only with time is everything possible. There are other auxiliary factors without which nothing can be done.

In this way our life goes on highlighting . . . that without a doubt, time both gives and takes. It gives life to new things and death to old ones. People go crazy when they are young; when they age past 50 or 60 years, it is not the same. 70 years ago the world was easier, time has passed and [the world has] changed: wars, famine, it rains and it doesn't rain, there is a calamity and then there is another. Those who currently believe that there is nothing to worry about are wrong. Who is holding back the Red tide so that its communist propaganda does not succeed? The Americans, they are the strong ones who are erecting strong walls [against the Red tide]. Some say we should not fear anything, neither war nor anything. Well, we seem to be so innocent that the only things missing are our little [angel] wings. My dear children, do not be so confident, live cautiously. You have your little house, who is going to encircle it with a wall to protect it from the enemies near and far who covet what is yours?

Receive this poor letter and do not forget your home.
Luz Moreno

⟶є९⟵

August 30 of 1951

To my beloved ausentes,

Beloved children. On the 29th of this month that is almost over, the month of September,[10] we received a letter that tells us that you are healthy—well thanks be to God. Hilario is the same as always . . . He has a plot of land but since the hail ruined it, he says that it is no longer any good. The one who writes, your old Papá Luz, continues with his palpitations and sometimes with an upset stomach, diarrhea, constipation, [or] headaches. [I am also] desperate because I cannot earn a nickel and do not feel like working. No one is asking me to bring [potting] soil because now there are many rancheros that bring it to them from the ranchos. It may be because they see me so old that they say that that man is history. Many people, of course those who have charity, give me ten or twenty cents. Or when I buy something they give me more than what I purchased; this brings me joy and sadness.

Juanito, it brings me much grief to know that you have not received notice about whether the Dollar you had sent Papá Luz had arrived. It arrived on the 14th of August, and that same day Papá Luz sent you a letter telling you so . . . You have many complaints about not receiving news; since I do not see everyone else's letters, I do not know what they send you. Chuy Orozco is heading your way to *el Norte*—who knows if he'll get there. With much difficulty he got his credential to enter the pool to become a bracero laborer, then off he went to Guadalajara for the selection process. Then to a place in California that is called Calexico. They will [decide who to contract in Calexico] through a rigorous medical exam. Each laborer has to pay their transportation [to Calexico]. How much will it cost from Guadalajara to Calexico? And if he does not get [chosen he will incur] another expense to come back to San Miguel or to go to you in Stockton.[11]

---

10. More than likely, Moreno meant August.

11. Moreno is referring to the lottery process that Mexico's Commission on Emigrant Worker Affairs organized to select workers for the Bracero Program. For a fuller account of the process see Henderson, *Beyond Borders*, 73–74.

Once there, Juan and Pancha, you will have to see what you do with him. Receive these matters and our regards and thanks for the Dollar that I received the 14th of August and for all the favors that this family receives from you.

Luz Moreno.

[P.S.]

What I wrote about Chuy, that he was going to *el Norte*: well he went to Guadalajara but he came back on the 29th. He arrived in San Miguel very sorry because there are many difficulties [in getting chosen to be a Bracero]. There are many difficulties and falsehoods in the proceedings.

September 11, 1951

Juan and Pancha, my beloved children.

Many people want to go to *el Norte*. The government does not have sufficient offices to serve the many aspiring Braceros. Even those of this house have been swept up [in the mania]. The 12th, Chilo left with all his documents in order; who knows if he will get there. They did not want Chuy because of his [young] age.

My beloved children, you can see the affliction that our separation causes me. Lolo also wants to go; who knows? In the end we may end up alone. . . .

We see how licentiousness is growing in movies and in the schools, as is injustice and robbery. If the world does not change, if it does not do penance to God, who made humanity to glorify Him, He will bring upon us cholera and many punishments until the perverse repent. The world cannot be redeemed because those who rule get together and can only think of defeating their enemies; they never think about forgiveness. Order is lost and while disorder exists we are obligating God to punish us.

We continue with our illnesses: palpitations and with [poor] digestion. I need my missing molars. Because no one calls me for soil, or anything else, I do not exercise and without exercise I am not hungry. I wake up well, but soon after I eat breakfast I get ill with headaches and [I am overcome] with such despair that I don't know what to do. The same with Hilario. No one else is ill. We await your arrival . . . as God wishes, you shall decide [whether you come]. I am not sure that I will live; I feel so many bad things that only God knows [whether I shall live]. Pray to God for this, your home.

At the pace that time passes it seems that it is injuring our nature, first one part, then another. It seems that the function of time is to diminish our energies in such a way that we see with pain the disappearance of our energies and in our limbs we feel many aches that put us on guard and kill us slowly and many times unexpectedly. Our desire is to recuperate what we lose through illnesses but many times we do not because of our poverty or because the medicines [we take] are not the appropriate ones. When we are in the midst of pain we wish the whole world to be moved [by our pain]. We think about the most friendly, most merciful person. We count the hours. We make calculations: will I get better with this remedy, like I did the last time [I was sick?] We look at our conscience. If something serious happens, what will be God's determination? Everything is hidden; what is not hidden are the effects of time, the lack of energy, the scorn of our own family members and those who used to hire us for work. [They say], "What is that old man going to do if he is not even able to carry his own bones?" The anxieties of an old man are very sad . . .

I am pleased by many of the things [that I have done] and I wish I had done more of those. But I have done many things that I am sorry for. Who has done purely good [in their life?] At no point does one see things in such a way as to see clearly their nature and their effects. Time gives counsel, but by the time it does so it is too late. Juan, my son, I am very grateful for what you

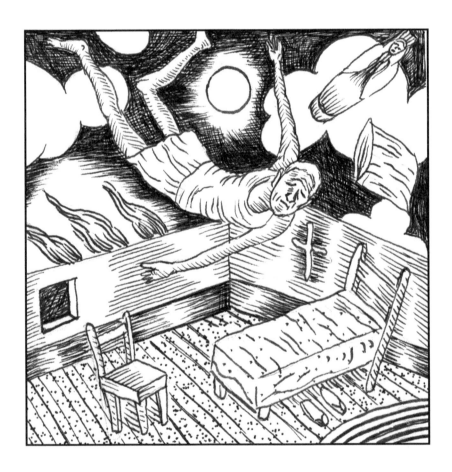

have done for me individually and for all of those of this family, so far. But if you are loath to speak with me with confidence it is because before your marriage I did not behave in a prudent manner, and this is what dissipated the confidence [between us.] Even though I have begged your pardon, I have not been able to erase my error. If your good will will allows, once more receive my supplication asking forgiveness for those affronts. My beloved children, Juan and Pancha, receive my sincere words. I am with the same illnesses.

Luz Moreno

September 27, 1951

To my ausentes,

Beloved children, I would like, at every instant to unburden the anxiety that I feel on these days that are, or at least used to be, joyous.[12] [Instead of joy], I saw disappear the hope I had in seeing my children during these days. In addition, and to deepen my sorrows, my Chilo has also gone. [All would be sorrow] were it not that I see that while Chilo is in the United States and he finds a little bit of interest in his life and he fears God, he will not get drunk. I also see that he will earn more money [over there], even though it will come at the cost of more privations. But what will happen to him in six months [when his Bracero contract is up]? What will I do without the pieces of my heart until they return? What I am going to do is make myself a heart of stone in order to put up with whatever God wants. You do what you have always done: write to me, talk to me, help me, and preserve my life with those demonstrations of love. In addition, let us ask God for help, patience, and a strong spirit [to face] adversity.

Sickness is with Hilario; the same as with Papá. They have given me injections, but my stomach remains ill . . . I pass the days and nights tossing and turning in my bed full of fleas and bed bugs thinking about a dark and uncertain future. I go to the rosary, I go to the plaza, [and] I see the people happy and full of energy. I remember my life, I see it in dreams. I see my little grandchildren. I see Chito's children: I see Sidonia, so big; Josefina and all the little girls; I see José, the only boy. I think about Chito, the father and Desideria, the mother. [I think about] Lolo's children: Miguel who already helps around the house; Lupe, so alive and enthusiastic about the burras; Coco carrying the infant. I do not see Victorina, because even though they have promised to bring her during these days, she has not

12. Reference to the fiestas of September.

arrived.[13] I see this, my darling family, and I ask myself: What will happen to this generation in the future? [What will happen] when my eyes can no longer see my beloved children? You my *amados ausentes*, you see my laments, the laments of your father that I offer to God in these last days of life so that He may forgive the faults I have committed in raising the children God has given me. Receive our memories, [and know that] I do not lose hope in seeing my *ausentes* some day.

Luz Moreno

~୧ୈ~

July 1, 1952

To my very beloved children,

Following the path to the place where we figure the beings who are the cause of our worry live, we heave a thousand sighs and ask the Angel that protects our family to take our exhalations to the place where those who are the cause our foolish restlessness live. Along with our regards go pieces of our hearts because the many calamities that affect the soul and body have come to us in a rush and have not left many healthy parts. Look at [my] old decaying body. Look at my soul that wishes nothing more than to leave its body in the company of the maggots. But I will die gazing towards the place where my absent children live, my lips uttering their sweet names. What may they be doing in these moments? What will they respond to my words? What judgment will they form upon seeing the disunity of brother against brother?

No one can live without thinking about one's death. All is chaos. Not one step is taken without fighting, quarreling, or haggling. There is no respect for anyone; there are no elders, [there are no] minors. This scandalous situation is passed onto the younger generation who sees the conflicts and continue them. What advantage could a brave person have over a cowardly one? A man over a woman? Man is armed and full of horror, fame, vices, and liberties. Strong among his friends and society, [man] believes the world is a paradise and that life is a gift. To him, night is as bright as day, and women are just a piece of common property who are at his disposal [and subject] to his desire. [To him,] Christianity seems to be a story in which Hell and eternal damnation, the immortality of the soul, and death as the key to eternal life, appear as fictions. Salvation is a business that is unimportant, and the Church is just a nuisance. "This type of life is good for living, but not for dying," said Luther. My dear children, this life ends but the one that follows is eternal.

13. The Victorina Luz is referring to is Isidoro Moreno's daughter.

On the 28th, we received a letter that informed us that you are fine. [You tell us] that the war in Korea still continues and that many of the injured come back miserable and hungry. That Russia has more weapons than the United States and that clothes, food, and other necessities are becoming expensive. Around here, well, we struggle with how expensive life is. People are more difficult, and the rich hold onto everything, even their surplus. They do not [give one piece] of firewood or allow anyone's animals onto their fields. Chito let six of his donkeys graze on the road and they got lost. Maize is 70 cents a kilo, hay is at 3 pesos a bundle. Milk is 80 cents a liter. There is hardly any pork and very little beef. Rain is abundant. The fields are looking quite green, and you can see lots of mushrooms . . .

Once again, I send my thanks for the Dollar you sent me and the other five that Chito gave me. May God give you lots of strength so that you can helps us. Hilario is still sick, and he looks rather skinny and pale; kind of like a piece of cotton, if you ask me. Is this the same mischievous child who was always getting into trouble? [The same person] who fled from his home [because] Papá Ypolito wanted to subjugate him and he ended up fighting in the revolution as a soldier in Villa's army?[14] [The man] who finally returned to San Miguel in [19]26. . .. and has been such a help to the family ever since?

Papá Luz feels a discomfort in his stomach, without being hungry or having diarrhea, or vomit. This started during the last week of June, in addition to my [injured] right leg that does not allow me to do much. Receive, my dear children, all of my affection and blessings, together with those of God's, and may you be happy all of your lives in that far-away land. Do not forget these old folks and these relatives and friends who long to see you again.

Luz Moreno

c. July 1, 1952

[My Beloved Children, Juan and Pancha,]

We have received many letters that you have kindly sent us. I had not answered any of them for many reasons. One reason that keeps me from writing back is that while I have never been worth anything, I matter much less now that I lie in my sad room, counting down the hours of the day and night in an ocean of fleas, with no hope except my beloved AUSENTES, knowing that there are very few days left for this poor old man, your Papá. All the signs, some visible and others invisible, [lead me to this conclusion]. Another reason that keeps

14. Hipólito Román was Hilario Román's father.

me from writing you back . . . is the envy, rancor, and hatred that many have taken up against me, accusing me of writing you pure negative gossip about them. Another reason that impedes such a natural [form] of communication is the jealousy, the rancor, and loathing that some family members have created against me because they believe that what I write to you is all bad. Another cause that impedes my complaints, my feelings, and my outcry from reaching the only ones who love me . . . is the weariness that I feel in all my body: my fingers cramp up, my only good eye, my right eye, gets blurry, with the other eye I can hardly make out anything. My misfortune is such that if my right eye were as dark as my left eye, I would lose all hope of seeing my beloved AUSENTES or of being able to walk by myself. I send you this news so that you can see that my complaints are not unfounded. The lack of necessities falls on my shoulders because I am the Father. The anger generated by household chores comes down on me because they see me laying about. If I contradict anything they say, they [unleash] their anger at me. What is lacking is understanding, charity, civilization, and education. With what integrity shall I welcome death? What hope do I have of any virtue, merit, reward, or salvation?

[Luz Moreno]

October 6, 1952

[Juan and Pancha,]

Every day the maladies make their victims lose hope of regaining health. Hilario is still sick. Life is not snatched away from you all at once; one's strength is extinguished a little at a time. Already Hilario is not the same person he was 50 years ago. He is not the same he was 25 years ago, nor 10 years ago, nor 5 years ago, nor 1 year ago. He is not even the same person he was 6 months ago, nor 3 months ago, nor 190 days ago, nor 50 days ago, not even twelve days ago. He is not even the same person he was yesterday. Every day, every hour, we go on creating the illusion that we are getting healthy. Yet when we move we can feel our body sway from one side to the other. What can this mean? It probably [means] that we are losing our blood, the thing that nourishes the nervous system and the whole organism. The digestive system needs healthy food and good medicine, but the stomach rejects even the most familiar and customary food. The heart palpitations are stronger, and sleep is more labored and lighter . . . It is strange how once [having been] the master of the house [Hilario] is now a poor, sickly old man for whom chicken must be fetched, even on Fridays when it is prohibited to eat meat. No one knows exactly how many days he has left in his life. Now think about this sad scene. See how all your sisters and

nieces and all the other people in this family are affected by his sickness, though not all of them to the same [degree]. His contributions are truly missed, especially the economic ones.

Papá Luz wants you to know that his illnesses continue. Don't you think that the principal reason for my illness is my age? If as a little boy they used to say I was afflicted with a donkey sickness, can you imagine the type of ailments that must affect me now? When I was younger, I used to be a cry-baby, this is why they said I had a donkey sickness. I swear that ever since [then] I have had a heart condition. In these past few days I have had some terrible dizzy spells along with heart palpitations and [a pain] in my knee. I will not trouble you anymore.

Luz Moreno[15]

15. Luz Moreno died on December 1, 1953. The last extant letter is from October 1952. This leaves a gap of about fourteen months in the correspondence between the letters we have and the time Luz Moreno passed away. While it is possible that Luz may have stopped writing after October 1952, it is far more likely that this part of the correspondence was lost or destroyed.

Luz Moreno.

Afterword

In the end, sadness is the slow death of the simple things,
those simple things that remain aching in one's heart.
One always returns to the places where you loved life,
only to realize that the things one loved are gone.
That's why, little girl don't leave longing to return,
because love is simple, and time devours the simple things
"Las Simples Cosas"

After Pancha left San Miguel el Alto in 1950, Luz Moreno swore that as long as he lived, no one in his family would follow her to the United States.[1] So, when Pancha and Juan returned for their first visit to San Miguel and Luz heard that they were going to ask for permission to take one of the Orozco children with them back to Stockton, he declared in no uncertain terms, and to any one who would listen, "She got married, God bless her, but none of my children will leave."[2] While even Luz could not keep his youngest son, Chilo, from going to pick cotton in the hot fields of Arizona as a bracero in 1951, everyone else stayed put until Papá Luz died.

After Luz Moreno died in 1953, all bets were off. In 1955 Pancha and Juan arrived in San Miguel for one of their visits. They came bearing gifts for everyone and determined to take their niece, Obdulia (Lula), back with them to Stockton. Lula, then twenty-five years old, was the natural choice. She was unmarried, had finished school, and did not have a steady job. Her brothers Jesús and José wanted to go to Stockton with their aunt and uncle, but Pancha and Juan never seriously considered taking either of them. They were men, and Pancha and Juan did not think they could be counted on to stay home and take care of them as they got older. Lula, whom Luz once described as "the tamed one, the harmless one, the obedient one,"[3] was seemingly more pliable. Unlike her *patas de perro* brothers,[4] Lula had never considered going to the United States. While not exactly happy in San Miguel, she had friends, a young red-headed man who was interested in a romantic relationship, and was making a little money by mending silk stockings for rich women who could afford such luxuries. She also earned money by using strands of hair to embroider initials and tiny images (smoking guns, packs of cigarettes, playing cards) on the handkerchiefs that young women gave as *prendas* (romantic keepsakes) to their boyfriends. She remembers that when Pancha and Juan arrived in San Miguel in 1955, they came with all the documents she needed to immigrate to the United States already in hand. They had thought of everything but getting her consent. Not that she ever felt it was her right to deny her aunt anything; Pancha had raised her and her brothers when their mother had died and then, over the past five years, had sent money to help support them. Still, she says, it would have been nice if someone had asked. No one did, so she spent the two months that Pancha and Juan stayed in San Miguel preparing for her new life in the United States. Six decades later, she recalls how she felt when she stepped into the bus that would deliver her to Stockton forty hours later, "I was neither happy nor sad. A little scared, but I knew I could lean on Pancha. I was close to her. Before she got married we slept on the same bed. Pancha made it OK. Besides, Juan had always described the United States as an immaculate country where the streets were clean and free of even the smallest tissue paper. Who would not want to live in a country like that?"[5]

After an exhausting trip, Lula, Pancha, and Juan arrived late at night to their home on East Washington Avenue, in the Latino neighborhood known as the Barrio del Chivo.[6] When Lula awoke the next morning she peeked out the window and saw a pile of soiled and torn mattresses in an empty lot in front of her house. As she wondered about what else Juan had embellished about her new country, she heard the plaintive wail of sirens and was amazed to see people running down the sidewalk. Pancha and Lula followed the crowd to the end of their street where they saw a house engulfed in flames. Lula had never seen a building on fire. As the fire trucks arrived and firefighters scrambled to extinguish the blaze, she and her aunt and many of her new neighbors stood frozen before the spectacle, their senses taking in the noise, smells, and sights of a small world in flames. The spell was broken when part of a wall collapsed on a pool of soot. The filthy water sprayed the crowd and baptized Lula as a member of her new community.[7]

The next day Lula went with Pancha to the cannery and began what would eventually be more than four decades of work sorting, washing, cutting, and canning the fruits and vegetables Americans consumed during their country's most prosperous decades. While Pancha always felt that her life was smaller, less significant, and more constricted in the United

States than it had been in San Miguel, Lula found herself free from the dynamics of an extended household where she had always been the orphaned ugly duckling: "she is too gangly," "her head is too big," "she is not very smart." She got her job in the cannery, learned to speak halting but entirely passable English, got her driver's license, and, after a couple of years, bought herself a car and the huge dollop of independence that came with it. Lula earned more money at the cannery than she made in Mexico, and she supplemented her wages by selling Jafra cosmetics, Stanley household products, and jewelry and children's clothes that she smuggled from Mexico. At night, she went to school and learned how cut hair, how to upholster sofas, how to make wigs and false eyelashes, and how to bake and decorate cakes. Lula sold these products and services to her friends and coworkers on credit. During the day she worked in the cannery or in the fields; in the evenings, after having dinner with Pancha and Juan, she would get in her car and deliver her products to her clients. In sum, she became an entrepreneur in a way she could not have in Mexico. Sure, she missed Mexico, but even today she refuses to go back to live in San Miguel, because, she says, "I cannot find myself there. I feel mute and dumb around everyone. Here I drive my own car, there I can't seem to walk without tripping."[8]

The money Lula and Pancha sent helped sustain the Moreno family with a steady stream of remittances that both quelled the family's episodic economic crises and fueled the desire of her more adventurous cousins and

Obdulia Orozco and Juanita Reyes working near Stockton during tomato planting season, c. 1955. Courtesy of Obdulia Orozco.

Obdulia and Pancha in front of home on Washington Ave in *El Barrio del Chivo*, Stockton, 1958.

siblings to move to the United States. Though her brother, Jesús (Chuy), never made it to the Promised Land, Lula's cousin, Sidonia, joined her in Stockton in 1956. Her youngest brother José migrated to Los Angeles in 1960. In 1958 Sidonia's father, Bonifacio (Chito), left San Miguel to live in Los Angeles. After slowly losing his ability to slaughter donkeys and pigs without being regulated by the government, Chito went to Los Angeles and worked in a leather tanning company in South Los Angeles. Once Chito established residency in the United States, he bought a home in East Los Angeles and arranged for his wife, Desideria, and the rest of his children (including Mage, Lupe, and José) to join him in Southern California. Eventually, nine of their twelve children moved to the United States; they settled in and around East Los Angeles, and worked in various light industry jobs. Later in life Chito used the money he earned working in the tannery to purchase the rancho (*La Tinaja*) his father, Luz, had been unceremoniously banished from in 1900.

Ysabel, Victorina, Ysidoro (Lolo), and Secundina stayed in San Miguel and never visited the United States. After his dispiriting six-month stint as a bracero worker in Arizona, Chilo never returned to work in the United States. He remained in San Miguel, where he provided for himself and his wife by playing bass in a musical group (Banda Capri) and making shoes. Employing the skills he learned under the tutelage of his Sinarquista uncle Gregorio, Chilo made custom shoes and cowboy boots made from snake, armadillo, and ostrich skin. He bought the skins in Guadalajara and sold his ostentatious footwear to the *Norteños* (Mexican immigrants to the United States), who seemed to be the only ones who had the money to pay for such luxuries. Cecilio Moreno eventually married and passed away a year after Pancha, in 2003.

Pancha returned to Mexico almost every year until 1994. That year, she suffered a series of strokes that kept her bedridden for the last eight years of her life. Because Juan had died in 1989, Lula, herself well on the way to becoming an old lady and still working in the canneries, became Pancha's caretaker. Lula refused to allow Pancha to go to a retirement facility, so she took care of her at home. Working at night and sleepwalking during the day, Lula, with the generous help of her friends, tended to her ailing aunt until 2002. On October 17 of that year, Pancha, 101 years old, Luz Moreno's muse, and the first and most precious link the Moreno/Orozco clan in the United States had to its past in San Miguel el Alto, died. Per Pancha's wishes, Lula had her body flown back to Mexico. There she was buried in San Miguel's municipal cemetery in a tomb on top of Juan, and near her father, Luz Moreno. Finally, five decades after she left, fifty years after

Gregorio Román, Sinarquista Chief burial, c. 1953. Courtesy of Obdulia Orozco.

her father had implored her to receive his memories, Pancha had returned to San Miguel. When asked whether she wants to be buried in Stockton, Obdulia Orozco replies that she wants to go back to San Miguel and be buried with Pancha: "I want to go to San Miguel. I would be lonely here."[9]

Gregorio Román, Sinarquist burial march, c. 1953. Courtesy of Obdulia Orozco.

In the sixty-six years since Pancha left her family in San Miguel, millions of transnational families have had to confront and negotiate the trade-offs that come with leaving and being left behind. By the early 1990s it was so common for Mexican families to have relatives living across what the anthropologists Roger Rouse calls the "transnational migrant circuit" that many observers, including Rouse, believed that a relatively permeable border, cheap air travel, and the use of modern communication technology allowed transnational families and communities "to maintain . . . spatially extended relationships as actively and effectively as the ties that link them to their neighbors."[10] In the aftermath of 9/11, economic crisis, and the resurrection of anti-immigrant xenophobia in the United States, many academics have soured on this assessment. They, including the anthropologist Leisy Abrego, argue that in in spite of a communications revolution that makes certain forms of personal interactions much easier and quicker than writing letters, a militarized border has made it increasingly difficult to "think of transnational families as single units that happen to be spread out spatially between the destination and home countries. To interpret transnational families as unproblematic split households that maintain communication seamlessly through electronics is to dismiss the painful reality in their day-to-day lives and in their patterned behaviors where it is evident that each individual family member is discretely present in a single and faraway space relative to loved ones."[11] Abrego and others have reasserted what Luz, Pancha, and millions of Mexicans have understood for a long time: jobs in the United States may help alleviate the worst effects of poverty in Mexico, but the material comfort that dollars sometimes provide impoverished families comes with a heavy emotional price tag that is barely mitigated by cell phones and Facebook.[12] Worse, the affective labor that lonely migrants expend to help tether themselves to their families has the contradictory—and in many ways injurious—effect of subsidizing a transnational machinery of migrant capitalism that generates billions of dollars in remittances for Mexico (about 22 billion in 2012) and billions more in profits, taxes, and savings in the United States.[13]

Max Frisch, a Swiss playwright and novelist, commented that when his country organized a guest worker program in the 1960s and 1970s it was hoping to get workers, but instead got human beings.[14] The difference between workers and human beings may be self-evident. It certainly seemed that way to Frisch who understood that unlike workers whose dehumanization makes them exploitable, cheap to maintain, and easy to dispose of, humans are messy, expensive, and transgressive beings who are much more than a collection of docile and utile human body parts.[15] Humans fall in love, they get hurt, they feel lonely; they want to feel included, and they want to give their children an education, health care, food, and housing. In the face of systems of economic exploitation that do not let this happen, and elite populations on both sides of the border that only want Mexicans for their manual labor, Mexicans in their various identities as Mexican Americans, Chicanos, Pochos, Communists, Anarchists, and Sinarquistas have organized, struck, sued, marched, and boycotted to reassert their humanity.[16] These often-dramatic actions appear in the pages of history books because they are the public acts of a people whose loving and rebellious spirit cannot help but assert the radical proposition that there is a difference between a human and worker.

Hidden from the pages of history books are the quieter affirmations of humanity, those simple exchanges that are the ones most vulnerable to the vagaries of time and space: expressions of love whispered in the dying moments of the evening sun, scribbled in ink that fades, written on paper that yellows, and remembered in memories that ashen. Luz Moreno wrote his letters to Pancha as memories committed to paper in the hope that she would return, that she would not forget him, that she would not forgo their religion, and that she would not neglect their family or their community. He hoped that his missives would serve as fragile, episodic reminders that she was more than Juan's wife, an overworked cannery worker, or a nameless immigrant. That always, and in spite of a devouring space that separated them from each other, and both of them from a moment in time when life seemed much easier, she was Pancha Moreno, his beloved daughter, and that he was more than an old, poor man who was dying a sad and lonely death.

Papá Luz emptied himself in his letters to propose a better version of himself, of Pancha, and of their family. His intimate missives were not intended for us. Yet here we are, reading the material remnants of the simple things that transpired between a father and his daughter and wondering about the millions of other ausentes whose memories we cannot receive, nor honor.

NOTES

ACKNOWLEDGMENTS

1. Alicia Azuela de la Cueva, "*Peace by Revolution:* Una Aproximación Léxio-Visual al México Revolucionario," *Historía Mexicana* LVI, no. 4 (2007): 1263–1307; Frank Tannenbaum, *Peace by Revolution: An Interpretation of Mexico,* illustrated by Miguel Covarrubias (New York: Columbia University Press, 1933); Stuart Chase, *Mexico: A Study of Two Americas,* illustrated by Diego Rivera (New York: The MacMillan Company, 1932); Carleton Beals, *Mexican Maze,* illustrated by Diego Rivera (New York: J. B. Lippincott, 1931); Issac Berliner, *City of Palaces* (1936), illustrated by Diego Rivera (Basking Ridge, NJ: Jacoby Press, 1996); Frances Toor, *A Treasury of Mexican Folkways,* illustrated by Carlos Merida (New York: Crown Publishers, 1947); John Steinbeck, *The Pearl,* illustrated by José Clemente Orozco (New York: Viking Press, 1947). Oscar Lewis's *Life in a Mexican Village: Tepoztlán Restudied* (1951) was illustrated by Alberto Beltrán. Beltrán also illustrated Ricardo Pozas Arciniega's anthropological classic *Juan Pérez Jolote: Biografía de un Tzotzil* (1952).
2. Carroll W. Pursell Jr., "Government and Technology in the Great Depression," *Technology and Culture* 20, no. 1 (1979): 163–164; Holly H. Mullin, "The Patronage of Difference: Making Indian Art Art, Not Ethnology," *Cultural Anthropology* 7, no. 4 (1992): 399; Mauricio Tenorio-Trillo, "Viejos gringos: radicales norteamericanos en los años trienta y su vision de México," *Secuencias, Revista de Historía y Ciencias Sociales* no. 21, (1991): 95–116; Helen Delpar, "Frank Tannenbaum: The Making of a Mexicanist, 1914–1933," *The Americas* 45, no. 2 (1988): 153–171.
3. Mauricio Tenorio-Trillo, *I Speak of the City: Mexico City at the Turn of the Twentieth Century* (Chicago: University of Chicago Press, 2012), 147–207; Helen Delpar, *The Enormous Vogue of Things Mexican: Cultural relations between and the United States and Mexico, 1920–1935* (Tuscaloosa: University of Alabama Press, 1992).

INTRODUCTION

1. In 1900 the life expectancy of a child born in rural Jalisco was thirty-seven years. Pancha's longevity was certainly aided by living the last fifty years of her life in the United States, where life expectancy was forty-years in 1900 and seventy-one in 1950. Robert McCaa, "The Peopling of Mexico from Origins to Revolution," in *A Population History of North America*, ed. Michael R. Haines and Richard H. Steckel (Cambridge: Cambridge University Press, 2000), 285.
2. Explaining the attraction that wrestling had for its audience, Roland Barthes wrote that it, like "the great solar spectacles, Greek drama and bullfights," produced "a light without shadow [that] generates an emotion without reserve."

Later in the essay, Barthes makes it clear that the rituals of religious faith (particularly, Christian rituals, beliefs, and symbols) inspired similar feelings: "It is as if the wrestler is crucified in broad daylight and in the sight of all. I have heard it said of a wrestler stretched on the ground: 'He is dead, little Jesus, there, on the cross,'" Roland Barthes, "The World of Wrestling," *Mythologies*, ed. and trans. Annette Lavers (New York: The Noonday Press, 1992), 15, 21.

3. On Mexican wrestling: Lourdes Grobet, *Lucha Libre: Masked Superstars of Mexican Wrestling*, (New York: Distributed Art Publishers, 2005); Heather Levi, *The World of Lucha Libre: Secrets, Revelations, and Mexican National Identity* (Durham, NC: Duke University Press, 2008).

4. "*Viva Cristo Rey, Viva Cristo Rey!/ el grito de guerra que enciende la tierra Viva Cristo Rey/ nuestro soberano Señor /nuestro capitan y campeon/ pelear por Él es todo un honor.*"Viva Cristo Rey! Viva Cristo Rey!/ This is the war's rally cry that inflames the earth/Viva Cristo Rey/ Our sovereign Lord/Our Captain and Champion/To fight for Him is a great honor. Written by Miguel Martínez during the Cristero Rebellion (1926–1929), the *Hymn to Christ the King* was sung during the Spanish Civil War (1936–1939) by the Catholic militias (*Requetés*) who fought for the Church and the King of Spain, Carlos.

5. The process by which Luz Moreno's letters made it to publication highlights the fact that, among other factors, the "underlying 'population' [of existing letters] is defined by preservers rather than writers or readers." Wolfgang Helbich and Walter D. Kamphoefner, "How Representative are Emigrant Letters? An Explorationof the German Case," in Letters Across Borders: The Epistolary Practices ofInternational Migrants, ed. Bruce S. Elliot, David A. Gerber, and Suzanne M. Sinke (New York: Palgrave Macmillan, 2006), 30. David Fitzpatrick, *Oceans of Consolation: Personal Accounts of Irish Migration to Australia* (Ithaca, NY: Cornell University Press, 1994), 28.

6. A similar stance is found in many of the photographs of *soldaderas* (female soldiers) taken during the Mexican Revolution. See Elena Poniatowska, *Las Soldaderas: Women of the Mexican Revolution*, trans. David Romo (El Paso: Cinco Puntos Press, 2006).

7. On women and the Cristero Rebellion see Jean, *La Cristiada: los cristeros*, vol. 3 (Mexico City: Siglo XXI Editores, 1993), 120–133; Kristina A. Boylan, "Gendering the Faith and Altering the Nation: Mexican Catholic Women's Activism, 1917–1940," in *Sex in Revolution: Gender, Politics, and Power in Modern Mexico*, ed. Jocelyn Olcott and Mary K. Vaughan (Durham, NC: Duke University Press, 2006), 199–222. For a first-hand accounts of other women's participation in the Cristiada see Concepción Alcalá, *El Diario de Concepción Alcalá: Recogidos Durante La Persecución Religiosa de 1926 a 1929*, n.d.; Josefina Arellano de Huerta, *Memorias: La Historia Cristera*. A critical review of both these documents can be found in Luis Gachuz-Meza, "Women, Freedom, and God: The Cristero Rebellion and the Work of Women in Small Towns of Los Altos," *Berkeley McNair Research Journal* no. 10 (2002),51–70

8. Obdulia Orozco, personal communication, March 22, 2002; Adrian A. Bantjes, "Saints, Sinners, and State-Formation: Local Religion and Cultural Revolution in Mexico," in *The Eagle and the Virgin: Nation and Cultural Revolution in Mexico, 1920–1940*, ed. Mary Kay Vaughan and Stephen E. Lewis (Durham, NC: Duke University Press, 2006), 146–148, 151–152; Boylan, "Gendering the Faith and Altering the Nation," 202–203.

9. Obdulia Orozco, personal communication, March 22, 2002.

10. Obdulia Orozco, personal communication, March 22, 2002. Apparently, the people of San Miguel were right. According to a team of German scientists, cows that are grazing or resting do align themselves on a north south axis: Sabine Begall, Julia Neef, Oldrich Vojtech, and Hynek Burda, "Magnetic Alignment in Grazing and Resting Cattle and Deer," *Proceedings of the National Academy of Sciences* 105, no. 36 (2008).

11. "Maybe [the letters] have lacked the respect or refinement that your position requires, but that is due to my ignorance and I ask that you forgive me. As soon as they see that I am about to write you a letter, they tell me not to put you on the spot with my rudeness." Letter from Luz Moreno to Pancha and Juan Rivera, April 12, 1950.

12. Obdulia Orozco, personal communication, March 22, 2002.

13. Eric Wolf, *Europe and the People Without History* (Berkeley: University of California Press, 1982); David A. Gerber, "What Is It We Seek to Find in First-Person Documents? Documenting Society and Cultural Practices in Irish Immigrant Writings," *Reviews in American History* 32, no.3 (2004): 306.

14. Gerber, "What is it We Seek to Find?," 312.

15. Given the almost unlimited potential that similar investigations could bring to the study of the Mexican diaspora to the United States, it is rather amazing that the study into the epistolary production of Mexican immigrants and their families remains as sorely underdeveloped as it is. Beyond two books and a couple of articles on the letters of recent undocumented immigrants, the epistolary history of the Mexican diaspora over the course of the twentieth century remains a tempting, yet largely ignored, low-hanging fruit. See Larry Siems, *Between the Lines: Letters Between Undocumented Mexican and Latin American Immigrants and Their Families and Friends* (Tucson: University of Arizona Press, 1992); Juan C. Guerra, *Close to Home: Oral and Literate Practices in a Transnational Mexicano Community* (New York: Teachers College Press, 1998).

16. On letters as physical artifacts that embody and represent certain aspects of the writer's class and emotions see Martha Hanna, "A Republic of Letters: The Epistolary Tradition in France during World War I," *American Historical Review* 108, no. 5 (2003): 1348; Cécil Dauphin, "Letter-Writing Manuals in the Nineteenth Century," in *Correspondence: Models of Letter-Writing from the middle Ages to the Nineteenth Century,* ed. Roger Chartier, Alain Boureau, and Célcile Dauphin, trans. Christopher Woodall (Princeton, NJ: Princeton University Press, 1997), 143.

17. Fitzpatrick, *Oceans of Consolation,* 28.

18. Fitzpatrick, *Oceans of Consolation*, 26; Wolfgang Helbich and Walter D. Kamphoefner, "How Representative are Emigrant Letters?," 29–31; David A. Gerber, *Authors of Their Lives: The Personal Correspondence of British Immigrants to North America in the Nineteenth Century* (New York: New York University Press, 2006), 218–219.

19. See, for example, Leisy Abrego, *Sacrificing Families: Navigating Laws, Labor, and Love Across Borders* (Redwood City, CA: Stanford University Press, 2014); Ana Elizabeth Rosas, *Abrazando el Espíritu: Bracero Families Confront the US–Mexico Border* (Berkeley: University of California Press, 2014).

20. Gerber, *Authors of Their Lives*, 208.

21. Eric Richards, "The Limits of the Australian Emigrant Letter," in *Letters Across Borders*, 60.

22. Fitzpatrick, *Oceans of Consolation*, 22, 26, 28.

23. Letter dated c. September, 1950.

24. On the debate about the "literary" quality of immigrant letters, see Gerber, *Authors of Their Lives*, 49–52.

25. Carlos Monsiváis, "Yes, Nor Do the Dead Speak, Unfortunately: Juan Rulfo," in *Mexican Postcards*, trans. John Kraniauskas (London: Verso, 2000), 57–58; Danny J. Anderson, "Introduction: The Ghosts of Comala: Haunted Meaning in *Pedro Páramo*," in *Pedro Páramo by Juan Rulfo*, trans. Margaret Sayers Peden (Austin: University of Texas Press, 2002), 7–11.

26. William E. French argues that there were many places a poor person could acquire literacy skills in Mexico other than in school and that "when it came to acquiring the level of literacy sufficient for [the task of writing a love letter], a little education went a long way." French bases this assessment on his own work on love letters written in the north of Mexico and on the work of Keith Breckenridge who studied the culture of literacy among southern Africa migrant workers. William E. French, *The Heart in the Glass Jar: Love Letters, Bodies, and the Law in Mexico* (Lincoln: University of Nebraska, 2015), 131; Keith Breckenridge, "Reasons for Writing: African Working Class Letter-Writing in Early Twentieth-Century South Africa," in *Africa's Hidden Histories: Everyday Literacy and Making the Self*, ed. Karin Barber (Bloomington, Indiana: Indiana University Press, 2006), 143–154.

27. This rough estimate is derived from Francisco Medina de la Torre's statement that in 1900 there were 3,125 people who could both read and write in the municipality. According to Leticia Gándara Mendoza, the population of the municipality in 1900 was 13,580. The literacy rate was surely higher—and probably closer to the 33 percent male literacy estimated by Mary Kay Vaughan for all of Mexico in 1910—if we only count citizens of the municipality who were older than six years old (like the 1895 census) or twelve years old (like 1910 census). Cecilio Moreno, personal communication, July 22, 2000. Francisco Medina de la Torre, "Apuntes geografícos, estadísticos e historicos del municipio de San Miguel el Alto: Estado de Jalisco, México," in *Estadisticas de Los Altos de Jalisco (1838–1908)*, ed. María Gracia Castillo and Jaime Olveda (Guadalajara Jalisco: Gobierno de Jalisco, Secretaria General, Unidad Editorial,1988), 135; Leticia Gándara Mendoza, "La evolución de una oligarquía: el caso de San Miguel el Alto, Jalisco," in *Política y sociedad en México el caso de los Altos de Jalisco*, Tomás Martínez Saldana and Leticia Gándara Mendoza (Mexico City: Centro de Investigaciones Superiores, Instituto Nacional de Antropologia e Historia 1976), 172; Mary Kay Vaughan, "Primary Education and Literacy in Nineteenth-Century Mexico: Research Trends, 1968–1988," *Latin American Research Review* 25, no. 1 (1990): 42–43.

28. Hanna, "A Republic of Letters," 1349.

29. David A. Gerber, "Forming a Transnational Narrative: New Perspectives on European Migrations to the United States." *The History Teacher* 35, no. 1 (2001): 68–71; Janet Gurkin Altman, *Epistolary: Approaches to a Form* (Columbus: Ohio State University Press, 1982), 120.

30. Gerber, *Authors of Their Lives*, 7–8.

31. These edits are indicated by ellipses.

32. On the issues that historian have grappled with when editing immigrant correspondence see Gerber, *Authors of Their Lives*, 53–56.

33. *Ausentes* is the word that Luz Moreno uses to refer to Pancha and her husband.

34. Nathaniel Philbrick, *Why Read Moby-Dick?* (New York: Viking, 2011), 43.

CHAPTER 1

1. On the history of Los Altos after the Mixtón War and the creation of a Spanish colonial society in the region see José Antonio Gutiérrez Gutiérrez, *Los Altos de Jalisco: Panorama historico de una region y de su sociedad hasta 1821* (Mexico City: Consejo Nacional para la Cultura y las Artes, 1991); José Antonio Gutiérrez Gutiérrez, *Jalostitlán a Través de los Siglos* (Aguascalientes: Universidad Autonoma de Aguascalientes, 1985); Andrés Fábregas Puig, *La formación histórica de una región: Los Altos de Jalisco* (Mexico City: Centro de Investigaciones y Estudios Superiores en Antropologia Social, 1986); Francisco Medina de la Torre, *San Miguel el Alto, Jalisco: biografía de un municipio* (Mexico City: Editorial Jus, 1967).

2. On the history of Los Altos see Gutiérrez Gutiérrez, *Los Altos de Jalisco.* On the history of animal husbandry in the region see Ramón María Serrera, *Guadalajara ganadera: estudio regional novohispano, 1760–1805* (Guadalajara, Jalisco: Consejo Consultivo para las Artes y la Cultura de Guadalajara, 1991).

3. Though the definition of a *rancho* varies from region to region, and from historian to historian, a *rancho* is typically understood to be a small to medium property that is owned and worked by one family. It is usually defined by academics in contradistinction to large *haciendas* that are privately owned but are usually worked by a dependent labor force (peons, sharecroppers, wage laborers) and the *ejido*, which, before the 1992 reform of Article 27 of the Constitution, was land owned by the government and worked by individuals and communities who had been given use of the land, but not ownership of it. On *ranchos* see Fábregas Puig, *La formación histórica de una región*; Jaime Espín and Patricia de Leonardo, *Economía y sociedad en los Altos de Jalisco* (Mexico: Centro de Investigaciones Superiores del Instituto Nacional de Antropologia e Historia, 1978); Frans J. Schryer, *The Rancheros of Pisaflores: The History of a Peasant Bourgeoisie in Twentieth-Century Mexico* (Toronto: University of Toronto Press, 1980); Luis González y González, *San José de Gracia: Mexican Village in Transition*, trans. John Upton (Austin: University of Texas Press: 1974).

4. For reasons I have yet to ascertain, the couple named two of their children Francisco. They distinguished one from the other with the diminutives Pancho and Panchillo.

5. "*O quieres mamá, o quieres mujer.*" Obdulia Orozco, personal communication, March 22, 2002.

6. Sharecroppers in Mexico are known as *medieros.* The word *medieros* comes from the Spanish word *medio*, or half. It accurately, though not exactly, describes the relationship between the landowner and the sharecropper. Though there is a range of agreements that can be worked out, usually the landowner provides the land, fertilizer, and the seed, while the sharecropper provides the labor and the tools to plant, tend to, and harvest the crop. After harvesting the product, the owner and the sharecropper share the harvest, usually 50–50. While Moreno chose to stay in San Miguel and work as a sharecropper, the lack of access to land forced many other rural workers to immigrate to the United States. For different versions of the *mediero* contract, see Gándara Mendoza, *La evolución de una oligarquía*, 173–174, 178, 191–192, 217–218; Espín and de Leonardo, *Economía y sociedad en los Altos de Jalisco*, 100–103; 233–240. According to Paul S. Taylor's analysis of wages in Arandas, the 37 cents Luz was paid to work for his family was fairly typical in the early part of the twentieth century. Paul S. Taylor, *A Spanish-Mexican Peasant Community; Arandas in Jalisco, Mexico* (Berkeley: University of California Press, 1933), 24.

7. Among the factors that engendered this lively market in land was the threat of land distribution made by successive revolutionary governments after 1920, the social and political upheaval (especially increased immigration) caused by the Cristero Rebellion (1926–1929), a population boom in the region, and a shift away from agricultural production to dairy production in the 1940s.

8. Gándara Mendoza points out that by 1974, 60 percent of the families in San Miguel owned land. This statistic is misleading because while 70.6 percent of the owners owned only one property (many of them 5 hectares or less), 2.4 percent of the municipality's land owners had five or more properties. See Gándara Mendoza, *La evolución de una oligarquía*, 198. Patricia de Leonardo points to similar trends in the Alteño municipality of Jalostitlán. Patricia de Leonardo, "El impacto del mercado en diferentes unidades de producción Municipio de Jalostitlán, Jalisico," in *Economía y sociedad en los Altos de Jalisco*, ed. Jaime Espín and Patricia de Leonardo. For the neighboring municipality of Arandas see Taylor, *A Spanish-Mexican Peasant Community*, 28–29.

9. Medina de la Torre, *San Miguel el Alto*, 230.

10. Statistics are for the states of Durango, Guanajuato, Jalisco Michoacán, San Luis Potosí, and Zacatecas. James A. Sandos and Harry E. Cross, "National Development and International Labour Migration: Mexico, 1940–1965," *Journal of Contemporary History* 18, no. 1 (1983): 46–47. For an analysis of population growth in a town in the Los Altos region see Taylor, *A Spanish-Mexican Peasant Community*, 9–13.

11. Ann L. Craig, *The First Agraristas: An Oral History of a Mexican Agrarian Reform Movement* (Berkeley: University of California Press, 1983), 35.

12. On the Cristero Rebellion see Jean Meyer, *The Cristero Rebellion: The Mexican People Between Church and State, 1926–1929*, trans. Richard Southern (Cambridge: Cambridge University Press, 1976); David C. Bailey, *Viva Cristo Rey! The Cristero Rebellion and Church–State Conflict in Mexico* (Austin: University of Texas Press, 1974); John Tutino, *From Insurrection to Revolution in Mexico: Social Bases of Agrarian Violence, 1750–1940* (Princeton, NJ: Princeton University Press, 1986); Jennie Purnell, *Popular Movements and State Formations in Revolutionary Mexico: The Agraristas and Cristeros of Michoacán* (Durham, NC: Duke University Press, 1999); Matthew Butler, *Popular Piety and Political Identity in Mexico's Cristero Rebellion: Michoacán, 1927–29* (Oxford: Oxford University Press, 2004).

13. Roberto Blancarte, "Intransigence, Anticommunism, and Reconciliation: Church/State Relations in Transition," in *Dictablanda: Politics, Work, and Culture in Mexico, 1938–1968*, ed. Paul Gillingham and Benjamin T. Smith (Durham, NC: Duke University Press, 2014), 70–71; Adrian Bantjes, "Idolatry and Iconoclasm in Revolutionary Mexico: The De-Christianization Campaigns, 1929–1940," *Mexican Studies/Estudios Mexicanos* 13, no. 1 (1997): 87–120; Adrian Bantjes, "Burning Saints, Molding Minds: Iconoclasm, Civic Ritual, and the Failed Cultural Revolution," in *Rituals of Rules, Rituals of Resistance: Public Celebrations and Popular Culture in Mexico*, ed. William H. Beezley, Cheryl English Martin, and William E. French (Wilmington, DE: Scholarly Resources Inc., 1999), 261–284.

14. In the nineteenth century, liberal politicians like Melchor Ocampo, Benito Juárez, and Miguel Lerdo de Tejada passed laws that directly threatened the Catholic Church's traditional economic, political, and cultural spheres of influence. The *Ley Juárez* (1855) abolished ecclesiastical and military *fueros* (exemptions) that had allowed priests and soldiers to avoid prosecution in civil courts. The *Ley Lerdo* (1856) prohibited the Church from owning or administering real property not used in the service of their daily mission, while the *Ley Iglesias* (1856) prohibited

priests from charging fees for baptisms, marriages, and funerals, and required that all of these important events be registered with civil authorities. These laws, and others permitting freedom of the press, assembly, mail, and mandating free and secular education, were enshrined in the Constitution of 1857 and were perpetuated in the Constitution of 1917.

15. Gilbert M. Joseph and Jürgen Buchenau, *Mexico's Once and Future Revolution: Social Upheaval and the Challenge of Rule since the Late Nineteenth Century* (Durham, NC: Duke University Press, 2013), 101–102.

16. Quoted in Enrique Krauze, *Mexico: Biography of Power*, trans. Hank Heifetz (New York: Harper Collins, 1997), 421.

17. According to Jean Meyer, 25 percent of Alteño landowners were small property holders. This group had a "massive" participation in the rebellion providing 10 percent of all Cristero rebels in Mexico. Meyer, *La Cristiada:los cristeros*, 17.

18. The Church agreed to end the civil war, register its priests with the state, and not teach religion in their schools. The Mexican government, then headed by Emilio Portes Gil (1928–1930), did not expunge the anticlerical provisions of the constitution. Instead, Portes Gil declared a general amnesty and promised not to enforce the anti-Church provisions of the constitution.

19. Pablo Yankelevich, *La educación socialista en Jalisco* (Guadalajara: Ediciones del D.E.P., 1985), 49–50.

20. Jean Meyer calculates that rebels assassinated one hundred teachers, mutilated two hundred, and burned scores of rural schools during *la Segunda*. Jean Meyer, "An Idea of Mexico: Catholics in the Revolution," in *The Eagle and the Virgin: Nation and Cultural Revolution in Mexico, 1920–1940*, ed. Mary Kay Vaughan and Stephen E. Lewis (Durham, NC: Duke University Press, 2006), 291; Victoria Lerner, *La educación socialista* (Mexico City: Colegio de México, 1979); Yankelevich, *La educación socialista en Jalisco*, 88–109; George C. Booth, *Mexico's School-Made Society* (Redwood City, CA: Stanford University Press, 1941).

21. Hugh Gerald Campbell, "The Radical Right in Mexico, 1929–1949" (PhD diss., University of California, Los Angeles, 1968), 212–220, 198–204; Blancarte, "Intransigence, Anticommunism, and Reconciliation," 72.

22. According to Jean Meyer, the word *Sinarquismo* is derived from the Greek *syn arch*, meaning "with authority, with power, with order." Meyer, "An Idea of Mexico," 291.

23. *La Legión* was formed in 1934 in reaction to Plutarco Calles's *Grito de Guadalajara*. For a good introduction to the Sinarquista movement see Jean Meyer, *El Sinarquismo: un fascismo mexicano? 1937–1947* (Mexico City: Editorial Joaquin Mortiz, 1979); Albert Michaels, "Fascism and *Sinarquismo*: Popular Nationalisms against the Mexican Revolution," *Journal of Church and State* 8 (Winter 1966): 234–250; Servando Ortoll, "Las Legiones, La Base y el Sinarquismo, tres organizaciones distintas y un sólo fin verdadero? (1929–1948)," in *La Política y el cielo: movimientos religiosos en el México contemporáneo,* ed. Luis Rodolfo Morán Quiroz (Guadalajara: Universidad de Guadalajara, 1990); Pablo Serrano Álvarez, "El ritual de un sacerdote sinarquista: Salvador Abascal," in *A dios lo que es de dios,* ed. Carlos Martínez Assad (Mexico City: Aguilar, Nuevo Siglo, 1994), 396–401; James Dormady, *Primitive Revolution: Restorationist Religion and the Idea of the Mexican Revolution, 1940–1968* (Albuquerque: University of New Mexico Press, 2011), 103–130.

24. The Sinarquista leadership was never of one mind on either the goals or means of the movement. Some accepted the truce between the Church and the government

and wanted to prosecute their resistance against the Revolution as a civic social movement. Other leaders, including Manuel Torres Bueno and Juan Ignacio Padilla, preferred to turn the UNS into a political party to contest the power of the official party at the ballot box. A third tendency, represented by the mystic Catholic Salvador Abascal, sought to use Catholicism as the basis for renovating the Catholic essence of the Mexican nation. See Laura Pérez Rosales, "Las mujeres sinarquistas: Nuevas adelitas en la vida política mexicana (1945–1948)," *Religión, política y sociedad: el sinarquismo y la iglesia en México: nueve ensayos,* ed. Rubén Aguilar V. and Guillermo Zermeño P (Mexico City: Universidad Iberoamericana, 1992), 174–175.

25. Blancarte, "Intransigence, Anticommunism, and Reconciliation," 72–74.
26. *El Sinarquista,* No. 38, Oct. 26, 1939. Cited by Nathan L. Whetten, *Rural Mexico* (Chicago: University of Chicago Press, 1948), 491.
27. Salvador Abascal (quoted by Hugh Campbell, *The Radical Right,* 238–239) was purged by the Sinarquista hierarchy in 1941 because his radical pronouncements scared moderates within the movement and threatened the tentative peace the Church had established with the Mexican State. For a discussion on Salvador Abascal see Serrano Álvarez, "El ritual de un sacerdote sinarquista."
28. Salvador Abascal, quoted in Campbell, *The Radical Right,* 246.
29. "*16 Puntos Basicos,*" *Historia Grafica del Sinarquismo,* ed. Comite Nacional de la Union Nacional *Sinarquista* n.d.; Whetten, *Rural Mexico,* Ch. XX; Meyer, *El Sinarquismo,* 139–179.
30. "*Ni en Moscú ni en el Norte nos espera la victoria feliz de nuestro afán/ Es de Cristo, es de Dios nuestra bandera y en las cumbres de México ondeará/ Tenga parte el obrero en las empresas y el labriego, la tierra en propiedad. Allá Marx con su mundo proletario!Proprietarios queremos! Y haya paz.*" *Himno de las Juventudes de Movimiento Nacional Sinarquista.* Laura Pérez Rosales, "Las mujeres sinarquistas," 169
31. "*Normas De Conducta Para Los Sinarquista,*" in *Historia Gráfica del Sinarquismo,* ed. Comite Nacional de la Union Nacional *Sinarquista* n.d.
32. Meyer, *El Sinarquismo, el cardenismo,* 61; Campbell, *The Radical Right,* 254, 260.
33. In 1939 Sinarquista militants were organized into two hundred municipal committees. By 1943, the Sinarquista movement had six hundred municipal committees. Meyer, *El Sinarquismo, el cardenismo,* 61–79.
34. Whetten, *Rural Mexico,* 502; Meyer, *El Sinarquismo, el cardenismo,* 77.
35. Pablo Serrano Álvarez, *La batalla de espiritu: el movimiento sinarquista en el Bajío (1932–1951) Volume 1* (Mexico City: Consejo Nacional para la Cultura y las Artes, 1992), 234; David J. Williams, "Sinarquismo in Mexico and the Southwest" (master's thesis, Texas Christian University, 1950).
36. Whetten was particularly impressed by the connection between the spectacular growth of the movement and state agrarian programs and policies that channeled less money from the Ejido Bank to the states—Guanajuato, Querétaro, Michoacán, Jalisco, and Guerrero—where Sinarquismo was the strongest. "Although 21.6 percent of the ejidatarios in the Republic are found in these five states, they received only 11.9 percent of the funds loaned to ejidatarios by the Ejido Bank in 1941." Whetten, *Rural Mexico,* 488. Historians Cross and Sandos see the neglect of the Bajío as a systematic part of the revolutionary government's attempt to prioritize the financial aid they made to areas (mostly in the North of Mexico) that would fund large agricultural units to feed the cities and fuel the industrial modernization of the economy. Harry E. Cross and James A. Sandos, *Across the Border: Rural Development in Mexico and Recent Mexican Migration to the United States* (Berkeley: Institute of Governmental Studies,

University of California, Berkeley, 1981); Timothy J. Henderson repeats this argument in *Beyond Borders: A History of Mexican Migration to the United States*, (Malden, MA: Wiley-Blackwell, 2011), 60–61; Michael Snodgrass, "Patronage and Progress: The Bracero Program from the Perspective of Mexico," in *Workers Across the Americas The Transnational Turn in Labor History*, ed. Leon Fink (New York: Oxford University Press, 2011), 253.

37. Jean Meyer notes that Sinarquismo's "absence is notable in the great cities: Mexico, Guadalajara, Monterrey, Veracruz and in the industrial corridor of Orizaba-Córdoba." Meyer, *El Sinarquismo, el cardenismo*, 65.

38. On the importance of León, Guanajuato, as the center of Catholic conservatism in the Bajío see Daniel Newcomer, *Reconciling Modernity: Urban State Formation in 1940s León, Mexico* (Lincoln: University of Nebraska Press, 2004).

39. The doctrinal inspiration for social Catholicism came from the encyclical *Rerum Novarum*. Issued by Pope Leo XIII on May 15, 1891, *Rerum Novarum* was written to address social conditions in the late nineteenth century that, according to the document, had exposed "the workers, each alone and defenseless, to the inhumanity of employers and the unbridled greed of competition." These conditions had not only subjected the working masses of the world to the "power of a few … exceedingly rich men who have laid a yoke almost of slavery on the unnumbered masses," but had pushed the workers to "cure this evil" by following Socialist doctrines and joining revolutionary movements. As Pope Leo XIII made clear in the encyclical, the answer to what was then commonly referred to as the "social question" was not revolution or revolutionary politics. In its stead the Catholic Church—co-opting an ideology of resistance and a set of organizational tools that had been popular in many parts of Europe during the nineteenth century (Catholic labor unions, schools, self-help societies, and mass forms of media, especially newspapers)—sought to resolve the real inequities of wealth produced by modern societies by calling for the united action of the Church, the state, the owners, and the workers. Pope Leo XIII argued that each sector of society had its natural place, its own set of rights, and its own reciprocal set of obligations in a strictly delineated social hierarchy. It followed that in contravention to the dictates of Socialist doctrine, a society could only function if this natural order, and Catholic morality, was respected and used as the basis for the social contract between classes. On social Catholicism see Manuel Ceballos Ramírez, *El catolicismo social: un tercero en discordia: Rerum novarum, la "cuestión social" y la movilización de los católicos mexicanos, 1891–1911* (Mexico City: El Colegio de Mexico, 1991).

40. Social Catholic activists employed these tactics of resistance for several decades, most importantly right before and during the Cristero Rebellion (1926–1929). Copy of flyer included in José de Jesús Ortega Martín, *San Miguel el Alto, Jalisco: Día, a día en la Revolución (1908–1918)* (San Miguel el Alto, Jalisco: 2010), 103.

41. Both the decrees and the two petitions are included in Ortega Martín, *San Miguel el Alto, Jalisco)*, 96–102.

42. Francisco Medina de la Torre, *San Miguel el Alto, Jalisco*, 144–147.

43. Ortega Martín, *San Miguel el Alto, Jalisco, día, a día,* 101.

44. The letter was written by José Guadalupe Rábago to the General Brigadier Chief of the 36th cavalry regiment and 3rd military sector located in Lagos de Moreno, Jalisco. Gregorio Román was arrested at this rally and was held in in the municipal jail until April 29, 1940. Archivo Historico San Miguel el Alto, Jalisco

(AHSMEAJ), Box 76, *Sección: Presidencial, Serie: Trabajo, Tránsito,Telégrafos,Turi smo, Traslado de Reos.*

45. The logic undergirding the Sinarquista's norms of conduct for women was in line with the ideology of early twentieth century Catholic Action organization in Mexico and in Europe. *Historia grafica del sinarquismo,* ed. Comite Nacional de la Union Nacional Sinarquista n.d.; Kristina A. Boylan, "Gendering the Faith and Altering the Nation," 201–202; Laura Pérez Rosales, "Las mujeres sinarquistas," 175.

46. "Era de ley" is the way her niece, Obdulia Orozco, described her. Literally, "she was of the law." Obdulia was using the phrase to describe Pancha's no-nonsense, honest personality. Obdulia Orozco, personal communication, April 25, 2012.

47. The Sinarquista attitude toward women and the roles they prescribed for them was the religious analogy of the roles that women as "natural" caretak-ers were expected to play in secular civil society. See Temma Kaplan, "Final Reflections: Gender, Chaos, and Authority in Revolutionary Times," in *Sex in Revolution: Gender, Politics, and Power in Modern Mexico,* ed. Jocelyn Olcott, Mary Kay Vaughan, and Gabriela Cano (Durham, NC: Duke University Press, 2006).

48. In addition to facilitating the birthing process, midwives in Mexico often stayed in the homes of their patients for many days after the birth of the child. Often in isolated rural areas, midwives cooked and cleaned and helped tend to the other children while the mother recuperated. Obdulia Orozco, personal communica-tion, March 26, 2002.

49. Patience A. Schell, "Of the Sublime Mission of Mothers of Families: The Union of Mexican Catholic Ladies in Revolutionary Mexico," in *The Women's Revolution in Mexico, 1910–1953,* ed. Stephanie Mitchell and Patience A. Schell (Lanham, MD: Rowman and Littlefield, 2007).

50. Bantjes, "Saints, Sinners, and State Formation," 147–148; Boylan, "Gendering the Faith and Altering the Nation," 201–204.

51. This was, as Matthew Butler has pointed out, especially true during the Cristero Rebellion and thereafter, when the crisis of the Church–State conflict opened up the possibility for lay Catholics to shoulder more responsibilities in the min-istry. Matthew Butler, "Revolution and the Ritual Year: Religious Conflict and Innovation in *Cristero* Mexico," *Journal of Latin American Studies* 38, no. 3 (2006): 465–490.

52. Patience A. Schell, *Church and State Education in Revolutionary Mexico City* (Tucson: University of Arizona Press, 2003), 183.

53. Schell, *Church and State Education,* 181.

54. Juan Rivera, Pancha's boyfriend who lived in the United States, sent the Sears catalogues to her. Obdulia Orozco, personal communication, March 26, 2002. On the importance of religious rituals to individual and communal identity see, Fernando Cervantes, "Mexico's 'Ritual Consent': Religion and Liberty from Colony to Post-Revolution," in *Faith and Impiety in Revolutionary Mexico,* ed. Matthew Butler (New York: Palgrave Macmillan), 70.

55. For information related to the demise of the Sinarquista movement, and their utopian society *La Colonia María Auxiliadora* see Salvador Abascal, *Mis recuer-dos: sinarquismo y Colonia María Auxiliadora: con importantes documentos de los archivos Nacionales de Washington (1935–1944)* (Mexico City: Tradición, 1980); Meyer, *El Sinarquismo, el cardenismo;* Pablo Serrano Álvarez, *La batalla de espiritu: el*

movimiento sinarquista en el Bajío (1932–1951) Volume II (Mexico City: Consejo Nacional para la Cultura y las Artes, 1992); Dormady, *Primitive Revolution*.

56. Luz lists the variety of jobs he and his children held in the letter dated May 10, 1951 in chapter 4: "El Miserable Pueblo."
57. Obdulia Orozco, personal communication, March 26, 2002.
58. Dawn Bohulano Mabalon, *Little Manila Is in the Heart: The Making of the Filipina/o American Community in Stockton, California* (Durham, NC: Duke University Press, 2013), 63–66; Carey McWilliams, *Factories in the Fields: The Story of Migratory Farm Labor in California* (Boston: Little, Brown and Company, 1939); Olive Davis and Sylvia Sun Minnick, *Stockton: Sunrise Port on the San Joaquin* (Woodland Hills, CA: Windsor Publications, 1984).
59. Davis and Minnick, *Stockton*, 84; Kitty Calavita, *Inside the State: The Bracero Program, Immigration, and the I.N.S.* (New York: Routledge, 1992), 1.
60. Obdulia Orozco, personal communication, March 26, 2002.
61. Obdulia uses the verb "*aparecer*" to describe Juan's return. Ibid.
62. Ibid.
63. Juan and Pancha had corresponded since the 1930s with Juan sending Pancha pages from the Sears catalogue and, according to Obdulia, small gifts like silk stockings, in his envelopes. Ibid.
64. Obdulia Orozco, personal communication, March 26, 2002.
65. See letter dated c. June 1950. William E. French explores the politics and culture of elopement, especially as it relates to literacy and love letters, in his book about love letters in Northern Mexico: *The Heart in the Glass Jar*, 26–32.
66. Mamá Cunda worked for one of the wealthiest women in San Miguel, Paula Padillo. Whenever the Padillo family hosted visiting dignitaries, Cunda was hired to make turkey mole. See letter dated c. June 27, 1950.
67. According to Obdulia Orozco, Juan's family had long abandoned the house. His parents had died and his sisters had all left San Miguel. The only reason Juan was able to sell the home was because Pancha had continued to pay the property taxes in his absence. Obdulia Orozco, personal communication, October 22, 2013.
68. Obdulia Orozco, personal communication, March 22, 2002
69. According to Obdulia Orozco, Pancha's first job in the United State was harvesting walnuts. One of her friends had invited her to work at a local orchard assuring Pancha that all she would have to do was pick up the walnuts that had fallen on the floor and place them in a sack. Pancha, eager to begin earning money, convinced Juan to let her work. The next morning Pancha's friend took her to the orchard where Pancha, like everyone else got down on her knees to gather the nuts. The only problem was that unlike everyone else, Pancha wore a dress. By lunch, with her knees bruised and bloodied, Pancha retreated to a shady tree. When her friend came over to invite her to join her for lunch, Pancha said, "No, thanks. I'll stay here. Just tell me which direction San Miguel is so I can cry facing my hometown." Obdulia Orozco, personal communication, April 10, 2014.
70. Because Juan appropriated each of her paychecks, giving her a weekly allowance, even supporting her family was more difficult. Obdulia Orozco, personal communication, April 10, 2014.
71. Taylor, *A Spanish-Mexican Peasant Community*. See also Craig *The First Agraristas*; Moisés González Navarro, *Cristeros y agraristas en Jalisco,* Vol. II (Mexico City: Colegio de México, Centro de Estudios Históricos, 2001); Moises González Navarro, *Cristeros y Agraristas en Jalisco,* Vol. III (Mexico City: Colegio de México, Centro de Estudios Históricos, 2003).

72. Meyer, *La Cristiada: los cristeros*, 267–271; Francisco Medina de la Torre, "Apuntes geográfícos, estadísticos e historicos del municipio de San Miguel el Alto: Estado de Jalisco, México," in *Estadisticas de Los Altos de Jalisco (1838–1908)*, ed. María Gracia Castillo and Jaime Olveda (Guadalajara: Gobierno de Jalisco, Secretaria General, Unidad Editorial,1988), 126, 129.

73. Letter from Luz Moreno to Pancha and Juan Rivera, April 8, 1950. On Bracero Program see Calavita, *Inside the State*; Ernesto Galarza, *Merchants of Labor: The Mexican Bracero Story* (Santa Barbara, CA: McNally and Loftin, 1964); Deborah Cohen, *Braceros: Migrant Citizens and Transnational Subjects in the Postwar United States and Mexico* (Chapel Hill: University of North Carolina Press, 2011); John Mraz and Jaime Vélez Storey, *Uprooted: Braceros in the Hermano Mayo Lens* (Houston: Arte Público Press, 1996); Taylor, *A Spanish-Mexican Peasant Community*.

74. Snodgrass, "Patronage and Progress."

75. Paul S. Taylor found in the early 1930s that the first person to leave the Alteño town of Arandas did so in 1905. In 1908 Francisco Medina de la Torre characterized *Sanmiguelenses* as a "hospitable, friendly and hardworking people who when they could not make a living in the municipality would go to live to other places." Medina de la Torre, though, was writing less about US-bound manual workers than about the horse and mule peddlers who traveled to places as far away as Central America, Cuba and New York to ply their hoofed merchandise. Medina de la Torre, "Apuntes geográfícos," 129.

76. The first *enganchador* in Arandas was a recruiter from the Santa Fe Railroad, who appeared in 1913. While Mexican workers mostly labored in agriculture and the construction and maintenance of railroads they did so over a large swath of the United States. In 1931 Paul S. Taylor found that the citizens of Arandas had worked in twenty-four North American states. Patricia Arias, Jorge Durand, "Estudios pioneros de la migración jalisciense," in *Paul S. Taylor y la migración jalisciense a Estados* Unidos, eds. Patricia Arias and Jorge Durand (Tepatitlán, Jalisco: Universidad de Guadalajara, Centro Universitario de los Altos, 2013), 15.

77. Las *reconcentraciones* was a tactic similar to the "strategic hamlets" used later in the century by the United States in Vietnam. See Taylor, *A Spanish-Mexican Peasant Community*, 38–40; Craig, *The First Agraristas*, 69–70. Jean Meyer, *La Cristiada:la guerra de los cristeros*, vol. 1 (Mexico City: Siglo Vientiuno, 1990), 175; Jim Tuck, *The Holy War in Los Altos: A Regional Analysis of Mexico's Cristero Rebellion* (Tucson: University of Arizona Press, 1982), 72–73.

78. One thousand people contracted smallpox in Arandas in 1928. José Antonio Gutiérrez Gutiérrez, *Jalostitlán a través de los siglos* (Aguascalientes: Universidad Autonoma de Aguascalientes, 1985), 252–256

79. *Excelsior*, October 5, 1927. Quoted by Jean Meyer, *La Cristiada: los cristeros, vol. 3* (Mexico: Siglo XXI Editores, 1993), 269.

80. Many of the *Alteños* who had not emigrated feared and envied the pretensions of their repatriated neighbors. Yet, as one informant reported to Paul S. Taylor, they eventually embraced this new culture and its material trappings: "They used to joke about them, and criticize their better clothing, but not now. Now they imitate them." Taylor, *A Spanish-Mexican Peasant Community*, 60; Snodgrass, "Patronage and Progress," 256–261; Juan Flores García, "Los braceros," in *Tepatitlán en el tiempo* (Tepatitlán, Jalisco: Juan Flores García, 1992), 12–13.

81. Consuelo Díaz Amador argues that this shift, prompted by the establishment of a Nestlé processing factory in the region, the paving of roads that connected Los Altos with Guadalajara, Jalisco and León, Guanajuato prompted land grab by the region's elites that squeezed unlucky rural workers (especially sharecroppers like Luz Moreno) to move into local municipal *cabeceras* (the centers of the municipal government), to large Mexican cities or to the United States. Consuelo Díaz Amador, "Los Altos de Jalisco: Transformación de una Región (1940–1980)," in *Política y región: Los Altos de Jalisco,* ed. Jorge Alonso and Juan García de Quevedo (Mexico City: Centro de Investigaciones y Estudios Superiores en Antropología Social, 1990), 40–42.

82. Over 165,000 Jalicienses worked as braceros from 1953 to 1964. According to demographer William W. Winnie, this figure that represents over thirty percent of the region's population in 1960. Winnie also includes in his calculations the Zacatecan municipalities of Nochistlán and Apulco. *La movilidada demográfica y sus incidencia en una region de fuerte emigración* (Guadalajara, Jalisco: Universidad de Guadalajara, 1984), 76–77.

83. The waves of movement out of the municipality are partially reflected in the population census. Between 1930 and 1940 the population of the municipality of San Miguel increased by 22.83 percent, largely due to the return of residents after the Cristero Rebellion. Between 1940 and 1950 immigration from the countryside and increased birth rates caused the population to increase by 9 percent, and by almost 20 percent between 1950 and 1960. This upward trend decisively ended in the 1960s and 1970s when the region experienced a drop in population of 16 and 21 percent, respectively. Most of this was due to outmigration to the United States and the large Mexican cities like Guadalajara and Mexico City. Consuelo Díaz Amador, "Los Altos de Jalisco: Transformación de una Región (1940–1980)," 41–45.

84. George Sánchez argues that we need to complicate our understanding of Mexican immigration by moving beyond seeing it as a phenomenon that is energized and conditioned solely by economic, political, and social push and pull factors. He highlights how immigration is also culturally conditioned by the practices and values that Mexicans bring with them from their places of origin. George Sánchez, *Becoming Mexican American: Ethnicity, Culture and Identity in Chicano Los Angeles, 1900–1945* (New York: Oxford University Press, 1993), 17–37; Snodgrass, "Patronage and Progress," 260.

85. This percentage reflects men who were eligible for the lottery because they met the age requirements. In reality, the number of men who were eligible was smaller (and hence the percentage of men who applied higher) because the list excluded skilled and employed laborers, as well as rural workers who had been given access to an ejido. In 1950 there were 1965 men in the municipality between the age of 20 and 39. *Séptimo Censo General de Población 6 de Junio de 1950, Estado de Jalisco,* 39

86. The municipal archive has documentation for only two bracero lotteries, 1947 and 1948. In 1947 688 men applied for 40 spots. In 1948, 325 men applied for 54 spots. The 1947 list of applicants includes their names and their addresses; the 1948 list also includes the men's age. We know that the bracero lottery continued at least through 1951 because Luz Moreno mentions it in his letters (August 30, 1951; October 22, 1951; October 25, 1951). Archivo Historico San Miguel el Alto,

Jalisco (AHSMEAJ) Box 76, *Sección: Presidencial, Serie: Trabajo, Tránsito, Telégrafos, Turismo, Traslado de Reos.*

87. In 1947 only 5.8 percent of the applicants received permission to become braceros; in 1948 it was 16.6 percent. If you include all the men who would have wanted to enter the lottery but could not (the employed, *ejidatarios*, those, like Luz Moreno's nephew Jesus Orozco, who were under twenty, and those who were over forty), the dimensions of the situation are clearer. Michael Snodgrass calculates that when you include immigrants who went to the United States without documentation, fully 30 percent of all working-age males from the state worked in the United States during the 1950s. Snodgrass, "Patronage and Progress," 256. Snodgrass bases this number on the work of Gloria Vargas y Campos, *El problema del bracero Mexicano* (thesis, Universidad Nacional Autonoma de México, 1964), 82–85.

88. Henderson, *Beyond Borders*, 72.

89. The next lines of the letter highlight how conflicted Luz felt about immigration to the United States. After lamenting the mania for dollars that he sees in his town, Luz tells Pancha that her sister wants Juan to bring her "two deep bowls to accommodate a lot of food and two flat plates . . . [and] Pancha to send her some cutlery." Letter is included in chapter 4.

90. Luis González, *San José de Gracia,* 219. Moreno and González's assessment is not hyperbolic. One of the unintended—but for many, especially rich American farmers, fortuitous—consequences of the Bracero Program was a dramatic rise in illegal immigration. Aided and abetted by capitalist interests in the United States and energized by the pluck and desperation of poor Mexican workers, the permanence of an illegal immigration system became one of the most important legacies of the Bracero Program. See Philip Martin, "There Is Nothing More Permanent Than Temporary Foreign Workers," in *Backgrounder* from *Center for Immigration Studies*, April 2001, www.cis.org/sites/cis.org/files/articles/2001/back501.pdf. About the optimism of the braceros and the positive attitude that many participants had about their experience in the Bracero Program, see Snodgrass, "Patronage and Progress," 259–260.

91. The term "epistolary embrace" is from Ernesto Che Guevara, *Latin American Diaries: The Sequel to the Motorcycle Diaries* (Melbourne: Ocean Press, 2011), 140.

92. Obdulia Orozco, personal communication, October 23, 2013.

CHAPTER 2

1. *Cuál de los dos amantes sufre más pena/el que se va o el que se queda/el que se queda/ se queda llorando/y el que se va, se va suspirando."*La Despedida."

2. *"Cuando Pancha se fue, nos quedamos ciegos."* Obdulia Orozco, personal communication, October 23, 2013.

3. On the distinction and historical relationship between space and place see Anthony Giddens, *The Consequences of Modernity* (Redwood City, CA: Stanford University Press, 1990), 17–21.

4. Giddens, *The Consequences of Modernity,* 18, 64, 21–28; David A. Gerber, "Forming a Transnational Narrative: New Perspectives on European Migrations to the United States." *The History Teacher* 35, no. 1 (2001): 71.

5. See letters October 25, 1951, July 23, 1952.

6. According to two of the earliest scholars to use letters to study the immigrant experience in the United States, all immigrant letters function, in form or another, "to manifest the persistence of familial solidarity in spite of the separation." William I. Thomas and Florian Znaniecki, *The Polish Peasant in*

Europe and America: A Classic Work in Immigration History, ed. Eli Zaretsky (Champaign: University of Illinois Press, 1995), 25. The study was originally published as a five-volume study between 1918–1920; Gerber, "Forming a Transnational Narrative," 69–71.

7. "Even though I have begged your pardon, I have not been able to erase my error. If your compassion will allow, once more receive my supplication asking forgiveness for those affronts" (September 11, 1951).

8. "Juan is an experienced man, an incomparable man, a man with a heart, with charity. He is a man of valor and energy who knows what to do, and who knows how to command" (c. September 1950).

9. "The qualities of his personality have been tested by the very people who most doubted his sincerity. It is rare for people who are united through marriage to [truly] care for each other, [yet] Juan is loved by most of this family" (c. September 1950).

10. Obdulia Orozco, personal communication, October 23, 2013.

11. The rest of the Moreno's did not follow suit. As both a commentary on his girth and an acknowledgment that he was an ominous presence in their life, they always referred to Juan as *Juanón*.

12. Gerber, "Forming a Transnational Narrative," 68.

13. William E. French writes that "letters seemed capable not only of delivering the message of love but also of extending the reach of their composer, who having touched the letter to write it, found in it the means for transmitting that touch, their feelings, their body to the object of their desire." While he was writing about the correspondence between lovers in northern Mexico during a slightly earlier point in time, his words capture a truth about Pancha and Luz and their correspondence. French, *The Heart in the Glass Jar*, 240.

14. "I imagine seeing you, my Panchita, very determinedly preparing lunch . . . or dinner for Juanito and I would like to know what type of food you are cooking at each meal. I wish I could eat a taco from your meal to see if that food harms me like the one from here." From the Collected Correspondence of Luz Moreno, 1950–1952: June 13, 1951. Other examples in this chapter see letters dated February 1951; August 7, 1951; c. November 18, 1951.

15. Daniel James, citing Christian Metz, writes that "photos are similar to funerals and other rituals in that they have the double function of remembering the dead but also remembering that they are dead and that life continues." Daniel James, *Doña María's Story: Life, History, Memory and Political Identity* (Durham, NC: Duke University Press, 2000), 149; Christian Metz, "Photography and Fetish," *October* 51, no. 34 (1985): 85.

16. Janet Gurkin Altman, *Epistolarity: Approaches to a Form* (Columbus: Ohio State University Press, 1982), 128–129. On haunting see Avery F. Gordon, *Ghostly Matters: Haunting and the Sociological Imagination* (Minneapolis: University of Minnesota Press, 1997).

17. Alicia Gojman de Backal and Laura Edith Bonilla, *Historia del Correo en México* (Mexico City: Miguel Angel Porrúa, 2000).

18. Martyn Lyons, "Love Letters and Writing Practices: On *Écritures intimes* in the Nineteenth Century," *Journal of Family History* 24, no. 2 (1999): 235.

19. Collected Correspondence of Luz Moreno, 1950–1952: March 13, 1951. What John Berger writes about songs can also be said about letters: "A song fills the present, while it hopes to reach a listening ear in some future somewhere. It leans forward, farther and farther. Without the persistence of this hope songs would

not exist. Songs lean forward." John Berger, "Some Notes on Song: The Rhythms of Listening," *Harper's Magazine*, February 2015, 64.

20. Luis González describes the importance of the church bells in the town of San José de Gracia, Michoacán in the following manner: "The sound of the church bells began in 1895, when Don Camilo Ocaranza cast them. From then on their knelling, pealing, tolling, ringing, clanging, chiming, and clanking told the parishioners what they should be doing any given time." *San José de Gracia: Mexican Village in Transition*, trans. John Upton (Austin: University of Texas Press, 1983), 90.

21. Agustín Yañez, *Yahualica* (Mexico City: n.p., 1946), 51–52.

22. Anthony Giddens writes about premodern conceptions of time: "The time reckoning which formed the basis of day-to-day life, certainly for the majority of he population, always linked time with place. No one could tell the time of day without reference to other socio-spatial markers: 'when' was almost universally either connected with 'where' or identified by regular natural occurrences." Giddens, *The Consequences of Modernity*, 17.

23. Adrian Bantjes, "Saints, Sinners, and State Formation: Local Religion and Cultural Revolution in Mexico," in *The Eagle and the Virgin: Nation and Cultural Revolution in Mexico, 1920–1940*, eds. Mary K. Vaughan and Stephen E. Lewis (Durham, NC: Duke University Press, 2006), 146–147; William A. Christian, Jr., *Local Religion in Sixteenth-Century Spain* (Princeton, NJ: Princeton University Press, 1981), 177; Fernando Cervantes, "Mexico's 'Ritual Consent': Religion and Liberty from Colony to Post-Revolution," in *Faith and Impiety in Revolutionary Mexico*, ed. Matthew Butler (New York: Palgrave Macmillan, 2007) 64, 70.

24. Obdulia Orozco, personal communication, October 22, 2013.

25. According to historian Vicki Ruíz, the cannery workers she interviewed spoke about time in terms of the fruit and vegetable they worked: "We met in spinach, fell in love in peaches and married in tomatoes." *Cannery Women, Cannery Lives: Mexican Women, Unionization, and the California Food Processing Industry, 1930–1950* (Albuquerque: University of New Mexico Press, 1987), 37.

26. "Juan and Pancha, you may have thought it strange that I did not take advantage of your visit to speak [with you]" (March 19, 1952).

27. "Long conversations bore me, that's why I don't look for friends." Collected Correspondence of Luz Moreno, 1950–1952: March 15,1951.

28. Carlos Monsiváis, *El género epistolar: Un homenaje a manera de carta abierta* (Mexico City: Miguel Angel Porrúa, 1991), 59; Rebecca Earle, "Introduction: Letters, Writers and the Historian," in *Epistolary Selves: Letters and Letter-Writers, 1600–1945*, ed. Rebecca Earle (Aldershot: Ashgate, 1999).

29. David M. Henkin argues, and this seems the case for Luz, that the postal culture of the United States not only created the opportunities to express certain intimacies, but the intimacies themselves. *The Postal Age: The Emergence of Modern Communication in Nineteenth-Century America* (Chicago: University of Chicago Press, 2006).

30. This was a common phenomenon among romantic correspondents in the love letters that Karen Lystra studied. Nathaniel Wheeler wrote to his girlfriend: "[I am] more *myself* as I sit here talking to you with the pen," while Eliza Trescot confessed to her love that "In writing I can express myself more easily than when I am with you." *Searching the Heart: Women, Men and Romantic Love in Nineteenth-Century America* (New York: Oxford University Press, 1989), 21, 26.

31. David A. Gerber writes that sending and receiving letters provided an entry into modernity and an introduction into bureaucratic organizations like the modern

postal system. Gerber, "Forming A Transnational Narrative," 71. This relationship, though, was fraught with anxiety about the honesty of postal workers and the efficiency of the system. In the context of the United States see William Merrill Decker, *Epistolary Practices: Letter Writing in America Before Telecommunications* (Chapel Hill: University of North Carolina Press, 1998), 58.

32. Interestingly, the late 1940s and 1950s marks the moment when, under the self-serving auspices of President Miguel Alemán (who had invested heavily in modernizing Acapulco and other tourist destinations for Americans), wealthy Mexicans begin to take flight with the development of a state-funded modern airline industry. John Sherman notes that while there were 90,000 airplane passengers in 1940, by the end of the Alemán era in 1952 there were 1 million. John Sherman, "The Mexican 'Miracle' and its Collapse," in *The Oxford History of Mexico*, ed. Michael C. Meyer and William H. Beezley (New York: Oxford University Press, 2000), 586.

33. Growing wings and taking flight is a common dream among immigrants and their families. Alicia R. Schmidt Camacho quotes Father Ademar Barilli, director of *Casa del Migrante, Tecún Umán* in Guatemala as saying, "Migrants would make wings if they had to." *Migrant Imaginaries: Latino Cultural Politics in the U.S.– Mexico Borderlands* (New York: New York University Press, 2008), 283.

34. Gerber, *Authors of Their Lives*, 92.

CHAPTER 3

1. *"Mira que Dios te Mira/Mira que te está mirando/Mira que te has de morir/Mira que no sabes cuando."* Medieval in origin, the refrain is popular across the Spanish speaking Catholic world.

2. Jose Vasconcelos, *La flama: los de arriba en la revolución, historia y tragedia* (Mexico City: Compañia Editorial Continental, 1959), 19.

3. Hispanophile intellectuals and politicians were reacting to the ideas and political programs of Mexico's *Indigenistas* who believed that the country's national identity was rooted in its Indian history and culture. José Orozco, *"Esos Altos de Jalisco*: Emigration and the Idea of Alteño Exceptionalism, 1926–1952" (PhD diss., Harvard University, 1998).

4. *"Vamos para los Altos,/donde son buenos cristianos/y por no perder la sangre/se casan primos-hermanos."* José Antonio Gutiérrez Gutiérrez, *Los Altos de Jalisco: panorama historico de una region y de su sociedad hasta 1821* (Mexico City: Consejo Nacional para la Cultura y las Artes, 1991), 187.

5. José López-Portillo y Weber, *La Conquista de la Nueva Galicia* (México: Talleres gráficos de la nación, 1935), 69; Matías de la Mota Padilla, *Historia de la conquista de Nueva Galicia* (Guadalajara: Instituto Jalisciencie de Antropología e Historia, Universidad de Guadalajara, 1973); José Antonio Gutiérrez Gutiérrez, *Los Altos de Jalisco*, 118–119; Francisco Alcalá Barba, *Sedentarización en la Zona de los Altos de Jalisco* (Tepatitlán, Jalisco: Consejo de Cronistas de Tepatitlán de Morelos, 1995).

6. Jean Meyer's classic study of the Cristero Rebellion popularized the narrative of the Cristeros (especially those of Los Altos) as ideologically motivated religious warriors. Meyer, *La Cristiada*, 3 vols. (Mexico City: Siglo XXI, 1973–74), but versions of these tropes can be found in Paul S. Taylor, *A Spanish-Mexican Peasant Community: Arandas in Jalisco, Mexico* (Berkeley: University of California Press, 1933),6–9; Ann L. Craig, *The First Agraristas: An Oral History of a Mexican Agrarian Reform Movement* (Berkeley: University of California Press, 1983),

19–23; Andrés Fábregas, "Los Altos de Jalisco: Características generals," in José Díaz, and Román Rodríguez, *El movimiento cristero: Sociedad y conflicto en los Altos de Jalisco* (Mexico City: Editorial Nueva Imagen CIS-INAH, 1979), 15–19; Stanley Robe, *Mexican Tales and Legends from Los Altos* (Berkeley: University of California Press, 1970), 30.

7. Jim Tuck, *The Holy War in Los Altos: A Regional Analysis of Mexico's Cristero Rebellion* (Tucson: University of Arizona Press, 1982), 10.

8. Matthew Butler, *Popular Piety and Political Identity in Mexico's Cristero Rebellion: Michoacán, 1927–29* (Oxford: Oxford University Press, 2004), 107–108.

9. Jean Meyer notes that up until the 1950s, fully one third of the population in Los Altos was involved in these organizations. "Perspectivas de análisis socio-histórico de la influencia de Guadalajara sobre su región," *Regiones y ciudades en América Latina*, eds, Jean Piel et al. (Mexico City: Sepsetentas, 1973), 161. In her study of the Cristero Rebellion in the neighboring state of Michoacán, Jennie Purnell compiles statistics that highlight the relatively high ration of churches, priests, and lay Catholic organization in Jalisco in the decades before the Cristero Rebellion. She also notes that because Jalisco had relatively few communities eligible to apply for land redistribution under the agrarian reform program, its peasants, especially those from Los Altos, were threatened by agrarianism. Religion and material interest reinforced each other and accounts for Alteño participation in the Cristiada. See Tables 4.2, 4.3, 4.4, and 4.5 in *Popular Movements and State Formation in Revolutionary Mexico: The Agrarista and Cristeros of Michoacán* (Durham, NC: Duke University Press, 1999), 92–106. For a case study of Alteño peasants who embraced the state's agrarian reform, see Craig, *The First Agraristas*, 1983.

10. Adrian Bantjes, Paul J. Vanderwood, and other historians prefer the term "local religion" to "popular" or "folk" religion because unlike these terms, "popular religion" does not treat the religious piety of nonelites as a separate and (usually) debased from of official or elite forms of religiosity. On the difference between popular and local religions see Vanderwood, *"Religion: Official, Popular, and Otherwise," Mexican Studies/Estudios Mexicanos* 16, no. 2 (2000): 416; Adrian Bantjes, "Religion and the Mexican Revolution: Toward a New Historiography," in *Religious Culture in Modern Mexico*, ed. Martin Austin Nesvig (Lanham, MD: Rowman and Littlefield Publishers, 2007), 226–227; William B. Taylor, *Magistrates of the Sacred: Priests and Parishioners in Eighteenth-Century* Mexico (Redwood City, CA: Stanford University Press, 1996); Alan Knight, "Superstitions in Mexico: From Colonial Church to Secular State," *Past and Present* 199, no. 3 (2008): 229–270; William A. Christian, Jr., *Local Religion in Sixteenth-Century Spain* (Princeton, NJ: Princeton University Press, 1981).

11. Although Luz Moreno was born and worked all his life in the countryside, he lived in the town of San Miguel el Alto and most likely would not have considered himself "rural folk." Adrian Bantjes, "Religion and the Mexican Revolution," 226.

12. Pamela Voekel, Bethany Moreton, and Michael Jo, "Vaya Con Dios: Religion and the Transnational History of the Americas," *History Compass* 5, no. 5 (2007): 1619.

13. The Virgin of Fátima appeared to three shepherd children on May 13, 1917. During biyearly visits, the Virgin shared with the children a vision of hell and a warning that God was readying himself to punish the earth with wars and famine. She conveyed to the children that in order to save the world and its human souls they had to, among other things, "consecrate Russia to my Immaculate Heart." Lúcia Santos, the only child to survive the Spanish flu epidemic

of 1918, elaborated on Fátima's warnings in 1936: "If my requests are heeded, Russia will be converted, and there will be peace; if not, she will spread her errors throughout the world, causing wars and persecutions of the Church. The good will be martyred; the Holy Father will have much to suffer; various nations will be annihilated. In the end, my Immaculate Heart will triumph. The Holy Father will consecrate Russia to me, and she shall be converted, and a period of peace will be granted to the world." This message helped Luz, and many anti-Communist political groups in the decades around the two world wars, create a sacred narrative of a world divided where, as the historian Mary Vincent writes, "Rome, and Mary, were ranged against the Soviet Union in a struggle between the redeemed and the fallen." Mary Vincent, *Catholicism in the Second Spanish Republic: Religion and Politics in Salamanca, 1930–1936* (Oxford: Clarendon Press, 1996), 101; Louis Kondor, ed., *Fátima in Lucia's own Words: Sister Lucia's Memoirs* (Fátima, Portugal: Secretariado dos Pastorinhos, 2007), 210; letter dated September 24, 1951.

14. 2 Peter 3:10.

15. For a particularly forceful example of the way Luz saw the history of the world as little more than the unfolding of God's intent, see letter circa June 1951.

16. See Spencer R. Weart, *Nuclear Fear: A History of Images* (Cambridge, MA: Harvard University Press, 1988); Frank Graziano, *The Millennial New World* (New York: Oxford University Press, 1999).Graziano mentions the recurring myth of Inkarrí (the Incan King figure that is a composite of Atahualpa the Incan emperor who was executed the Spanish in 1533 and Túpac Amaru neo-Incan leader who was decapitated by the Spanish in 1572) as one example of these Cold War millennial movements. In the early 1970s, Quechua-speaking adherents looked forward to a millennial kingdom because it was then that Inkarrí would return and there would "be no hunger, no, wars, no atomic bomb." Graziano, *Millennial New World*, 189.

17. Graziano, *The Millennial New World*, 17.

18. On Tomochic, see Paul J. Vanderwood, *The Power of God Against the Guns of Government: Religious Upheaval in Mexico at the Turn of the Nineteenth Century* (Redwood City, CA: Stanford University Press, 1998), 15.

19. Salvador Abascal, *Mis recuerdos: sinarquismo y Colonia María Auxiliadora: con importantes documentos de los archivos Nacionales de Washington (1935–1944)* (Mexico City: Tradición, 1980).

20. Letter circa September, 1950; Graziano, *The Millennial New World*, 69.

21. "I would like for us to die together; but no, we will die as God wishes." Circa April 1951. Letter is in chapter 4, "El Miserable Pueblo."

22. Moreno always referred to the Soviet Union as "Russia."

23. The proverb is generally attributed to Don Álvaro de Luna of Castile, Duke of Trujillo (1388–1453) who on a hunting trip encountered a beggar whose eyes had been gouged out by crows he had lovingly raised. The Duke's response "*Cría cuervos y te sacarán los ojos*," is the source of the proverb.

24. William Merrill Decker develops the idea of the difference between absence and incomplete presence in writing about the correspondence of John Winthrop (1587–1649), the seventeenth-century governor of the Massachusetts Bay Colony, to his family in England. *Epistolary Practices: Letter Writing in America before Telecommunications* (Chapel Hill: University of North Carolina Press, 1998), 71.

25. Letter found in chapter 2.

26. In his spiritual-geographic understanding of the world, Luz was very much in line with early modern Spanish understanding of the world as a "homogenous Christendom with an infidel fringe." J. H. Parry, *The Spanish Theory of Empire in the Sixteenth Century* (New York: Octagon Books, 1974), 13. Also quoted in Graziano, *The Millennial New World*, 22.

27. On the concept of "Big Gods" and their role in creating prosocial, large human communities see Ara Norenzayan, *Big Gods: How Religion Transformed Cooperation and Conflict* (Princeton, NJ: Princeton University Press, 2013).

28. As a matter of habit, and a reflection of his position at the top of the Great Chain Being, God generally deputized his angels and saints to make, as Paul J. Vanderwood writes, "His plans, desires, and anger known to His adherents." Vanderwood, *The Power of God Against the Guns of Government*, 55.

29. Anthony Giddens, *The Consequences of Modernity* (Redwood City, CA: Stanford University Press, 1990), 11, 124–125.

30. Jack Goody makes the point that the "co-existence of the scientific and the supernatural remains a feature of contemporary societies." Jack Goody, *The Theft of History* (Cambridge: Cambridge University Press, 2006), 16.

31. Luis González, *San José de Gracia: Mexican Village in Transition*, trans. John Upton (Austin: University of Texas Press, 1983), 111.

32. Adrian Bantjes notes that Mexican Guadalupanismo "an alternative Catholic source of Mexican nationalism." Adrian Bantjes, "Religion and the Mexican Revoluiton," 224. On the role of saints and the Virgin de Guadalupe as divine intercessors between humanity and God see Taylor, *Magistrates of the Sacred*, 277–300.

33. Jeanette Rodríguez, "Guadalupe: The Feminine Face of God," in *Goddess of the Americas: Writings on the Virgin of Guadalupe*, ed. Ana Castillo (New York: Riverhead Books, 1996).

34. "Lupita" is the diminutive for of "Guadalupe," and is often used by Mexicans as a term of endearment for the Virgin of Guadalupe. Jeanette Rodríguez writes that the Virgin of Guadalupe offers Mexico's spiritually orphaned the belief "that we are lovable and capable, that we belong, that we can grow and be transformed, and that there is as reason to live and a reason to hope. Rodríguez, "Guadalupe," 29.

35. Cécile Dauphin also notes that letter-writing resembled prayer in "its effort to transcend absence. "Letter-Writing Manuals in the Nineteenth Century," 132.

36. John Berger writes about prayer: "And Prayer in most, if not all, religions, temples, and churches is double-faced. It can endlessly reiterate dogma or it can articulate hope. And which function it accomplishes doesn't necessarily depend on the place or circumstances where the prayer is being prayed. It depends on the stories of those praying." John Berger, "Some Notes on Song: The Rhythms of Listening," *Harper's Magazine*, February 2015, 68.

37. Carlos Monsiváis, "Forward: When Gender Can't be Seen amid the Symbols: Women and the Mexican Revolution," in *Sex in Revolution: Gender, Politics, and Power in Modern Mexico*, eds. Jocelyn Olcott, Mary K. Vaughan, and Gabriela Cano (Durham, NC: Duke University Press, 2006), 12.

38. This is not to imply that the partisans of each tradition were hermetically sealed from the influences of the other tradition's holy books. Luz read the newspaper every day, and many of Mexico's most anticlerical zealots were quite familiar with and often acted in accordance with teachings of the Bible. Knight,

"The Mentality and Modus Operandi of Revolutionary Anticlericalism," 30; Graziano, *The Millennial New World*, 20.

39. Vanderwood, "Religion: Official, Popular, and Otherwise," 427. Letters circa September 1950, circa December 1950, and September 10, 1951.

40. For example, in his first letter to Pancha he advises her to "take care of that precious treasure that is your faith; with it, and the practice of all the virtues, you will be great in the eyes of God" (April 8, 1950).

41. For historiographies on religion in the era of Mexican Revolution see Matthew Butler's "A Revolution in Spirit? Mexico, 1910–1940," in *Faith and Impiety in Revolutionary Mexico* ed. Matthew Butler (New York: Palgrave Macmillan, 2007), 1–20. For an excellent historiographic essay popular religion in Latin America see Reinaldo L. Román and Pamela Voekel, "Popular Religion in Latin American Historiography," in *The Oxford Handbook of Latin American History*, ed. José C. Moya (New York: Oxford University Press, 2011); Voekel, Moreton, and Jo, "Vaya Con Dios," 1619–1620, 1622.

CHAPTER 4

1. *"El miserable pueblo"* is the term the Luz uses to refer to poor and oppressed people of the world. It can be literally translated as the "downtrodden people;" but a better translation might be the "wretched of the earth."

2. Pulque is a traditional fermented drink made from the juices of the maguey plant. Obdulia Orozco, personal communication, October 15, 2013.

3. In spite of the nationalist rhetoric that President Miguel Aleman (1946–1952) used, the level of investment by North American economic interests, as John Sherman notes, "reached proportions similar to, if not greater than, that under [Porfirio] Diaz." John Sherman, "The Mexican 'Miracle' and its Collapse," in *The Oxford History of Mexico*, ed. Michael C. Meyer and William Beezley (New York: Oxford University Press, 2000), 544. Here Sherman in citing Lorenzo Meyer's book *Mexico and the United States in the Oil Controversy, 1917–1942*, trans. Muriel Vasconcellos (Austin: University of Texas Press, 1977).

4. For an analysis of the rise of a postrevolutionary political elite in Los Altos see, Leticia Gándara Mendoza, *"La evolución de una oligarquía: el caso de San Miguel el Alto, Jalisco,"* in *Política y sociedad en México: el caso de los Altos de Jalisco*, ed. Tomás Martínez Saldaña and Leticia Gándara Mendoza (Mexico City: Centro de Investigaciones Superiores, Instituto Nacional de Antropología e Historia, 1976).

5. From 1946 to 1950 Mexico's economic sputtered as the price of its principal exports declined after the end of World War II. Wages dropped, and unemployment increased, especially as thousands of now redundant braceros returned home. The beginning of the Korean War in 1950 initiated an economic recovery. Gilbert M. Joseph and Jürgen Buchenau, *Mexico's Once and Future Revolution: Social Upheaval and the Challenge of Rule since the Late Nineteenth Century* (Durham, NC: Duke University Press, 2013). 154.

6. Luis González writes that the poor of San José the Gracia, Michoacán evinced a similar attitude toward the rich: "Out in the country what counted was experience—not whether or not you had gone to a good school. In fact, educated people were inept when it came time to raising crops and handling cattle. They didn't know how to do anything. They couldn't drive a team of oxen or do any of the other chores in the cornfield . . . for them there was no talent but manual dexterity, and no wisdom beyond their own empirical knowledge. Thus, they considered themselves more intelligent than their masters." *San José de Gracia: Mexican Village in Transition* (Austin: University of Texas Press, 1983) 188–189.

7. Gillingham and Smith, eds., *Dictablanda: Politics, Work, and Culture in Mexico, 1938–1968* (Durham, NC: Duke University Press, 2014), 4.

8. Héctor Aguilar Camín and Lorenzo Meyer, *In the Shadow of the Mexican Revolution: Contemporary Mexican History, 1910–1989*, trans. Luis Alberto Fierro (Austin: University of Texas Press, 1993, 162.

9. According to Jeffrey Bortz and Marcos Aguilar, wages in Mexico City hit their nadir in the late 1940s and did not recover until the late 1960s. "Earning a Living: A History of Real Wages Studies in Twentieth Century Mexico," *Latin American Research Review* 41, no. 2 (2006): 126. Cited by Robert F. Alegre, "*Las Rieleras*: Gender Politics, and Power in the Mexican Railway Movement, 1958–1959," *Journal of Women's History* 23, no. 2 (2011): 165.

10. Joseph and Buchenau, *Mexico's Once and Future Revolution*, 156; Aguilar Camín and Meyer, *In the Shadow of the Mexican Revolution*, 164.

11. See essays in *Fragments of a Golden Age: The Politics of Culture in Mexico Since 1940*, eds. Gilbert M. Joseph, Anne Rubenstein, and Eric Zolov (Durham, NC: Duke University Press, 2001; Jean Franco, *The Decline and Fall of the Lettered City: Latin America in the Cold War* (Cambridge, MA: Harvard University Press, 2002); Gillingham and Smith, eds., *Dictablanda*.

12. See Elena Poniatowska, *Massacre in Mexico*, trans. Helen R. Lane (Columbia: University of Missouri Press, 1991); Paco Ignacio Taibo II, '*68* trans. Donald Nicholson-Smith (New York: Seven Stories Press, 2004).

13. Daniel Cosío-Villegas, "Mexico's Crisis," in *American Extremes*, trans. Américo Paredes (Austin: University of Texas Press, 1964), 3–27.

14. José Iturriaga, "México y su crisis histórica," *Cuadernos Americanos*, May–June 1947: 21–37, cited in Thomas Benjamin, *La Revolución: Mexico's Great Revolution as Memory, Myth, and History* (Austin: University of Texas Press, 2000) 157. Jesús Silva Hertzog, the former director of the School of Economics at the National University, took the argument to its logical extreme by pronouncing the Revolution dead; "La Revolución Mexicana es ya un Hecho Historíco," *Cuadernos Americanos*, September–October, 1949, 7–16 in *Is the Mexican Revolution Dead?*, 2nd ed., ed. Stanley R. Ross (Philadelphia: Temple University Press, 1975).

15. Jean Franco characterizes Mexico's incomplete modernity as "tenuous moment when what had once been imagined as an organic community, as a social body, becomes irrevocably fragmented and no longer representable in a teleological narrative." Jean Franco, *The Decline and Fall of the Lettered City*, 137. Franco is referring to the novels of Paraguayan Augusto Roa Basto and Mexican Juan Rulfo. Octavio Paz, "*El poeta Buñuel*," *Nuevo Cine* 4–5 (1961): 48.

16. Luz feared that the Russians would bomb Stockton. Looking at how peripheral Stockton is to world events now, it is hard to imagine that during World War II, because of the military munitions factories and shipbuilding facilities that were located there, Juan and Pancha's town, as historian Olive Davis writes, "was considered the number one military target in California in case of enemy attack." Olive Davis, *Stockton: Sunrise Port on the San Joaquin* (Woodland Hills, CA: Windsor Publications, 1984), 82.

17. David Fitzgerald, *How Mexico Manages its Migration* (Berkeley: University of California Press, 2009; Benedict Anderson, *Imagined Communities: Reflections on the Origin and Spread of Nationalism* (London: Verso, 1990) 13, 24–28. James Dormady, *Primitive Revolution: Restorationist Religion and the Idea of the Mexican Revolution, 1940–1968* (Albuquerque: University of New Mexico Press, 2011), 111.

18. Paul Gillingham and Benjamin T. Smith quote the Mexican cartoonist political cartoonist Abel Quezada (1920–1991) ("Mexico remained 'the best place to watch history from the ringside seats'") to make the point that "in Mexico the Cold War largely failed to inspire what Greg Grandin has termed the "politicization and internationalization" of everyday life." "Introduction: The Paradoxes of Revolution," *Dictablanda*, 24.

19. Héctor Aguilar Camín and Lorenzo Meyer, *In the Shadow of the Mexican Revolution: Contemporary Mexican History, 1910–1989* trans. Luis Alberto Fierro (Austin: University of Texas Press, 1993), 164.

20. Stephen Niblo discusses a wide range of corruption strategies in chapter 5, "The Politics of Corruption," in *Mexico in the 1940s: Modernity Politics, and Corruption* (Wilmington, DE: Scholarly Resources, 1999), 253–309. The corruption of local elite who sold spots in the Bracero lottery, especially in the Los Altos region, is discussed by Michael Snodgrass in "Patronage and Progress: The Bracero Program from the Perspective of Mexico," in *Workers Across the Americas The Transnational Turn in Labor History*, ed. Leon Fink (New York: Oxford University Press, 2011).

21. For an analysis of the rise of a postrevolutionary political elite in Los Altos see, Leticia Gándara Mendoza, "*La evolución de una oligarquía: El caso de San Miguel el Altos, Jalisco*," in *Política y sociedad en México: El caso de Los Altos de Jalisco*, ed. Tomás Martínez Saldaña and Leticía Gándara Mendoza (Mexico City: Centro de Investigaciones Superiores-Instituto Nacional de Antropolgía e Historia, 1976). Jaime Espín and Patricia de Leonardo, *Economía y sociedad en los Altos de Jalisco* (Mexico City: CIS-INAH, 1978), 237–279. For a comedic take on the culture of PRI corruption in the Mexican provinces, see Luis Estrada's 1999 movie *La Ley de Herodes* (Herod's Law).

22. The municipal government was in the hands of San Miguel's elite families who during this period are linked to Jalisco's Governor, Jesús González Gallo (1947–1953) through Miguel Moreno Padilla. González Gallo was from the Alteño town of Yahualica, and Moreno Padilla was born in San Miguel el Alto. They were friends and conservative political allies who opposed Lázaro Cardenas's liberal reforms. Moreno Padilla was a Senator in Mexico City (Diputado Federal) when González Gallo was President Manuel Avila Camacho's personal secretary (1940–1946). See Leticia Gándara Mendoza, "*La evolución de una oligarquía*," 182, 256–258, 271.

23. Paul J. Vanderwood highlights the dilemma that Tomochic's citizens were put into when the Porfirian state started to require to register births, weddings and deaths with the civil government and imposed on them taxes on all the cattle they slaughtered. *The Power of God Against the Guns of Government* (Redwood City, CA: Stanford University Press, 1998), 62.

24. The parish priest that Luz is most likely writing about is Manuel F. Flores, who came to the parish in 1946. According to Luis Median Ascensio, the organ that Flores was gathering money for was not purchased until 1954. Francisco Medina de la Torre and Luis Medina Ascensio, *San Miguel el Alto, Jalisco: Biografía de un municipio* (Mexico City: Editorial Jus, 1967), 176.

25. Jean Meyer, *El Sinarquismo, el cardenismo y la iglesia, 1934–1947* (Mexico City: Tusquets Editores, 2003), 162.

26. On "pious anticlericalism" see Ruth Behar, "The Struggle for the Church: Popular Anticlericalism and Religiosity in Post-Franco Spain," in *Religious Orthodoxy and Popular Faith in European Society*, ed. Ellen Badone

(Princeton, NJ: Princeton University Press, 1990), 77; Adrian A. Bantjes, "Saints, Sinners, and State Formation: Local Religion and Cultural Revolution in Mexico," in *The Eagle and the Virgin: Nation and Cultural Revolution in Mexico, 1920–1940,* ed. Mary Kay Vaughan and Stephen E. Lewis (Durham, NC: Duke University Press, 2006), 144.

27. Matthew Butler, *Popular Piety and Political Identity in Mexico's Cristero Rebellion: Michoacán, 1927–29* (New York: Oxford University Press, 2004), 168–169, and "Revolution and the Ritual Year: Religious Conflict and Innovation in *Cristero* Mexico," *Journal of Latin American Studies* 38, no. 3 (2006): 465–490.

28. According to Jose Cutiliero and Joyce Riegelhaupt, this is what distinguishes "pious anticlericalism" from "secular anticlericalism," which expresses anti-Church or antireligion sentiments. Joyce Riegelhaupt, "Popular Anti-Clericalism and Religiosity in pre-1974 Portugal," in *Religion, Power and Protest in Local Communities: The Northern Shore of the Mediterranean,* ed. Eric R. Wolf (Berlin: Mouton, 1984), 96–97; José Cutileiro, *A Portuguese Rural Society* (Oxford: Clarendon Press, 1971).

29. Richard Sennett and Jonathan Cobb, *The Hidden Injuries of Class,* (New York: Vintage Books, 1972).

CHAPTER 5

1. Translated into English and published in the United States in 1962 as *Child of the Dark: The Diary of Carolina Maria de Jesus,* trans. David St. Clair (New York: E.P. Dutton, 1962).

2. Robert M. Levine, "The Cautionary Tale of Carolina Maria de Jesus," *Latin American Research Review* 29, no. 1 (1994): 55–83. David St. Clair, "Translator's Preface to *Child of the Dark*," in *Child of the Dark: The Diary of Carolina Maria de Jesus* (New York: E.P. Dutton, 1962).

3. In 1958 when she met Audalio Danta, the newspaper reporter who would eventually edit and publish *Child of the Dark,* de Jesus had been writing for three years and had filled twenty-six notebooks with her diary and fantasy fiction. St. Clair, "Translator's Preface to *Child of the Dark*," 12.

4. Robert M. Levine and José Carlos Bom Meihy, *The Life and Death of Carolina Maria de Jesus* (Albuquerque: University of New Mexico Press, 1995), 67.

5. De Jesus's mother was a cleaning lady at a local brothel in the northeastern city of Sacramento, Brazil. Carolina Maria attended school because a woman named Maria Leite, the wife of a local landowner and a follower of a spiritualist cult, paid for her school, in part to make penance for the fact that her ancestors had owned slaves. Levine and Meihy, *Life and Death,* 24, 36.

6. De Jesus, *Child of the Dark,* 28.

7. De Jesus, *Child of the Dark,* 29; Levine, Meihy, *Life and Death,* 41–42.

8. De Jesus, *Child of the Dark,* 40.

9. Keeping a diary is an interesting and seductive activity, in the abstract. It is often much easier to want to keep a diary (to think that one should keep a daily account of ones life and world) than it actually is to do so. Louis Menand, commenting about diarists who were much more privileged than Carolina Maria de Jesus, writes that keeping a diary demands a combination of persistence that is 1) fueled by "vanity and self-importance"; 2) facilitated by a level of neurosis that allows the individual to "confess rather than repress" their "unconsummated longings and petty humiliations"; and 3) enabled by a hope that one's words will justify or exculpate (redeem) one's life to an unseen, but sympathetic, father

figure. Louis Menand, "Woke Up This Morning: Why do we Read Diaries?" *The New Yorker*, December 10, 2007.

10. Levine, Meihy, *The Life and Death*, 141.

11. De Jesus, *Child of the Dark*, 30.

12. De Jesus, *Child of the Dark*, 24.

13. The accusations hurled at Luz Moreno and Carolina Maria de Jesus are interesting for at least two reasons: 1) in societies were literacy is limited, reading and writing are often treated as forms of (often dangerous) magic; 2) women (witches) and old people (warlocks, wizards) are traditionally seen as bearers of magical powers. Walter J. Ong, *Orality and Literacy: The Technologizing of the World* (London: Methuen, 1982), 93.

14. "Around here, as soon as someone sees that I am about to write you a letter, they tell me, 'Papá, do not write to them any more, you just worry Juan and Pancha. You are very rude'" (December 4, 1950).

15. Frank Salomon and Mercedes Niño-Mucia describe the suspicion that literacy engenders in the Peruvian highland communities they study in the following manner: "Heavy reading seems to Tupicochans at once admirable and suspect, because it implies ambition in bad as well as good senses. Also because voluntary solitude is off the normal behavioral track, solitary reading may be misinterpreted as snobbish rejection of sociability, or private scheming." *The Lettered Mountain: A Peruvian Village's Way with Writing* (Durham, NC: Duke University Press, 2011), 146.

16. "Do not doubt, though, that this interest in your gifts [has created] envy. [Indeed], because I write to you often and ask you about things I want to know, they accuse me of being indiscreet" (September 6, 1951). David Fitzpatrick, "Irish Emigration and the Art of Letter-Writing," in *Letters Across Borders: The Epistolary Practices of International Migrants*, eds. Bruce S. Elliot, David A. Gerber, and Suzanne M. Sinke (New York: Palgrave Macmillan, 2006), 97.

17. On this point see Miguel Angel Vargas, "Epistolary Communication between Migrant Workers and their Families," in *Letters Across Borders,* 133.

18. Paul S. Taylor explores this remittance culture and its effects in his study of the neighboring Alteño town of Arandas during the 1930s. Taylor, *A Spanish-Mexican Peasant Community*, 32–34.

19. Luz describes the desire for dollars and the urge to go work in the United States as a collective mania. See letter October 22, 1951.

20. It took about seven days for a letter to be delivered. This means that shortest time it could take for either party to get a response to an inquiry was two weeks. October 9, 1951, August 25, 1951 in the Collected Correspondence of Luz Moreno, 1950–1952.

21. On letters and their relationship to oral communication see Janet Gurkin Altman, *Epistolarity: Approaches to Form* (Columbus: Ohio State University Press, 1982), 134–135; Fitzpatrick, "Irish Emigration and the Art of Letter-Writing," 102–103; Ong, *Orality and Literacy*.

22. William E. French comments on the ability of the love letter to "if not conjure the missing correspondent, then to act as a medium for delivering their touch, to make their presence manifest." French, *The Heart in the Glass Jar*, 175.

23. Reading letters in public is a common feature of migrant correspondence circuits around the world. William E. French, "'I Am Going to Write You a Letter': Coplas, Love Letters, and Courtship Literacy," in *Mexico in Verse: A History of Music, Rhyme,*

and *Power*, ed. Stephen Neufeld and Michael Matthews (Tucson: University of Arizona Press, 2015), 175; Hanna, "A Republic of Letters," 1349.

24. Unlike many immigrant correspondences, Pancha's letters were not read in public to members of the community who were not part of the Moreno family. Samuel L. Bailey and Franco Ramella, eds., *One Family, Two Worlds: An Italian Family's Correspondence Across the Atlantic, 1901–1922*, trans. John Lenaghan (New Brunswick, NJ: Rutgers University Press, 1988), 14.

25. Obdulia Orozco, personal communication, October 22, 2013

26. This distinction is not meant to imply that Luz was more self-reflexive, self-aware, or intelligent than Secundina. Nor am I endorsing Walter J. Ong's proposition that literacy necessarily leads to a fixed set of qualitative changes in the ability of individuals and cultures to express self-awareness, self-reflexivity, or historical consciousness. What I am noting is that Luz was better able than Secundina, mostly because he wanted to and worked hard at it, to use literacy to express some of the qualities of mind that Ong and other assert mark a break between literacy and orality. Unfortunately, because none of Pancha's letters have survived, we cannot make any assertion about her relationship with her literacy—although it must be noted that because she was writing letters to Juan since he left San Miguel c. 1918, she was, of all of the Morenos, the most practiced at keeping a long-distance, long-term correspondence. Ong, *Orality and Literacy*, 82–84, 100; Gerber, *Authors of Their Lives*, 74–77; French, *The Heart in the Glass Jar*, 7–10.

27. C. August 1951, Collected Correspondence of Luz Moreno, 1950–1952.

28. Obdulia Orozco, personal communication, March 15, 2015.

29. Gerber, *Authors of Their Lives*, 75–76.

30. On how letters create a space for the creation of an idealized self see French, *The Heart in the Glass Jar*, 15.

31. On how letter-writing encouraged and facilitated this modern form of consciousness see Jurgen Habermas, *The Structural Transformation of the Public Sphere: An Inquiry Into a Category of Bourgeois Society*, trans. Thomas Burger (Cambridge, MA: MIT Press, 1991); Gerber, "Forming a Transnational Narrative," 61–78; Ann Goldberg, "Reading and Writing Across the Borders of Dictatorship: Self-Censorship and Emigrant Experience in Nazi and Stalinist Europe," in *Letters Across Borders: The Epistolary Practices of International Migrant*, ed. Bruce S. Elliot, David A. Gerber, and Suzanne M. Sinke (New York: Palgrave Macmillian, 2006), 166–167.

32. Using Michel Foucault as his guide, John Comaroff notes: "The *self* was viewed as a divided entity . . . On the one hand, it was the core of subjectivity: 'I' the center from which a person looked out and acted on the world. On the other, it was an object: 'me, myself,' something of which 'I' could become (self)conscious. . . . The partibility of the self—later to reappear as a 'scientific' principle in among other things, Freudian psychology—also manifested itself in the 'natural' oppositions of mind and body, spirit and essence, consciousness and being, which came to loom so large in post-enlightenment thought." In "Images of Empire, Contests of Conscience: Models Colonial Domination in South Africa," *American Ethnologist* 16, no. 4 (1989): 661–685; Jean and John Comaroff, *Of Revelation and Revolution: Christianity, Colonialism, and Consciousness in South Africa, Vol. 1* (Chicago: Chicago University Press, 1991); Anderson, *Imagined Communities*, 30–31; letter from Luz Moreno to Pancha and Juan Rivera, c. February 6, 1951.

33. Gerber, "Forming A Transnational Narrative," 68.

34. On this point it is instructive to compare Luz Moreno's letter to the writings of Concepción Alcalá, *El Diario de Concepción Alcalá: Recogidos Durante La Persecución Religiosa de 1926 a 1929* and Josefina Arellano de Huerta, *Memoirs: La Historia Cristera*. A critical review of both these documents can be found in Luis Gachuz-Mesa, "Women, Freedom, and God: The Cristero Rebellion and the Works of Women in Small Towns of Los Altos," *Berkeley McNair Research Journal* no. 10 (2002): 51-70.

35. On these issues see Angel Rama, *The Lettered City*, trans. John Charles Chasteen (Durham, NC: Duke University Press, 1996); Frank Salomon and Mercedes Niño-Mucia, *The Lettered Mountain;* French, "The Lettered Countryside," in *The Heart in the Glass Jar*.

36. The citizens of San José de Gracia, Michoacán were drawn out of their isolation during the late nineteenth century by "winds from the outside world" that blew into their town in the form of the Catholic newspaper, *El País*. In many ways Luz's literacy, like the many changes that *El País* introduced to San José de Gracia, was the fruit of Mexican social Catholic efforts to produce and disseminate newspapers and other forms of printed materials since the 1870s. Ironically, the often antimodern newspapers fostered the creation of Catholic versions of very modern forms of communications, communities, and forms of consciousness. See Luis González, *San José de Gracia: Mexican Village in Transition* trans. John Upton (Austin: University of Texas Press, 1982, 99–101; Christopher Clark, "The 'New Catholicism' and the European Culture Wars," in *Culture Wars: Secular-Catholic Conflict in Nineteenth-Century Europe,* ed. Christopher Clark and Wolfram Kaiser (Cambridge: Cambridge University Press, 2003), 23–24.

37. In still another letter, Luz expresses dismay to Pancha because his love of newspapers and his commitment to inform her about what he reads has created so much conflict in his family. "It is not my intention to deceive or frighten anyone; everyone should believe and do what they want or can do. Me, they have me pegged for a simpleton because I believe what the newspapers say; [they say] that it is a waste to give them my money because I am so poor. I see that lately more newspapers are being sold. Why should that be? War is ugly in and of itself, not because the newspapers tell us it is" (c. 1951).

38. Letter Found in chapter 4.

39. Terry Pinkard, *Hegel: a Biography* (Cambridge: Cambridge University Press, 2000), 241–242. Cécile Dauphin also notes that letter-writing resembled prayer in "its effort to transcend absence. "Letter-Writing Manuals in the Nineteenth Century," 132.

40. The phrase "men of bookish bent" is from Salamon and Niño-Murcia, *The Lettered Mountain*, 147. It is similar to how Angel Rama uses the term *"letrados"* in his study of literacy and the city *The Lettered City.*

41. *Rerum Novarum* is the foundational text of the social Catholic movement. The encyclical was the Church's response to socialist ideologies that called for class struggle as the method for ameliorating the poverty and social misery created by unfettered capitalism and industrialization. In it Pope Leo XIII called for class harmony as the basis of social justice. This class harmony was to be grounded in a series of reciprocal rights and obligations to ensure that both the sanctity of private property and the amelioration of the "misery and wretchedness pressing so unjustly on the majority of the working class." Manuel Ceballos Ramírez, *El catolicismo social, un tercero en discordia: Rerum novarum, la "cuestión social" y*

la movilización de los católicos mexicanos, 1891–1911 (Mexico City: El Colegio de México, 1991).

42. Information in this section comes from the website for the municipal government of San Miguel el Alto, accessed March 31, 2015, www.sanmiguelelalto.gob.mx/personajes-ilustres/63-jes%C3%BAs-delgado.html.

43. Victoriano Ramírez's remains were eventually interred in the catacombs Delgado designed.

44. Stanley L. Robe, *Mexican Tales and Legends from Los Altos* (Berkeley: University of California Press, 1970), 55, 58; Stanley L. Robe and Mariano Azuela, *Azuela and the Mexican Underdogs* (Berkeley: University of California Press, 1979), 225–230.

45. Obdulia Orozco, personal communication, March 15, 2015

46. De Jesus, *Child of the Dark*, 37–38.

47. De Jesus, *Child of the Dark*, 35.

48. Of the Sinarquista newspaper *Orden*, Luz wrote: "Desiring that you be up to date on the latest news, I send you some newspapers that will give you some good information. This newspaper swears to publish only the truth, just as any individual who joins Sinarquismo swears before God to defend the Christian faith, even if it costs them their life. It is the newspaper that speaks frankly without beating around the bush or [inspiring] fear. It publishes the good things the government does, as well as the bad. It is the defender of the rights and justice of Mexican people. It is like a beacon of light in the midst of the dense and dark ignorance of most of its children" (August 30, 1952).

49. Carolina wrote of her diary entries: "There will be those who reading what I write will say—this is untrue. But misery is real." De Jesus, *Child of the Dark*, 47.

CHAPTER 6

1. Luz was born in 1877. The life expectancy of a person born in rural Jalisco in 1880 was thirty-four years. McCaa, "The Peopling of Mexico from Origins to Revolution," 285.

2. Philippe Ariès, *The Hour of Our Death*, trans. Helen Weaver (New York: Knopf, 1981); Carlos M. N. Eire, *From Madrid to Purgatory: The Art and Craft of Dying in Sixteenth-Century Spain* (Cambridge: Cambridge University Press, 1995); Pamela Voekel, *Alone Before God: The Religious Origins of Modernity in Mexico* (Durham, NC: Duke University Press, 2002); Martina Will de Chaparro and Miruna Achim, "From the Here to the Hereafter: An Introduction to Death and Dying," in *Death and Dying in Colonial Spanish America*, ed. Martina Will de Chaparro and Miruna Achim (Tucson: University of Arizona Press, 2011).

3. This is a problem of sources as most of what we know about the elite comes from written sources produced by the elite (wills, last testaments etc.) or assumed to be read by them (prayer books). Juan Pedro Viqueira, "El sentimiento de la muerte en el México ilustrado del siglo XVIII a través de dos textos de la época," *Relaciones 2*, no. 5 (1981): 27–62.

4. Letter is in chapter 4. The possibility of sudden death (*mors repentina*) and or dying alone was one of the biggest threats to the consummation of a good death. See Claudio Lomnitz, *Death and the Idea of Mexico* (Brooklyn, NY: Zone Books, 2005), 265–266; Drew Gilpin Faust, *This Republic of Suffering: Death and the American Civil War* (New York: Knopf, 2008), 16–18; Ariès, *The Hour of Our Death*, 28.

5. Twentieth-century novelists and philosophers like Juan Rulfo, José Revueltas, and, most influentially, Octavio Paz, have written imaginatively about the attitudes of poor Mexicans toward death. While sympathetic, they have tended

to opaque rather than clarify the matter by emphasizing the supposed ironic fatalistic attitude of Mexico's poor toward death. Paz famously wrote that the Mexican was "seduced by death"; he "jokes about it, caresses it, sleeps with it, celebrates it; it is one of his favorite toys and his most steadfast love." José Revueltas's *Human Mourning*, trans. Roberto Crespi (Minneapolis: University of Minnesota Press, 1990); Juan Rulfo, *Pedro Páramo*, trans. Margaret Sayers Peden (New York: Grove Press, 1994); Octavio Paz, "The Day of the Dead," in *The Labyrinth of Solitude*, trans. Lysander Kemp, Yara Milos, and Rachel Phillips Belash (New York: Grove Press, 1985), 57–58; Barbara Brodman, *The Mexican Cult of Death in Myth, Art and Literature* (Bloomington, IN: iUniverse, 2011); Lomnitz, *Death and the Idea of Mexico*, 20–21.

6. Barbara Myerhoff, *Number Our Days* (New York: Dutton, 1978), 251.

7. Myerhoff, *Number Our Days*, 107–108.

8. Gerber, et al., "What Is It We Seek to Find?," 313.

9. Barbara Myerhoff, "Life History Among the Elderly: Performance, Visibility, and Re-membering," in *Remembered Lives: The Work of Storytelling, Ritual, and Growing Older*, ed. Marc Kaminsky (Ann Arbor: University of Michigan Press, 1992). I was directed to this work, as to *Number Our Days*, by Daniel James's book *Doña María's Story: Life, History, Memory and Political Identity* (Durham, NC: Duke University Press, 2000).

10. Rulfo, *Pedro Páramo*, 4. On the importance of nostalgia to sustaining a sense of self and continuity in the face of old age and the prospect of death see Gerber, *Authors of Their Lives*, 118–119.

11. Myerhoff has written that these "opportunities for appearing" are "an indispensible ingredient of being itself, for unless we exist in the eyes of others, we may come to doubt even our own existence." "Life History among the Elderly," 233.

12. "Their decline isolates them. . . . That is the hardest thing—the tacit isolation of the ageing and dying from the community of the living, the gradual cooling of their relationships to people to whom they were attached, the separation from human beings in general, who gave them meaning and security." Norbert Elias, *The Loneliness of the Dying*, trans. Edmund Jephcott (New York: Continuum, 2001), 2.

13. Obdulia Orozco, personal communication, October 15, 2013.

14. Henri Bergson, *Laughter: An Essay on the Meaning of the Comic*, trans. Cloudesley Brereton and Fred Rothwell (Kobenhavn, Demark: Green Integer, 1999).

15. Along with his worries about his body, Luz worried about his fading memories and the oblivion this portended: "I would like to have more life, for my limbs to be reenergized, and for my forehead to shine with more clarity the memories of this life that seem to fade away with the most minor disturbances of time" (October 20, 1952). Letter is in chapter 3.

16. "The scorn that an old man suffers should be attributed to the passage of time. The old man sees the specter of death approaching him; and although both young and old await death, it is more imminent for the old man. The sacred scripture says, 'Rise before a bedridden person and give honor to the old and dying'" (February 15, 1951).

17. C. February 1951, Collected Correspondence of Luz Moreno, 1950–1952.

18. Oscar Lewis, *Life in a Mexican Village: Tepoztlán Restudied* (Urbana: The University of Illinois Press, 1951), 411.

19. Nancy Scheper-Hughes, *Death Without Weeping: The Violence of Everyday Life in Brazil* (Berkeley: University of California Press, 1993), 158.

20. See letter dated c. February 1951.

21. "A man in his house is the king. In his kingdom he must have vassals, and these will be his children. Not his wife; because her nature is the same as his she shares the same crown. They are rooted and united in such a way that only death can separate these two beings" (letter c. September 1950). Letter included in chapter 2.

22. On cryptomatriarchy see Myerhoff, *Number Our Days*, 245. See also Matthew C. Gutman, *The Meanings of Macho: Being a Man in Mexico City* (Berkeley: University of California Press, 1996), 17.

23. In the abject way he expressed his spent manhood, Luz was, very much, a Mexican man—or at least the Mexican man that appeared in the Ranchero music of the era. For example, compare his letters on this matter with a common trope of Mexican popular music found in songs like *La Llorona*, "*ayer maravilla fui/llorona/ y ahora ni sombra soy*"; *Gritenme Piedras del Campo* by Cuco Sánchez, "*A veces me siento un sol/Y el mundo me importa nada/Luego despierto y me río (2x)/Soy mucho menos que nada*," and almost the whole of José Alfredo Jiménez's oeuvre.

24. The effect that immigration had on women's familial responsibilities, specifically in the era of the Bracero Program, is explored by Ana Elizabeth Rosas in her book *Abrazando el Espíritu: Bracero Families Confront the U.S Mexico Border* (Oakland: University of California Press, 2014); George J. Sánchez, *Becoming Mexican American: Ethnicity, Culture and Identity in Chicano Los Angeles, 1900–1945* (New York: Oxford University Press, 1993), 23.

25. Letters dated April 23, 1951 and July 1, 1952.

26. Letter dated December 4, 1950. Included in chapter 5.

27. Myerhoff, *Number Our Days*, 46.

28. See David A. Gerber's discussion of psychoanalyst Erik Erickson's ideas about identity formation and the importance of the somatic, the interpersonal, and the societal in grounding an evolving and continuous identity of self. Gerber, *Authors of Their Lives*, 65–66.

29. This insight hinges on the work of Mary Douglas, who famously noted: "Just as it is true that everything symbolizes the body. . . so it is equally true that the body symbolizes everything else." Mary Douglas, *Purity and Danger: An Analysis of the Concepts of Pollution and Taboo* (New York: Routledge, 2003), 123; Nancy Scheper-Hughes and Margaret M. Lock, "The Mindful Body: A Prolegomenon to Future Work in Medical Anthropology," *Medical Anthropology Quarterly* 1, no. 1 (1987): 29.

30. On the Mexican supposed indifference to death, see Lomnitz, *Death and the Idea of Mexico*, 405.

31. "'When I was a young man,' Carlos Fuentes confesses, 'I wrote to live. Now, at 54, I write not to die. Like Scheherazade in the *Arabian Nights*, I'll live as long as I have another story to tell.'" Arthur Holmberg, "Carlos Fuentes Turns to Theater," *New York Times*, June 9, 1982, www.nytimes.com/1982/06/06/theater/carlos-fuentes-turns-to-theater.html.

32. "Because death is infinitely a loving act. "Alberto Quintero Álvarez. Epigraph to José Revueltas's *Human Mourning*, trans. Roberto Crespi (Minneapolis: University of Minnesota Press, 1990).

AFTERWORD

1. Obdulia Orozco, personal communication, March 26, 2002.

2. Ibid.

3. May 10, 1951. Letter included in chapter 4.

4. *Patas de perro*, literally "dog paws," is a Mexican colloquialism that is used to describe someone who has wanderlust.

5. Obdulia Orozco, personal communication, January 23, 2015.

6. El Barrio del Chivo (the Goat Neighborhood) was a mostly working-class Mexican community that was torn down in 1960 to build the Crosstown Freeway. Residents of the neighborhood hold annual reunions at local parks to honor the community that one reporter wrote was "lost as if it were the Atlantis of Stockton." Emil Guillermo, "Barrio Chivo Readies for 20th Reunion," last modified August 27, 2005, www.recordnet.com/article/20050827/ENT/50827004.

7. Obdulia Orozco, personal communication, January 23, 2015.

8. Ibid.

9. Obdulia Orozco, personal communication, June 8, 2015.

10. Roger Rouse, "Mexican Migration and the Social Space of Postmodernism," in *Diaspora* 1, no. 1 (1991): 13.

11. Leisy J. Abrego, *Sacrificing Families: Navigating Laws, Labor, and Love Across Borders* (Redwood City, CA: Stanford University Press, 2014), 23.

12. "The distance that separates us provides for us and takes away from us. It provides us with the means to arrive at and find ourselves in a place where it is easier to find a job. [This job] may be troublesome, [but] it pays better than in Mexico. It takes away from us because it deprives us of communication that is timely" (October 25, 1951 in chapter 4). Joanna Dreby, *Divided by Borders: Mexican Migrants and their Children* (Berkeley: University of California Press, 2010); Rosas *Abrazando el Espíritu*; Jennifer Cole and Deborah Lynn Durham, *Generations and Globalization: Youth, Age, and Family in the New World Economy* (Bloomington: University of Indiana Press, 2007).

13. Rosas, *Abrazando el Espíritu*, 7–8.

14. "We called for workers, and there came human beings." Quoted by Calavita, *Inside the State*, 6.

15. In a very real way, the history of immigration from Mexico to the United States since the end of the nineteenth century is one long playing out of a seemingly interminable oscillation between state-sponsored programs that bring Mexican workers to fill gaps in the American labor force and social, political reactions that expel them when it becomes evident that they are human beings with physical, social, and emotional needs. Hence the contract labor system of the 1910s and 1920s begat Repatriation in the 1930s, which begat the Bracero program in the 1950s, which begat Operation Wetback in the 1950s, which begat the Border Industrialization Program in the 1960s, and so on. This history is ably covered in Henderson, *Beyond Borders*.

16. Zaragosa Vargas presents a good overview of these struggles in his book *Crucible of Struggle: A History of Mexican Americans from Colonial Times to the Present Era.* (New York: Oxford University Press, 2010).

BIBLIOGRAPHY

Abascal, Salvador. *Mis recuerdos, sinarquismo y Colonia María Auxiliadora (1935–1944): con importantes documentos de los Archivos Nacionales de Washington.* Mexico City: Tradición, 1980.

Abrego, Leisy J. *Sacrificing Families: Navigating Laws, Labor, and Love Across Borders.* Redwood City, CA: Stanford University Press, 2014.

Achim, Miruna, and Martina Will de Chapparo. "From the Here to the Hereafter: An Introduction to Death and Dying." In *Death and Dying in Colonial Spanish America,* edited by Miruna Achim and Martina Will de Chaparro, 1–27. Tucson: University of Arizona Press, 2011.

Aguilar Camín, Héctor, and Lorenzo Meyer. *In the Shadow of the Mexican Revolution: Contemporary Mexican History, 1910–1989.* Translated by Luis Alberto Fierro. Austin: University of Texas Press, 1993.

Alcalá Barba, Francisco. *Sedentaricación en la Zona de los Altos de Jalisco.* Tepatitlán, Jalisco: Consejo de Cronistas de Tepatitlán de Morelos, 1995.

Alcalá, Concepción. *El Diario de Concepción Alcalá: Recogidos Durante La Persecución Religiosa de 1926 a 1929.* n.d.

Alegre, Robert. "Las Rieleras: Gender Politics, and Power in the Mexican Railway Movement, 1958–1959." *Journal of Women's History* 23, no. 2 (2011): 162–186.

Altman, Janet Gurkin. *Epistolarity: Approaches to a Form.* Columbus: Ohio State University Press, 1982.

Amador, Consuelo Díaz. "Los Altos de Jalisco: Transformación de una Región (1940–1980)." In *Política y región: Los Altos de Jalisco,* edited by Jorge Alonso and Juan García de Quevedo, 35–70. Mexico City: Centro de Investigaciones y Estudios Superiores en Antropología Social, 1990.

Anderson, Benedict. *Imagined Communities: Reflections on the Origin and Spread of Nationalism.* London: Verso, 1990.

Anderson, Danny J. "Introduction: The Ghosts of Comala: Haunted Meaning in *Pedro Páramo.*" In *Pedro Páramo by Juan Rulfo,* translated by Margaret Sayers Peden, 7–11. Austin: University of Texas Press, 2002.

Arias, Patricia, and Jorge Durand. "Estudios pioneros de la migración jalisciense." In *Paul S. Taylor y la migración jalisciense a Estados Unidos,* edited by Patricia Arias and Jorge Durand, 13–34. Tepatitlán, Jalisco: Universidad de Guadalajara, Centro Universitario de los Altos, 2013.

Ariès, Philippe. *The Hour of Our Death.* Translated by Helen Weaver. New York: Knopf, 1981.

Azuela de la Cueva, Alicia. "Peace by Revolution: Una Aproximación Léxio-Visual al México Revolucionario." *Historía Mexicana* 56, no. 4 (2007): 1263–1307.

Backal, Alicia Gojman de, and Laura Edith Bonilla. *Historia del correo en México*. Mexico City: Miguel Angel Porrúa, 2000.

Bailey, David C. *Viva Cristo Rey! The Cristero Rebellion and the Church–State Conflict in Mexico*. Austin: University of Texas Press, 1974.

Baily, Samuel L., and Franco Ramella, eds. *One Family, Two Worlds: An Italian Family's Correspondence Across the Atlantic, 1901–1922*. Translated by John Lenaghan. New Brunswick, NJ: Rutgers University Press, 1988.

Bantjes, Adrian. "Religion and the Mexican Revolution: Toward a New Historiography." In *Religious Culture in Modern Mexico*, edited by Martin Austin Nesvig, 223–254. Lanham, MD: Rowman and Littlefield, 2007.

Bantjes, Adrian. "Burning Saints, Molding Minds: Iconoclasm, Civic Ritual, and the Failed Cultural Revolution." In *Rituals of Rules, Rituals of Resistance: Public Celebrations and Popular Culture in Mexico*, edited by William H. Beezley, Cheryl English Martin, and William E. French, 261–284. Willmington, DE: Scholarly Resources Inc., 1999.

Bantjes, Adrian A. "Saints, Sinners, and State-Formation: Local Religion and Cultural Revolution in Mexico." In *The Eagle and the Virgin: Nation and Cultural Revolution in Mexico, 1920–1940*, edited by Mary K. Vaughan and Stephen E. Lewis, 137–156. Durham, NC: Duke University Press, 2006.

Bantjes, Adrian A. "Idolatry and Iconoclasm in Revolutionary Mexico: The De-Christianization Campaigns, 1929–1940." *Mexican Studies-estudios Mexicanos* 13, no. 1 (1997): 87–102.

Barthes, Roland. "The World of Wrestling." In *Mythologies*, translated by Annette Lavers, 15–26. New York: The Noonday Press, 1992)

Beals, Carleton, and illustrator Diego Rivera. *Mexican Maze*. Philadelphia: J. B. Lippincott, 1931.

Begall, Sabine, Julia Neef, Oldrich Vojtech, and Hynek Burda. "Magnetic Alignment in Grazing and Resting Cattle and Deer." *Proceedings of The National Academy of Sciences* 105, no. 36 (2008): 13451–13455. doi:10.1073/pnas.0803650105.

Behar, Ruth. "The Struggle for the Church: Popular Anticlericalism and Religiosity in Post-Franco Spain." In *Religious Orthodoxy and Popular Faith in European Society*, ed. Ellen Badone, 76–112. Princeton, NJ: Princeton University Press, 1990.

Benjamin, Thomas. *La Revolución: Mexico's Great Revolution As Memory, Myth and History*. Austin: University of Texas Press, 2000.

Berger, John. "Some Notes on Song: The Rhythms of Listening." *Harper's Magazine*, February 2015.

Bergson, Henri. *Laughter: An Essay on the Meaning of the Comic*. Translated by Cloudesley Shovell Henry Brereton and Fred Rothwell. København: Green Integer, 1999.

Berliner, Issac. *The City of Palace*. Philadelphia: Jacoby Press, 1966.

Blancarte, Roberto. "Intransigence, Anticommunism, and Reconciliation: Church/State Relations in Transition." In *Dictablanda: Politics, Work, and Culture in Mexico, 1938–1968*, edited by Paul Gillingham and Benjamin T. Smith, 70–88. Durham, NC: Duke University Press, 2014.

Booth, George C. *Mexico's School-Made Society*. Redwood City, CA: Stanford University Press, 1941.

Bortz, Jeffrey, and Marcos Aguilar. "Earning a Living: A History of Real Wages Studies in Twentieth Century Mexico." *Latin American Research Review* 41, no. 2 (2006): 112–138.

Boylan, Kristina A. "Gendering the Faith and Altering the Nation: Mexican Catholic Women's Activism, 1917–1940." In *Sex in Revolution: Gender, Politics, and Power in Modern Mexico*, edited by Jocelyn Olcott and Mary K. Vaughan, 199–222. Durham, NC: Duke University Press, 2006.

Brading, David. *The First America*. Cambridge: Cambridge University Press, 1993.

Breckenridge, Keith. "Reasons for Writing: African Working Class Letter-Writing in Early Twentieth-Century South Africa." In *Africa's Hidden Histories: Everyday Literacy and Making the Self*, edited by Karin Barber, 143–154. Bloomington: Indiana University Press, 2006.

Brodman, Barbara. *The Mexican Cult of Death in Myth, Art and Literature*. Bloomington, IN: iUniverse, 2011.

Butler, Mathew. "Revolution and the Ritual Year: Religious Conflict and Innovation in Cristero Mexico." *Journal of Latin American Studies* 38, no. 3 (2006): 565–490.

Butler, Matthew. *Popular Piety and Political Identity in Mexico's Cristero Rebellion: Michoacán, 1927–29*. Oxford: Oxford University Press, 2004.

Butler, Matthew. "Introduction: A Revolution in Spirit? Mexico, 1910–40." In *Faith and Impiety in Revolutionary Mexico*, edited by Matthew Butler, 1–20. New York: Palgrave Macmillan, 2007.

Calavita, Kitty. *Inside the State: The Bracero Program, Immigration, and the I.N.S.* New York: Routledge, 1992.

Campbell, Hugh Gerald. "The Radical Right in Mexico, 1929–1949." PhD diss., University of Califorina, Los Angeles, 1968.

Ceballos Ramírez, Manuel. *El catolicismo social: un tercero en discordia : Rerum novarum, la "cuestión social" y la movilización de los católicos mexicanos, 1891–1911*. Mexico City: El Colegio de México, 1991.

Cervantes, Fernando. "Mexico's 'Ritual Consent': Religion and Liberty from Colony to Post-Revolution." In *Faith and Impiety in Revolutionary Mexico*, edited by Matthew Butler, 57–74. New York: Palgrave Macmillan, 2007.

Chase, Stuart. *Mexico: A Study of Two Americas*. New York: MacMillan, 1932.

Christian, Jr., William A. *Local Religion in Sixteenth-Century Spain*. Princeton, NJ: Princeton University Press, 1981.

Clark, Christopher. "The 'New Catholicism' and the European Culture Wars." In *Culture Wars Secular–Catholic Conflict in Nineteenth-Cen-tury Europe*, eds. Wolfram Kaiser and Christopher M. Clark, 11–46. Cambridge: Cambridge University Press, 2003.

Cohen, Deborah. *Braceros: Migrant Citizens and Transnational Subjects in the Postwar United States and Mexico*. Chapel Hill: University of North Carolina Press, 2011.

Cole, Jennifer, and Deborah Lynn Durham. *Generations and Globalization: Youth, Age, and Family in the New World Economy*. Bloomington: Indiana University Press, 2007.

Comaroff, Jean, and John L. Comaroff. *Of Revelation and Revolution: Christianity, Colonialism, and Consciousness in South Africa 1 1*. Chicago: University of Chicago Press, 1991.

Comaroff, John L. "Images of Empire, Contests of Conscience: Models Colonial Domination in South Africa." *American Ethnologist* 16, no. 4 (1989): 661–685.

Comite Nacional de la Union Nacional Sinarquista. *Historia gráfica del sinarquismo*. Unión Nacional Sinarquista Comité Nacional, n.d.

Cosío-Villegas, Daniel. "Mexico's Crisis." In *American Extremes: (Extremos De América)*, translated by Américo Paredes, 3–27. Austin: University of Texas Press, 1964.

Craig, Ann L. *The First Agraristas: An Oral History of a Mexican Agrarian Reform Movement*. Berkeley: University of California Press, 1983.

Cross, Harry E., and James A. Sandos. *Across the Border: Rural Development in Mexico and Recent Migration to the United States*. Berkeley: Institute of Governmental Studies, University of California, Berkeley, 1981.

Cutileiro, José. *A Portuguese Rural Society*. Oxford: Clarendon Press, 1971.

Dauphin, Cécile. "Letter-Writing Manuals in the Nineteenth Century." In *Correspondence: Models of Letter-Writing from the Middle Ages to the Nineteenth Century*, edited by Roger Chartier, Alain Boureau, and Cécile Dauphin, translated by Christopher Woodall, 112–157. Princeton, NJ: Princeton University Press, 1997.

Davis, Olive, and Sylvia Sun Minnick. *Stockton: Sunrise Port on the San Joaquin*. Woodland Hills, CA: Windsor Publications, 1984.

Decker, William Merrill. *Epistolary Practices Letter Writing in America Before Telecommunications*. Chapel Hill: University of North Carolina Press, 1998.

Delpar, Helen. *The Enormous Vogue of Things Mexican Cultural Relations between the United States and Mexico, 1920–1935*. Tuscaloosa: University of Alabama Press, 1992.

Delpar, Helen. "Frank Tannenbaum: The Making of a Mexicanist, 1914–1933." *The Americas* 45, no. 2 (1988): 153–171.

Dormady, Jason. *Primitive Revolution: Restorationist Religion and the Idea of the Mexican Revolution, 1940–1968*. Albuquerque: University of New Mexico Press, 2011.

Douglas, Mary. *Purity and Danger: An Analysis of the Concepts of Pollution and Taboo*. New York: Routledge, 2002.

Dreby, Joanna. *Divided by Borders: Mexican Migrants and Their Children*. Berkeley: University of California Press, 2010.

Díaz Román Rodríguez, José. *El movimiento cristero: Sociedad y conflicto en los Altos de Jalisco*. Mexico City: Editorial Nueva Imagen CIS-INAH, 1979.

Earle, Rebecca. "Introduction: Letters, Writers and the Historian." In *Epistolary Selves: Letters and Letter-Writers, 1600–1945*, edited by Rebbecca Earle, 1–12. Aldershot: Ashgate, 1999.

Eire, Carlos M. N. *From Madrid to Purgatory: The Art and Craft of Dying in Sixteenth-Century Spain*. Cambridge: Cambridge University Press, 1995.

Elias, Norbert. *The Loneliness of the Dying*. Translated by Edmund Jephcott. New York: Continuum, 2001.

Fábregas Puig, Andrés. *La formación histórica de una región: los Altos de Jalisco*. Mexico City: Centro de Investigaciones y Estudios Superiores en Antropología Social, 1986.

Fitzgerald, David. *A Nation of Emigrants How Mexico Manages Its Migration*. Berkeley: University of California Press, 2009.

Fitzpatrick, David. *Oceans of Consolation: Personal Accounts of Irish Migration to Australia*. Ithaca, NY: Cornell University Press, 1994.

Fitzpatrick, David. "Irish Emigration and the Art of Letter-Writing." In *Letters Across Borders: The Epistolary Practices of International Migrants*, edited by Bruce S. Elliott, David A. Gerber, and Suzanne M. Sinke, 97–106. New York: Palgrave Macmillan, 2006.

Flores García, Juan. "Los braceros." In *Tepatitlán en el tiempo*. Tepatitlán, Jalisco: Juan Flores García, 1992.

Franco, Jean. *The Decline and Fall of the Lettered City Latin America in the Cold War*. Cambridge, MA: Harvard University Press, 2002.

French, William E. *The Heart in the Glass Jar: Love Letters, Bodies, and the Law in Mexico*. Lincoln: University of Nebraska Press, 2015.

French, William E. "'I Am Going to Write You a Letter': Coplas, Love Letters, and Courtship Literacy." In *Mexico in Verse: A History of Music, Rhyme, and Power*, edited by Stephen Neufeld and Michael Matthews, 145–180. Tucson: University of Arizona Press, 2015.

Gachuz-Mesa, Luis. "Women, Freedom, and God: The Cristero Rebellion and the Works of Women in Small Towns of Los Altos." *Berkeley McNair Research Journal* no. 10 (2002): 51–70.

Galarza, Ernesto. *Merchants of Labor: the Mexican Bracero Story*. Santa Barbara, CA.: McNally and Loftin, 1964.

Gerber, David A. *Authors of Their Lives: The Personal Correspondence of British Immigrants to North America in the Nineteenth Century*. New York: New York University Press, 2006.

Gerber, David A. "Forming a Transnational Narrative: New Perspectives on European Migrations to the United States." *The History Teacher* 35, no. 1 (2001): 61–78.

Gerber, David A., Kerby A. Miller, Arnold Schrier, Bruce D. Boling, and David Doyle. "What Is It We Seek to Find in First-Person Documents? Documenting Society and Cultural Practices in Irish Immigrant Writings." *Reviews in American History* 32, no. 3 (2004): 305–316.

Gibson, Charles. *The Aztecs Under Spanish Rule: A History of the Indians of the Valley of Mexico, 1519–1810*. Redwood City, CA: Stanford University Press, 1964.

Giddens, Anthony. *The Consequences of Modernity*. Redwood City, CA: Stanford University Press, 1990.

Gillingham, Paul, and Benjamin T. Smith, eds. *Dictablanda: Politics, Work, and Culture in Mexico, 1938–1968*. Durham, NC: Duke University Press, 2014.

Gilpin Faust, Drew. *This Republic of Suffering: Death and the American Civil War*. New York: Knopf, 2008.

Goldberg, Ann. "Reading and Writing across the Borders of Dictatorship: Self-Censorship and Emigrant Experience in Nazi and Stalinist Europe." In *Letters Across Borders The Epistolary Practices of International Migrants*, edited by Bruce S. Elliott, David A. Gerber, and Suzanne M. Sinke, 158–174. New York: Palgrave Macmillan, published in association with the Carleton Centre for the History of Migration, 2006.

Goody, Jack. *The Theft of History*. Cambridge: Cambridge University Press, 2006.

Gonzalez, Luis. *San José de Gracia: Mexican Village in Transition*. Translated by John Upton. Austin: University of Texas Press, 1982.

González Navarro, Moisés. *Cristeros y agraristas en Jalisco Vol. 2*. Mexico City: El Colegio de México, Centro de Estud. Históricos, 2001.

González Navarro, Moisés. *Cristeros y agraristas en Jalisco Vol. 3 Vol. 3*. Mexico City: El Colegio de México, Centro de Estud. Históricos, 2003.

Gordon, Avery F. *Ghostly Matters: Haunting and the Sociological Imagination*. Minneapolis: University of Minnesota Press, 1997.

Graziano, Frank. *The Millennial New World*. New York: Oxford University Press, 1999.

Grobet, Lourdes. *Lucha Libre: Masked Superstars of Mexican Wrestling*. New York: Distributed Art Publishers, 2005.

Guerra, Juan C. *Close to Home: Oral and Literate Practices in a Transnational Mexicano Community*. New York: Teachers College Press, 1998.

Guevara, Che. *Latin American Diaries: The Sequel to the Motorcycle Diaries*. Melbourne: Ocean Press, 2011.

Guillermo, Emil. "Barrio Chivo Readies for 20th Reunion." *Recordnet.com*, August 27, 2005. www.recordnet.com/article/20050827/ENT/50827004.

Gutiérrez Gutiérrez, José Antonio. *Los Altos de Jalisco: panorama histórico de una región y de su sociedad hasta 1821*. Mexico City: Consejo Nacional para la Cultura y las Artes, 1991.

Gutiérrez Gutiérrez, Jose Antonio. *Jalostitlán a través de los siglos*. Aguascalientes: Universidad Autonoma de Aguascalientes, 1985.

Gutmann, Matthew C. *The Meanings of Macho: Being a Man in Mexico City*. Berkeley: University of California Press, 1996.

Gándara Mendoza, Leticia. "La evolución de una oligarquía: El caso de San Miguel el Altos, Jalisco." In *Política y sociedad en México: El caso de Los Altos de Jalisco*, edited by Tomás Martinez Saldaña and Leticia Gándara Mendoza, 149–279. Mexico City: Centro de Investigaciones Superiores-Instituto Nacional de Antropolgía e Historia, 1976.

Habermas, Jürgen. *The Structural Transformation of the Public Sphere: An Inquiry Into a Category of Bourgeois Society*. Translated by Thomas Burger. Cambridge, MA: MIT Press, 1991.

Hanna, Martha. "A Republic of Letters: The Epistolary Tradition in France During World War I." *American Historical Review* 108, no. 5 (2003): 1338–1361.

Helbich, Wolfgang and Walter D. Kamphoefner. "How Representative are Emigrant Letters? An Exploration of the German Case." In *Letters Across Borders The Epistolary Practices of International Migrants*, edited by ed. Bruce S. Elliot, David A. Gerber, and Suzanne M. Sinke, 29–55. New York: Palgrave Macmillan, published in association with the Carleton Centre for the History of Migration, 2006.

Henderson, Timothy J. *Beyond Borders: A History of Mexican Migration to the United States*. Malden, MA: Wiley-Blackwell, 2011.

Henkin, David M. *The Postal Age The Emergence of Modern Communications in Nineteenth-Century America*. Chicago: University of Chicago Press, 2006.

Holmburg, Arthur. "Carlos Fuentes Turns to Theater." *New York Times*, June 9, 1982. www.nytimes.com/1982/06/06/theater/carlos-fuentes-turns-to-theater.html.

Iturriaga, José. "México y su crisis histórica." *Cuadernos Americanos*, May/June 1947, 21–27.

James, Daniel. *Doña María's Story: Life History, Memory, and Political Identity*. Durham, NC: Duke University Press, 2000.

Jesus, Carolina Maria de. *Child of the Dark: The Diary of Carolina Maria De Jesus*. trans. David St. Clair. New York: E. P. Dutton, 1962.

Joseph, Gilbert M., and Jürgen Buchenau. *Mexico's Once and Future Revolution: Social Upheaval and the Challenge of Rule Since the Late Nineteenth Century*. Durham, NC: Duke University Press, 2013.

Joseph, Gilbert M., Anne Rubenstein, and Eric Zolov. *Fragments of a Golden Age: The Politics of Culture in Mexico Since 1940*. Durham, NC: Duke University Press, 2001.

Kafka, Franz. *Letters to Milena*. New York: Schoken Books, 1990.

Kaplan, Temma. "Final Reflections: Gender, Chaos, and Authority in Revolutionary Times." In *Sex in Revolution: Gender, Politics, and Power in Modern Mexico*, edited by Jocelyn Olcott, Mary K. Vaughan, and Gabriela Cano, 261–276. Durham, NC: Duke University Press, 2006.

Knight, Alan. "The Mentality and Modus Operandi of Revolutionary Anticlericalism." In *Faith and Impiety in Revolutionary Mexico*, edited by Matthew Butler, 21–56. New York: Palgrave Macmillan, 2007.

Knight, Alan. "Superstition in Mexico: From Colonial Church to Secular State." *Past & Present* 199, no. 3 (2008): 229–270.

Kondor, Fr. Louis, ed. *Fátima in Lucia's own Words: Sister Lucia's Memoirs*. Fátima, Portugal: Secretariado dos Pastorinhos, 2007.

Krauze, Enrique. *Mexico: Biography of Power: A History of Modern Mexico, 1810–1996*. Translated by Hank Heifetz. New York: HarperCollins, 1997.

Leonardo, Patricia de. "El impacto del mercado en diferentes unidades de producción Municipio de Jalostitlán, Jalisico." In *Economía y sociedad en los Altos de Jalisco*, edited by Patricia de Leonardo and Jaime Leonardo Espín Díaz, NEED. Mexico City: Centro de Investigaciones Superiores del Instituto Nacional de Antropología e Historia, 1978.

Leonardo, Patricia de, and Jaime Leonardo Espín Díaz. *Economía y sociedad en los Altos de Jalisco*. Mexcio: Centro de Investigaciones Superiores del Instituto Nacional de Antropología e Historia, 1978.

Lerner, Victoria. *La educación socialista*. Mexico City: Colegio de México, 1979.

Levi, Heather. *The World of Lucha Libre: Secrets, Revelations, and Mexican National Identity*. Durham, NC: Duke University Press, 2008.

Levine, Robert M., and José Carlos Sebe Bom Meihy. *The Life and Death of Carolina Maria De Jesus*. Albuquerque: University of New Mexico Press, 1995.

Levine, Robert M. "The Cautionary Tale of Carolina Maria de Jesus." *Latin American Research Review* 29, no. 1 (1994): 55–83.

Lewis, Oscar, and Alberto Beltrán. *Life in a Mexican Village: Tepoztlán Restudied*. Urbana: University of Illinois Press, 1951.

Lockhart, James. *The Nahuas After the Conquest: A Social and Cultural History of the Indians of Central Mexico, Sixteenth Through Eighteenth Centuries*. Redwood City, CA: Stanford University Press, 1992.

Lomnitz-Adler, Claudio. *Death and the Idea of Mexico*. Brooklyn, NY: Zone Books, 2005.

López-Portillo y Weber, José. *La Conquista de la Nueva Galicia*. Mexico City: Talleres gráficos de la nación, 1935.

Lyons, Martyn. "Love Letters and Writing Practices: On Écritures intimes in the Nineteenth Century." *Journal of Family History* 24, no. 2 (1999): 232–239.

Lystra, Karen. *Searching the Heart: Women, Men, and Romantic Love in Nineteenth-Century America*. New York: Oxford University Press, 1989.

Mabalon, Dawn Bohulano. *Little Manila Is in the Heart: The Making of the Filipina/ o American Community in Stockton, California*. Durham, NC: Duke University Press 2013.

Martin, Philip. "There Is Nothing More Permanent Than Temporary Foreign Workers." *Backgrounder, Center for Immigration Studies*, April 2001. www.cis.org/sites/cis.org/files/articles/2001/back501.pdf.

McCaa, Robert. "The Peopling of Mexico from Origins to Revolution." In *A Population History of North America*, edited by Michael R. Haines and Richard H. Steckel, 241–304. Cambridge: Cambridge University Press, 2000.

McWilliams, Carey. *Factories in the Field: The Story of Migratory Farm Labor in California*. Boston: Little, Brown, 1939.

Medina de la Torre, Francisco. "Apuntes geográficos, estadísticos e historicos del municipio de San Miguel el Alto:Estado de Jalisco, México." In *Estadísticas de Los Altos de Jalisco (1838–1908)*, edited by Mária Gracia Castillo and Jaime Olveda, NEED. Guadalajara: Gobierno de Jalisco, Secretaría General, Unidad Editorial, 1988.

Medina de la Torre, Francisco, and Luis Medina Ascensio. *San Miguel el Alto, Jalisco: biografía de un municipio*. Mexico City: Editorial Jus, 1967.

Menand, Louis. "Woke Up This Morning: Why Do We Read Diaries?" *The New Yorker*, December 10, 2007.

Metz, Christian. "Photography and Fetish." *October* 34, no. 3 (1985): 81–90.

Meyer, Jean A. *El sinarquismo: un fascismo mexicano? 1937–1947*. Mexico City: Editorial J. Mortiz, 1979.

Meyer, Jean A. *La Cristiada: Los Cristeros, vol. 3*. Mexico City: Siglo XXI Editores, 1993.

Meyer, Jean A. *The Cristero Rebellion: The Mexican People Between Church and State, 1926–1929*. Translated by Richard Southern. Cambridge: Cambridge University Press, 1976.

Meyer, Jean. *El Sinarquismo, el cardenismo y la iglesia, 1934–1947*. Mexico City: Tusquets Editores, 2003.

Meyer, Jean. *La Cristiada. 1,*. Mexico City: Siglo Vientiuno, 1990.

Meyer, Jean. "Perspectivas de análisis sociohistórico de la influencia de Guadalajara sobre su región." In *Regiones y ciudades en América Latina*, edited by Jean Piel et al., 148–168. Mexico City: Sepsetentas, 1973.

Meyer, Jean. "An Idea of Mexico: Catholics in the Revolution." In *The Eagle and the Virgin: Nation and Cultural Revolution in Mexico, 1920–1940*, edited by Mary K. Vaughan and Stephen E. Lewis, 281–296. Durham, NC: Duke University Press, 2006.

Meyer, Lorenzo. *Mexico and the United States in the Oil Controversy, 1917–1942*. Translated by Muriel Vasconcellos. Austin: University of Texas Press, 1977.

Michaels, Albert. "Fascism and Sinarquismo: Popular Nationalisms against the Mexican Revolution." *Journal of Church and State* 8 (Winter 1966): 234–250.

Monsiváis, Carlos. "Yes, Nor Do the Dead Speak, Unfortunately: Juan Rulfo." In *Mexican Postcards*, translated by John Kraniauskas, 57–70. London: Verso, 2000.

Monsiváis, Carlos. *El género epistolar: Un homenaje a manera de carta abierta*. Mexico City: Miguel Angel Porrúa, 1991.

Monsiváis, Carlos. "Forward: When Gender Can't Be Seen Amid the Symbols: Women and the Mexican Revolution." In *Sex in Revolution: Gender, Politics, and Power in Modern Mexico*, edited by Jocelyn Olcott, Mary K. Vaughan, and Gabriela Cano, 1–20. Durham, NC: Duke University Press, 2006.

Moreno, Julio. *Yankee Don't Go Home! Mexican Nationalism, American Business Culture, and the Shaping of Modern Mexico, 1920–1950*. Chapel Hill: University of North Carolina Press, 2003.

Mota Padilla, Matías Angel de la. *Historia del reino de Nueva Galicia en la América septentrional*. Guadalajara: Instituto Nacional de Antropología e Historia, Universidad de Guadalajara, 1973.

Mraz, John and Jaime Vélez Storey. *Uprooted: Braceros in the Hermano Mayo Lens*. Houston: Arté Publico Press, 1996.

Mullin, Molly H. "The Patronage of Difference: Making Indian Art 'Art, Not Ethnology.'" *Cultural Anthropology* 7, no. 4 (1992): 395–424.

Myerhoff, Barbara. *Number Our Days*. New York: Dutton, 1978.

Myerhoff, Barbara. "Life History among the Elderly: Performance, Visibility, and Remembering." In *Remembered Lives: The Work of Ritual, Storytelling, and Growing Older*, ed. Marc Kaminsky, 231–247. Ann Arbor: University of Michigan Press, 1992.

Newcomer, Daniel. *Reconciling Modernity Urban State Formation in 1940s León, Mexico*. Lincoln: University of Nebraska, 2004.

Ngai, Mae M. *Impossible Subjects: Illegal Aliens and the Making of Modern America*. Princeton, NJ: Princeton University Press, 2004.

Niblo, Stephen R. *Mexico in the 1940s: Modernity, Politics, and Corruption*. Wilmington, DE: Scholarly Resources, 1999.

Norenzayan, Ara. *Big Gods: How Religion Transformed Cooperation and Conflict.* Princeton, NJ: Princeton University Press, 2013.

Ong, Walter J. *Orality and Literacy: The Technologizing of the Word.* London: Methuen, 1982.

Orotoll, Servando. "Las Legiones, La Base y el Sinarquismo, tres organizaciones distintas y un sólo fin verdadero? (1929–1948)." In *La Política y el cielo: movimientos religiosos en el México contemporáneo,* edited by Luis Rodolfo Morán Quiroz, 73–118. Guadalajara: Editorial Universidad de Guadalajara, 1990.

Orozco, José. *"Esos Altos De Jalisco!:* Emigration and the Idea of Alteño Exceptionalism, 1926–1952". Phd. diss., Harvard University, 1998.

Ortega Martín, José de Jesús. *San Miguel el Alto, Jalisco: Día, a día en la Revolución (1908–1918).* San Miguel el Alto, Jalisco, 2010.

Parry, J. H. *The Spanish Theory of Empire in the Sixteenth Century.* New York: Octagon Books, 1974.

Paz, Octavio, and Rachel Phillips Belash. "The Day of the Dead." In *The Labyrinth of Solitude,* translated by Lynsander Kemp and Yara Milos, 47–64. New York: Grove Press, 1985.

Paz, Octavio. "El poeta Buñuel." *Nuevo Cine,* no. 4–5 (1961): 46–48.

Philbrick, Nathaniel. *Why Read Moby-Dick?* New York: Viking, 2011.

Pinkard, Terry P. *Hegel: A Biography.* Cambridge: Cambridge University Press, 2000.

Poniatowska, Elena. *Massacre in Mexico.* Translated by Helen R. Lane. Columbia: University of Missouri Press, 1991.

Poniatowska, Elena, and David Dorado Romo. *Las Soldaderas: Women of the Mexican Revolution.* El Paso: Cinco Puntos Press, 2006.

Pozas, Ricardo. *Juan Pérez Jolote: biografía de un tzotzil.* Mexico City: Fondo de Cultura Económica, 1952.

Purnell, Jennie. *Popular Movements and State Formation in Revolutionary Mexico: The Agraristas and Cristeros of Michoacán.* Durham, NC: Duke University Press, 1999.

Pursell Jr., Carroll W. "Government and Technology in the Great Depression." *Technology and Culture* 20, no. 1 (1979): 162–174.

Pérez Rosales, Laura. "Las mujeres sinarquistas: Nuevas adelitas el la vida política mexicana, (1945–1948)." In *Religión, política y sociedad: el sinarquismo y la iglesia en México : nueve ensayos,* edited by Rubén Aguilar V. and Guillermo Zermeño P., 169–193. MexicoCity: Universidad Iberoamericana, 1992.

Rama, Angel. *The Lettered City.* Translated by John Charles Chasteen. Durham, NC: Duke University Press, 1996.

Revueltas, José. *Human Mourning.* Translated by Roberto Crespi. Minneapolis: University of Minnesota Press, 1990.

Richards, Eric. "The Limits of the Australian Emigrant Letter." In *Letters Across Borders The Epistolary Practices of International Migrants,* edited by Bruce S. Elliott, David A. Gerber, and Suzanne M. Sinke, 56–74. New York: Palgrave Macmillan, published in association with the Carleton Centre for the History of Migration, 2006.

Riegelhaupt, Joyce. "Popular Anti-Clericalism and Religiosity in pre-1974 Portugal." In *Religion, Power, and Protest in Local Communities: The Northern Shore of the Mediterranean,* edited by Eric R. Wolf, 93–116. Berlin: Mouton, 1984.

Robe, Stanley Linn. *Mexican Tales and Legends from Los Altos.* Berkeley: University of California Press, 1970.

Robe, Stanley Linn, and Mariano Azuela. *Azuela and the Mexican Underdogs.* Berkeley: University of California Press, 1979.

Rodríguez, Jeanette. "Guadalupe: The Feminine Face of God." In *Goddess of the Americas: La Diosa De Las Américas : Writings on the Virgin of Guadalupe*, edited by Ana Castillo, 25–31. New York: Riverhead Books, 1996.

Román, Reinaldo, and Pamela Voekel. "Popular Religion in Latin American Historiography." In *The Oxford Handbook of Latin American History*, edited by Jose C. Moya, 254–287. New York: Oxford University Press, 2011.

Rosas, Ana Elizabeth. *Abrazando El Espíritu: Bracero Families Confront the US–Mexico Border*. Berkeley: University of California Press, 2014.

Ross, Stanley R. *Is the Mexican Revolution Dead?* , 2nd ed. Philadelphia: Temple University Press, 1975.

Rouse, Roger. "Mexican Migration and the Social Space of Postmodernism." *Diaspora* 1, no. 1 (1991): 8–23.

Ruíz, Vicki. *Cannery Women, Cannery Lives Mexican Women, Unionization, and the California Food Processing Industry, 1930–1950*. Albuquerque.: University of New Mexico Press, 1987.

Rulfo, Juan. *Pedro Páramo*. Translated by Margaret Sayers Peden. New York: Grove Press, 1994.

Salomon, Frank, and Mercedes Niño-Murcia. *The Lettered Mountain: A Peruvian Village's Way with Writing*. Durham, NC: Duke University Press, 2011.

Sandos, James A., and Harry E. Cross. "National Development and International Labour Migration: Mexico 1940–1965." *Journal of Contemporary History* 18, no. 1 (1983): 43–60.

Sánchez, George J. *Becoming Mexican American: Ethnicity, Culture, and Identity in Chicano Los Angeles, 1900–1945*. New York: Oxford University Press, 1993.

Schell, Patience A. "Of the Sublime Mission of Mothers of Families: The Union of Mexican Catholic Ladies in Revolutionary Mexico." In *The Women's Revolution in Mexico, 1910–1953*, edited by Stephanie Mitchell and Patience A. Schell, 187–203. Lanham, MD: Rowman and Littlefield, 2007.

Schell, Patience A. *Church and State Education in Revolutionary Mexico City*. Tucson: University of Arizona Press, 2003.

Scheper-Hughes, Nancy. *Death Without Weeping The Violence of Everyday Life in Brazil*. Berkeley: University of California Press, 1993.

Scheper-Hughes, Nancy, and Margaret M. Lock. "The Mindful Body: A Prolegomenon to Future Work in Medical Anthropology." *Medical Anthropology Quarterly* 1, no. 1 (1987): 6–41.

Schmidt Camacho, Alicia R. *Migrant Imaginaries: Latino Cultural Politics in the U.S.– Mexico Borderlands*. New York: New York University Press, 2008.

Schryer, Frans J. *The Rancheros of Pisaflores: The History of a Peasant Bourgeoisie in Twentieth-Century Mexico*. Toronto: University of Toronto Press, 1980.

Sennett, Richard, and Jonathan Cobb. *The Hidden Injuries of Class*. New York: Vintage Books, 1972.

Serrano Alvarez, Pablo. *La batalla del espíritu : el movimiento sinarquista en el Bajío (1932–1951)*, vol. 1. Mexico City: Consejo Nacional para la Cultura y las Artes, 1992.

Serrano Alvarez, Pablo. *La batalla del espíritu: el movimiento sinarquista en el Bajío (1932–1951)*, vol. 2. Mexico City: Consejo Nacional para la Cultura y las Artes, 1992.

Serrano Álvarez, Pablo. "El ritual de un sacerdote sinarquista: Salvador Abascal." In *A dios lo que es de dios*, edited by Carlos Martínez Assad, NEED. Mexico City: Aguilar, Nuevo Siglo, 1994.

Serrera Contreras, Ramón María. *Guadalajara ganadera: estudio regional novohispano, 1760–1805*. Guadalajara, Jalisco: Consejo Consultivo para las Artes y la Cultura de Guadalajara, 1991.

Sherman, John. "The Mexican 'Miracle' and its Collapse." In *The Oxford History of Mexico*, edited by Michael C. Meyer and William H. Beezley, 537–568. New York: Oxford University Press, 2000.

Siems, Larry. *Between the Lines: Letters Between Undocumented Mexican and Central American Immigrants and Their Families and Friends*. Tucson: University of Arizona Press, 1992.

Silva-Hertzog, Jesús. "La Revolución mexicana es ya un hecho históríco." *Cuadernos Americanos*, September/October 1949, 7–16.

Snodgrass, Michael. "Patronage and Progress: The Bracero Program from the Perspective of Mexico." In *Workers Across the Americas: The Transnational Turn in Labor History*, edited by Leon Fink, 245–266. New York: Oxford University Press, 2011.

Steinbeck, John, and José Clemente Orozco. *The Pearl*. New York: Viking Press, 1947.

Taibo II, Paco Ignacio. *'68*. Translated by Donald Nicholson-Smith. New York: Seven Stories Press, 2004.

Tannenbaum, Frank, and Miguel Covarrubias. *Peace by Revolution; An Interpretation of Mexico*. New York: Columbia University Press, 1933.

Taylor, Paul S. *A Spanish-Mexican Peasant Community; Arandas in Jalisco, Mexico*. Berkeley: University of California Press, 1933.

Taylor, William B. *Magistrates of the Sacred: Priests and Parishioners in Eighteenth-Century Mexico*. Redwood City, CA: Stanford University Press, 1996.

Tenorio-Trillo, Mauricio. *I Speak of the City: Mexico City at the Turn of the Twentieth Century*. Chicago: University of Chicago Press, 2012.

Tenorio-Trillo, Mauricio. "Viejos gringos: radicales norteamericanos en los años trienta y su vision de México." *Secuencias, Revista de Historía y Ciencias Sociales*, no. 21 (1990): 95–116.

Thomas, William Isaac, and Florian Znaniecki. *The Polish Peasant in Europe and America: A Classic Work in Immigration History*. Edited by Eli Zaretsky. Urbana: University of Illinois Press, 1996.

Toor, Frances, Carlos Mérida, and Luis Márquez. *A Treasury of Mexican Folkways: The Customs, Myths, Folklore, Traditions, Beliefs, Fiestas, Dances, and Songs of the Mexican People*. New York: Crown Publishers, 1947.

Tuck, Jim. *The Holy War in Los Altos: A Regional Analysis of Mexico's Cristero Rebellion*. Tucson: University of Arizona Press, 1982.

Tutino, John. *From Insurrection to Revolution in Mexico: Social Bases of Agrarian Violence, 1750–1940*. Princeton, NJ: Princeton University Press, 1986.

Vanderwood, Paul J. *The Power of God Against the Guns of Government: Religious Upheaval in Mexico at the Turn of the Nineteenth Century*. Redwood City, CA: Stanford University Press, 1998.

Vanderwood, Paul J. "Religion: Official, Popular, and Otherwise." *Mexican Studies/Estudios Mexicanos* 16, no. 2 (2000): 411–441.

Vargas y Campos, Gloria R. "El problema del bracero mexicano." Tesis (licenciatura en economía), Universidad Nacional Autónoma de México, 1964.

Vargas, Miguel Angel. "Epistolary Communication between Migrant Workers and their Families." In *Letters Across Borders The Epistolary Practices of International Migrants*, edited by Bruce S. Elliott, David A. Gerber, and Suzanne M. Sinke, 124–140. New York: Palgrave Macmillan, 2006.

Vargas, Zaragosa. *Crucible of Struggle: A History of Mexican Americans from Colonial Times to the Present Era*. New York: Oxford University Press, 2010.

Vasconcelos, José. *La flama; los de arriba en la revolución, historia y tragedia*. Mexico City: Compañía Editorial Continental, 1959.

Vasconcelos, José. *La raza cosmica: mision de la raza Iberoamericana, Argentina y Brasil*. Mexico City: Espasa-Calpe, 1966.

Vaughan, Mary Kay. "Primary Education and Literacy in Nineteenth-Century Mexico: Research Trends, 1968–1988." *Latin American Research Review* 25, no. 1 (1990): 31–66.

Vincent, Mary. *Catholicism in the Second Spanish Republic: Religion and Politics in Salamanca, 1930–1936*. Oxford: Clarendon Press, 1996.

Viqueria, Juan Pedro. "El sentimiento de la muerte en el México ilustrado del siglo XVIII a través de dos textos de la época." *Relaciones* 2, no. 5 (1981): 27–62.

Voekel, Pamela. *Alone Before God: The Religious Origins of Modernity in Mexico*. Durham, NC: Duke University Press, 2002.

Voekel, Pamela, Bethany Moreton, and Michael Jo. "Vaya Con Dios: Religion and the Transnational History of the Americas." *History Compass* 5, no. 5 (2007): 1604–1639.

Weart, Spencer R. *Nuclear Fear: A History of Images*. Cambridge, MA: Harvard Universtiy Press, 1988.

Whetten, Nathan L. *Rural Mexico*. Chicago: University of Chicago Press, 1948.

Williams, David J. "Sinarquismo in Mexico and the Southwest." Master's thesis, Texas Christian University. 1950.

Winnie, William W. *La movilidada demográfica y sus incidencia en una region de fuerte emigración*. Guadalajara, Jalisco: Universidad de Guadalajara, 1984.

Wolf, Eric R. *Europe and the People Without History*. Berkeley: University of California Press, 1982.

Yankelevich, Pablo. *La educación socialista en Jalisco*. Guadalajara: Ediciones del D.E.P., 1985.

Yañez, Agustín. *Yahualica*. Mexico City: n.p., 1946.

INDEX

Page numbers in italics indicate photographs. Page numbers followed by f indicate illustrations.

from materialism, 99–100
of Moreno, Chilo, 197
in old age, 179–80
of Rivera, Pancha, 73, 186
survival, 108, 139–141

technology, 64
of postal service, 49, 50
Ten Norms of Conduct for Sinarquistas, 26, 31, 222n45
Tostado, Lupe, 52
tradition, 5
transportation, 143
travel
blessing on, 75–78
difficulty with, 79
Truman, Harry S., 171, 171n9
Tuck, Jim, 84

unemployment
of Moreno, Chito, 190
in San Miguel, 146
union, 163
La Unión Nacional Sinarquista (UNS), 6, 24
Union of Mexican Catholic Ladies, 31
United States. *See also* "El Norte"; Stockton
as beneficiary of immigration, 210
Bracero Program in, 10, 26, 35, 38–40
Communism impact on, 100
economy of, 39
immigration to, 36–39
in Korean War, 170–71
life in, 80
materialism of, 56, 132
poverty impacted by jobs in, 210
religious beliefs of, 94–95
as Rome, 100–101
Russia relationship with, 79
UNS. *See* Unión Nacional Sinarquista
US. *See* United States

Vasconcelos, José, 83
Vega, José Reyes, 163

Villa, Pancho, 22, 43
Viqueira, Juan Pedro, 179
Virgin of Guadalupe, 89, 163
visitation
anticipation for, 75–76, 80, 145
as contraband, 190
desire for, 135
encouragement for, 173
obstruction from, 144, 186
of Rivera, Pancha, 53–54
"Viva Cristo Rey! Viva Cristo Rey!," 4

weather
in context, 142
guidance and, 103
Western Attitudes Towards Death (Ariès), 19
Whetten, Nathan, 26
Wolf, Eric, 8
work, 21
in corn production, 188
corruption in, 112
of family, 111–12, 137–138
health and, 71
of Márquez, Sidonia, 111
of Moreno, Chilo, 111, 207
of Moreno, Chito, 67, 111, 127
of Moreno, Lolo, 111
of Moreno, Victorina, 111, 137
of Moreno, Ysabel, 111
opportunity for, 145
of Orozco, Chuy, 111, 124
of Orozco, José, 111
of Orozco, Lula, 204–5
of Rivera, Juan, 71–73, 136
of Rivera, Pancha, 36–37, 93, 107, 112, 126, 223n69
World War II, 35, 94
wrestling, 2–3

Yañez, Agustín, 51

Zapata, Emiliano, 22

José Orozco, editor, translator.

José Lozano, illustrator.